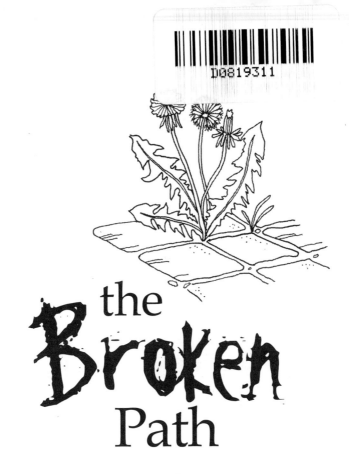

the Broken Path

How Catholic Bishops Got Lost in the Weeds of American Politics

Judie Brown

Manufactured in the United States of America

ISBN 978-1-4507-9669-9

Dedication

This book would never have become
a reality had it not been for two
of the most important men in my life:
my husband, Paul, who has always
encouraged me to be consistent in never
backing away from the truth, and my
spiritual mentor for a quarter century,
Father Denis O'Brien, MM,
who persisted in reminding me,
"Don't talk to walls!"

The Broken Path:
How Catholic Bishops Got Lost in the Weeds of American Politics

Contents

Foreword

One of the advantages of growing old (I am now 88) is that one has the opportunity to see and experience it all. I was born a Catholic and I grew up a Catholic. I have experienced the Church from pew to pulpit. Always an avid reader (I was a freshman in high school when I subscribed to *Time* magazine back when it was published by Henry Luce and was eminently readable), I tried to know everything about what was going on in the world.

The Catholic world of my youth was the world of Bing Crosby's *Going My Way*. It was a world in which bishops did not tolerate nonsense in the Church and were not afraid to take controversial stands. I remember Christopher E. Byrne, bishop of Galveston, making a 1946 endorsement of a proposed legalization of horse racing in Texas saying, "Watching horses race is a morally good and pleasurable thing!" Now that took courage in a state that was dominated by Baptists at the time. Then, shortly afterward, Cardinal Francis Spellman, archbishop of New York, condemned the movie *Baby Doll* and called on all Catholics to boycott the movie.

As I write this, I am mindful that today is July 25, 2011, the 43rd anniversary of Pope Paul VI's encyclical, *Humanae Vitae*. I remember my astonishment when 27 priests of the Archdiocese of Washington publicly dissented from the magisterial teaching of the pope's encyclical. I applauded when Cardinal O'Boyle suspended the priests, but was shocked when, on April 1, 1971, Cardinal John Wright, then prefect of the Congregation of Clergy, to whom the priests had appealed, overruled Cardinal O'Boyle and directed the reinstatement of the dissenting priests.

Two years later, in 1973, the Church was confronted with the U.S. Supreme Court decision, *Roe v. Wade*. I had only been a bishop for two years at that time, yet Archbishop Carroll appointed me director of pro-life activities for the Province of Miami. I soon became aware that the willingness to confront error as shown by Cardinal O'Boyle and Cardinal Spellman was a thing of the past.

In 1990, when I was bishop of Corpus Christi, I followed the procedure I subsequently outlined in my essay, "A Twelve Step Program for Bishops," and issued three decrees of excommunication against an abortionist doctor and two women who ran aborturaries. Shortly thereafter, as a member of the NCCB/USCC Pro-Life Activities Committee, I attended a meeting of the committee. After we had finished the business of our agenda, I asked the chairman, Cardinal John O'Connor, if I could explain to the committee what had happened in Corpus Christi that led to the three excommunications. For some 30 minutes I spoke to a committee that included seven bishops, Cardinals O'Connor, Mahony, and Law, and a dozen or so priests and laity. At the conclusion of my presentation I said that I would be happy to answer any questions. After about five minutes of very painful and embarrassing silence, Cardinal O'Connor said, "Well, if there is no further business, this meeting of the committee is adjourned."

In retrospect, I can only conclude that my presentation of the facts surrounding the Corpus Christi excommunications was a source of embarrassment to the cardinals and bishops present, since they were surely faced with the same problems I had had to face in Corpus Christi. My presentation must have been a challenge to them as to why they had not done the same thing in their own dioceses.

How do we explain the apparent lack of courage and unwillingness on the part of most of the bishops of the United States to face up to the challenges increasingly posed to the Church by our secular society—not only regarding life issues, but now also by same-sex "marriage"?

That is the question Judie Brown courageously poses for all Catholics in the United States—clergy and laity alike. Judie Brown has probably experienced more frustration in dealing with the American hierarchy than most of us. Therefore, this book is a welcome addition to the debate and hopefully it will help point the way to solutions.

Bishop Rene Gracida

Acknowledgments

In the years leading up to the final preparation of this volume I learned so much from many great Catholic men—each of whom is a priest faithful to truth without apology. Among them are Pope Saint Pius X, Pope Pius XI, Pope Pius XII, Pope Paul VI, Pope John Paul II, and Pope Benedict XVI. There are also Cardinals John J. O'Connor and Raymond Burke and Bishops Robert Vasa, Thomas Olmsted, Fabian Bruske-witz, Joseph Martino, Rene Gracida, and John Yanta. There are Fathers William Kuchinsky; Thomas Eu-teneuer; Paul Marx, OSB; John Hardon, SJ; Anthony Brankin; James Farfaglia; Charles Brown; James Buckley, FSSP; and others I have sadly forgotten at the moment.

Brilliant friends and co-workers have taught me so much. Many are noted in this volume, but I want to especially thank Debi Vinnedge, Ione Whitlock, and Elizabeth Wickham, Ph.D.

I mastered an understanding of the difference between Catholic ethics and fake bioethics from Professor Dianne Irving, M.S., Ph.D., and Professor C. Ward Kischer. Their patience in consistently correcting my errors is appreciated in ways that these few words cannot convey.

I value now and always the constructive criticism and wise counsel from my husband; my three children; James W. Sedlak; David Brandao; Mickey O'Hare; Michael Hichborn; Rita Diller; Rob Gasper; the creative genius of recently deceased Craig Kapp; and my mentor, Mildred Faye Jefferson, M.D.

Finally, the nitty-gritty of getting this volume into a coordinated format that looks like a readable book would never have happened without so many members of the team at American Life League, including Susan Ciancio, Bonnie Seers, Paul Rondeau, Karen Williams, Bridget Carroll, Stephanie Hopping, and my public policy partners.

Over the course of the five years it took me to gather the courage to sit down and actually do this, my husband kept gently nudging me to move forward. I hesitated until one day, during a conversation with him, I realized that I too could be accused of being part of the problem if I failed to come up with a roadmap that guides the way out of the tragic situation confronting Catholics in America today.

So here it is, and Mr. Brown, I do thank you. Your love and persistence has paid off. Thanks be to God.

Introduction

Current events have made it impossible to continue to ignore the serious consequences that come into play when religious leaders or their representatives confuse religion with politics. It is no secret that the leadership of the United States Conference of Catholic Bishops (USCCB), for example, has taken the moral currency of Catholic doctrine and, to a large degree, squandered it on securing seats at the table of the political and cultural powerbrokers in America. Such actions are both hypocritical and destructive to the credibility of the Church and its teaching. Further, there is no doubt that many individual Catholics have been alienated from the Church in the process.

First came the near silence during a political process that resulted in the election of the most pro-abortion, anti-Catholic individual in the history of the United States— President Barack Hussein Obama. Then there was the pomp and circumstance of this president receiving an honorary degree from the prestigious University of Notre Dame, an allegedly Catholic institution of higher learning. Additionally, the health care reform debate and the law's subsequent passage consumed much of the USCCB's time, energy, and dollars—for all of the wrong reasons.

It is obvious that something quite disturbing has happened to Catholic identity in the United States. Catholic structures, such as schools and hospitals, have grown dependent on government financial support. Catholic priests have grown more responsible for fundraising to retire building debts than for enriching the souls of parishioners entrusted to their fatherly care. And bishops have had to confront the media's challenges and the painful reality of dealing with attorneys to resolve sex abuse cases and the like.

And the beat goes on.

In each of these situations, as with so many over the past decade, many bishops have appeared more like liberal politicians rather than Catholic shepherds with a clear message. To make matters worse, these men have spokespeople and lobbyists who further muddy the waters and confuse Catholic doctrine with political posturing. Most of them appear to prefer the game of politics that is fundamentally grounded in the not-so-Catholic idea of compromise.

For its own sake, of course, there is nothing wrong with political compromise. That's what politics is all about. But when political posturing is used to water down or misrepresent Catholic teaching, an immense problem results.

Whether the subject is how the Catholic hierarchy should relate to such topics as the election process, legislative questions, sexual abuse cases, honorary degrees, or funerals for the deceased, there is a common thread that ties all of these things together. That unbroken cord should be the undeniable truth that the teachings of the Church are not malleable, but are constant and true in every case where faith and morals exist in the culture. When that thread is broken or frayed, the path to truth takes a detour, and Catholic teachings become subject to abuse, refutation, misrepresentation, and marginalization. The results are not pretty.

The Broken Path: How Catholic Bishops Got Lost in the Weeds of American Politics is an analysis of this growing tendency among Catholic leaders to take the focus off Christ and put it instead on secular approaches to current trends in American social and political life.

The involvement of the United States Conference of Catholic Bishops in the health care reform debates has made it quite easy to define the reasons, the motives, and the results of a hierarchy that is largely—but not totally—political first and Catholic second.

As one examines the complicit role a variety of bishops played in the passage of a bill that defies every principle of Catholic social teaching, it becomes obvious that there is a fundamental crisis in the Church today that is not only troublesome but antithetical to all that it means to be Catholic. I might go so far as to suggest that it is monumental in scope and devastating to Catholic identity.

As shepherds serving in direct lineage with Christ's first apostles, the Catholic bishops have a solemn responsibility to feed their people the spiritual nourishment necessary for the flock to grow in its love of Christ, to teach people to grow in devotion to biblical truth, and to teach a respect for the traditions and magisterial teachings of the Catholic Church. In other words, even now in the twenty-first century, it is not idealistic to point out that the primary and singularly exclusive role of Catholic bishops and, by extension, their ordained priests and deacons, is to strengthen Catholic people in their faith by setting the example in their words and in their deeds.

Believe it or not, nowhere in Church documents can we find a definition of the ordained priest as partisan politician, lobbyist, or labor leader. According to the *Catechism of the Catholic Church,* it is a clear and well-documented teaching that, as citizens of this great nation, every Catholic—whether ordained or lay—has a role to play in the electoral and political process. But first and foremost, he must remain true to his Catholic faith. The involvement in this process does not and should not require a single one of us to bend as Catholics, or to twist or deny Catholic teaching in order to suit a certain political ideology.

As Catholics in America, our primary goal must focus on bringing Christ to the public square and standing firmly on the truths taught to us as Catholics. In doing so, we make our voices and Christ's teaching heard in the malaise of American politics and public life. We can and should do this without ever feeling that part of our task is to embrace what is contradictory to or even slightly dissimilar to the laws of God and the teachings of the Church. To do so would be to suggest that our identity as Catholics really has little to do with our public lives outside the church on Sunday morning.

To be clear, we Catholics should proudly stand as witnesses to what is right and just. For, without justice, there can be no charity, no sound government, and no peace. While this vision of Catholics in public life has become increasingly blurred, it is never too late to adjust the picture and get things back into focus.

Today it is nearly impossible to distinguish the Catholic American from any other American. This is unhealthy, not only for the Church, but for America as well. This book will attempt to diagnose the reasons why this dilemma—which is actually a monstrous crisis—occurred, and what it will take to correct it.

The unity of purpose that inspired Christopher Columbus to put his stake in the ground and proudly announce the arrival of Christianity has become disfigured and, at times, unrecognizable. We want to identify why this is so and apply some common sense to repairing it.

At the outset we must make one thing very clear. There will be those who will decry this work as just another attempt to *criticize* the Catholic bishops and spread false information among the faithful and the secular world. Such allegations are nothing new. They are but an extension of the gobbledygook I have had to live with for many years. Ever since the first campaign I led calling on Catholic bishops to obey Church law in their dealings with pro-abortion Catholics in public life and to make sure such people were denied Holy Communion, I have been a thorn in the side of many bishops.

Certain bishops have told me that the interpretation of Catholic Church law is not any of my business and that they have their own lawyers to guide their decisions. I have been told that, when we as lay people make a public point of suggesting that the Church law in question should be obeyed, we are acting in disrespect and doing nothing but creating an unwelcome disturbance. This is a not-so-polite way of telling us to mind our own business.

I have been told that our persistent requests that the bishops courageously stand on the laws of the Church is nothing more than denigrating the office of bishop. I have been told that a bishop is the one to decide what needs to be done and when action is needed. I have been excoriated, ignored, and made to feel humiliated for being honest with more than a few members of the hierarchy.

But the real problem has nothing to do with how a particular bishop views what is explained, documented, and exposed by a simple woman like me. The problem is not how a bishop speaks to me—or any Catholic for that matter. My task is not to create disunity, but to shine a light on what is true according to Catholic teaching versus what is being peddled by some as a new pabulum-like strain of Catholic mush!

Real unity like that imagined by Christopher Columbus begins with absolute truth, not political rhetoric.

The problem is that far too many Catholic bishops have chosen to avoid, deny, or otherwise ignore what is fundamentally their first and primary responsibility—the saving of souls.

An ordained priest, including Catholic bishops, cannot enrich the lives of his flock and help people get to heaven by lobbying for a piece of legislation. But he can teach them how to confront the world and bring Christ into it.

An ordained priest, including Catholic bishops, cannot feed the hungry soul when he is more interested in playing footsie with politicians. Such bishops may not realize that by foregoing the photo op and using that time to formulate messages that will strengthen his flock, he can achieve a level of spiritual success far outweighing public accolades or honors bestowed by mere men.

An ordained priest, including Catholic bishops, cannot spread the Good News on Sunday and then, on Monday, decide to ignore the impudence of the Nancy Pelosis, Joe Bidens, and Chris Matthews of the world. To do so is to create confusion, to alienate people who are fed up with the contradictions they see and hear, and to betray the sacred trust of Christ through whom all power and goodness flows.

There is a time and a place for standing up and being counted—not because the world cannot wait to hear what you have to say, but because to do less is to become part of a growing problem that, in this case, is currently confronting the American Catholic Church. Many good Catholic bishops and priests are doing just that—and so is this grandmother.

As we begin this examination into the whys and where-fores of the decay I see occurring within the Church today, and discover anew the antidote that already exists, let me respond to all those who will disparage this work by setting the record straight right now: I am not going to stand or walk on a broken path and continue to watch souls go the wrong way. I love being Catholic and I want others to see why. It is my sincere hope that this book straightens the path for those who are concerned about what is at stake when a Catholic bishop or his spokespeople get lost in the weeds of American politics.

The Broken Path

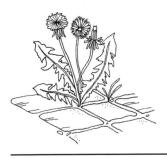

1

CHAPTER ONE:
How It All Began

[I]f anybody wishes to be considered a real Catholic, he ought to be able to say from his heart the selfsame words which Jerome addressed to Pope Damasus: "I, acknowledging no other leader than Christ, am bound in fellowship with Your Holiness; that is, with the chair of Peter. I know that the Church was built upon him as its rock, and that whosoever gathereth not with you, scattereth."

– Pope Leo XIII,
  Testem Benevolentiae Nostrae, 1899

What the Church teaches about sinners

The history of man's failure to live up to God's expectations goes all the way back to the first human beings, Adam and Eve.

In their case, their inability to follow a simple directive given to them by God Himself ultimately affected all of us in a negative way. Choosing not to obey God's one request of them, but preferring instead to believe the serpentine devil, was where it all began. That decision represents the first act of exercising one's freedom of choice. That single act resulted in a permanent condition we Catholics understand as original sin. Aside from Jesus Christ, who is both human and divine, only one human being born since that event has not been marked by the tendency to sin—our Blessed Mother Mary.

This is why Christ, driven by His love for mankind, instituted the seven sacraments of the Church. Each is a divine gift given to us to help us get to heaven one day. The first of these is the sacrament of baptism. When we are baptized, the mark of original sin is washed away and we have a clean slate, though we still retain the tendency toward sin. Once we reach the age of reason, usually around seven years of age, we are prepared by our parents and teachers to receive the sacraments of penance and Holy Communion.

From that point forward, whenever we do commit sin, we have the opportunity to confess those sins by taking advantage of the sacrament of penance—more commonly known today as the sacrament of reconciliation. Baptism, penance, and all the sacraments are designed to affirm in our hearts and souls the reality of how much God loves every single human being.

The Catholic Church teaches that, with the exception of Jesus Christ and our Blessed Mother, there is no such thing as a perfect or flawless human being. Every single one of us is capable of sinning, and thus offending God. Each of us can, by our words or deeds, travel down the wrong path. And we can also lead others into error by setting a bad example. There are numerous ways in which we, as adult Catholics, can mislead those who look to us for guidance or for the truth about what it means to be a Catholic.

A structure of sin is part of the human condition; this is made manifest in daily life by a willingness to do what is comfortable or convenient rather than a desire to obey the laws of God. This human tendency is the part of our nature that is a direct result of that first sin.

A recognition of this fact preyed heavily on my mind as I sat down to write this book. It is obvious that we dare not cast stones at others, but rather must stick to the facts that are evident and clearly available to everyone. Because we name names throughout this volume, we realize that those who dislike what is said here will say we are casting judgment on our fellow Catholics.

However, we have taken care to address only the ACTIONS of certain individuals, to explain what is erroneous or evil about these actions, and to attempt to provide a positive antidote. The human being in question can only be judged by God. Without passing judgment on the individual, we can examine his actions—and learn from his mistakes.

Now that we understand these few basic facts about human beings and the faulty judgment of Adam and Eve, we can move forward to the subject of the decline of the moral authority and credibility of many of the Catholic bishops and their various bureaucracies.

Background

How the American Catholic Church arrived at this current state of affairs is not all that easy to explain. Volumes have been written about it and multitudinous commentaries have been published. Yet there remains still a void—an absence of understanding about why so many are suffering so deeply because of these problems.

We will begin with an explanation of the history of the Catholic Church in America to help us wade through the current morass. We can actually start with Christopher Columbus—a Catholic explorer with a mission.

Columbus was neither a Catholic bishop nor a priest. But as a Catholic who had been properly educated he had many goals; among them was one that was specifically defined by his identity as a Catholic. Catholic historians tell us that, when Christopher Columbus discovered a new land, he was inspired not only by the challenge of discovery but by his faith in God. One of Columbus's chief ambitions was to "spread the good news of salvation and convert the natives to Christianity" in each new territory he encountered.[1] And, throughout Columbus's published writings, this missionary theme is found.

As we know, once his discovery of the North American continent had occurred, it took a while for the first adventurous people to actually set sail and come to this new land. Among them were the Spanish colonists who followed Columbus, and the Pilgrims who, though not Catholic, had a strong sense of faith and a desire to rid themselves and their families of the oppressive conditions they had left behind. They sought freedom to practice their religion without government intrusion. At the time, they were the pioneers not only of the territories that opened up before them but of separation of Church and state.

Not long after the country began to take shape and the founding fathers set forth their principles, the Catholic Church in America began to grow. In the beginning it was not in any way victimized by the politics of the day.

1899—Rome makes a statement

Over time, however, that all changed. The role of the Catholic Church in the context of the American experience became challenging, at least as far as the Vatican was concerned. As early as the late 1800s Rome was reminding American bishops that, while the Catholic population should be assimilated into the culture of this still young America, the integration of Catholics into the culture should not necessitate altering anything fundamental to the identity of the Church and its people.[2]

In 1899 Pope Leo XIII, concerned about the possibility of some American prelates and theologians diluting the teachings of the Church, addressed an entire encyclical to the problem.

Pope Leo XIII's encyclical, *Testem Benevolentiae Nostrae (Concerning New Opinions, Virtue, Nature and Grace, with Regard to Americanism)*, was addressed to Cardinal James Gibbons, the leader of the American Catholic bishops at the time.[3] The encyclical dealt with two very important aspects of the Church and its teachings.

The first point Pope Leo XIII made dealt with the unchangeable nature of the magisterial teachings of the

Church, which are based on biblical teaching and Catholic tradition. Magisterial teaching[4] refers to doctrinal pronouncements from the pope on matters of faith and morals. Catholic tradition[5] refers to those practices and teachings of the doctors of the Church and pronouncements made by Church councils which expound and expand in many cases on fundamental Catholic teaching and biblical principles.

The reason for Pope Leo XIII's letter is that certain concerns had come to his attention. Apparently there had been some erroneous interpretations of Catholic teaching which necessitated his involvement to the extent he deemed wise at the time. It is for this reason that he urged the bishops to either avoid or, due to the circumstances, change the manner in which Catholic doctrine was being imparted to the faithful.

The second point Pope Leo XIII made was that the Church is not in any way similar to manmade organizations such as corporations, clubs, or governments—be they democratic or dictatorial. While manmade laws can be amended, debated, or subjected to perverted interpretations, such is not the case with the Catholic Church and its doctrine—including its laws. As the bride of Christ, the Church has received the deposit of faith from God and, as such, is entrusted with these teachings.

However, Pope Leo XIII realized that even though fundamental truth never changes, there were American Catholics in positions of authority who would disagree and misrepresent those very truths for a wide variety of questionable purposes.

Pope Leo XIII knew there were some Catholics who were suggesting that if certain Church teachings could be modified or avoided, the result would be that more people might be enticed to join the Catholic Church. While the pope made it clear that the Church is always concerned about souls and bringing those of different faiths, or no faith, to know and understand Catholic teaching, he emphasized the fact that the Church cannot make concessions in what it teaches in order to accommodate those who disagree with Catholic doctrine. Nobody has the authority to do that. The pope pointed out that the Church is a divine society and, unlike the Church, all other social human organizations can and do "depend simply on free will and choice of men."

The most remarkable thing about the warnings Pope Leo XIII gave to the American bishops in 1899 is that his words were not only pertinent to that time but also prophetic. It is clear in hindsight that the problem he defined as "Americanism" more than 100 years ago became larger as time passed.

Fast forward to 1965

The modern day American Catholic Church is still, in many instances, suffering from the very same type of internal deconstruction that provoked Pope Leo XIII to write his encyclical. The absence of a leadership committed to cohesive teaching is the core problem. To pinpoint a moment in time when the current divorce between unified teaching and opinions about those teachings occurred isn't really all that hard.

It was the juxtaposition of Vatican Council II in 1965 with the ensuing 1968 encyclical letter, *Humanae Vitae,* by Pope Paul VI, that provided impetus to the runaway false teaching trend.

On the one hand, there was a Vatican Council which was being misinterpreted and misapplied to suit the agendas of the liberal wing of Catholic thought in America. Catholics were receiving mixed messages about what Vatican Council II documents actually allowed or implemented. What was happening was literally a replacement of the facts contained in those documents with a wide variety of personal beliefs being pronounced by those who thought themselves "experts."[6]

Then there was *Humanae Vitae,* which came just three short years later.[7] This encyclical was issued as these same liberal-minded churchmen were publicly saying the Church's teachings on birth control were going to change forever. When *Humanae Vitae* was issued and did not change Catholic teaching, these dissident moral theologians, led by

Father Charles Curran, issued a rebellious statement which was published in the *Baltimore Sun*.[8] These mavericks ignored the truth contained in that encyclical and proceeded to misrepresent the teaching, misinterpret it, and deceive the people of the Church about what the teaching meant. It was at this point that the current decline in Catholic consistency emerged with an enormous impact of a totally negative nature.

This failure of many ordained Catholic priests to teach the fullness of truth started slowly but escalated as cultural attitudes—including those of Catholics—moved farther and farther away from Catholic moral teaching and closer to moral subjectivity. While we could define this breakdown in doctrinal communication in any number of ways, the bottom line is that the result has been devastating.

There were too many priests, bishops, and theologians eating the forbidden fruit, enjoying it, and passing it along.

Democracy as Catholicism

As Americans, many Catholics—ordained and lay—have for more than a century made an effort to apply a style of democratic or secular thinking to what is profoundly Catholic. Such an application is clearly impossible since the infallible teachings of the Church in matters of faith and morals are not malleable, are not subject to polling results, and are not ever going to be different—no matter what the moderate wing of the Church says about it.

The role of Catholic priests, including bishops and Catholic theologians, is to guard the teachings of the Church and share them with the flock—absent political correctness. But in today's world every teaching can, depending on who is speaking about it, be laced with personal opinion and innuendo. The reason is that there are many who have been entrusted with defending truth, but who find it more comfortable to dissent or manipulate that truth. In other words, love for the truth contained in those teachings has been replaced, in many quarters, by love of self.

Alas, those Catholic people who have been subjected to such balderdash don't even realize these days that what they are hearing, learning, and repeating is far afield from what is actually genuine Catholic teaching.

To make this point a bit clearer, let us use an example from everyday life. Let's say that someone chooses to commit a grave act such as murder. According to the manmade laws in this country, the perpetrator is always guilty of the same moral offense regardless of who he is or the situation involved. Though presumed innocent until tried by a jury of his peers and sentenced by a judge in a court of law, his crime, once confirmed, is never anything less than the taking of the life of a human being. But if a jury or a judge can redefine his act as something that did not result in the death of a person, then all of a sudden murder is no longer always and in every case an act that results in death. Preposterous, of course, but it makes my point. There are no gray areas when it comes to murder.

In the same way, there are no gray areas when it comes to teaching Catholic doctrine set forth by God as articulated in the Bible and as carried forward by the Church in its magisterial teaching and tradition.

It may seem that we are oversimplifying, but as we will learn in this book, there are some things that are unchanging and very easy to comprehend. It is human beings who create confusing, complicated scenarios by suggesting that nothing is ever black and white.

Autonomy as an end in itself

Many who have analyzed the current situation plaguing the Catholic Church agree that part of the problem is best defined as personal autonomy—the ability to be free to choose to do whatever one wishes as long as nobody else is harmed.

There is nothing wrong with autonomy per se, but it should not be divorced from the natural law. In other words, even though we have the freedom to make choices for ourselves, we should consider the rightness and wrongness of the choice in the context of a higher law before making a decision. Adam and Eve must have done this before choosing the serpent's advice as being more appealing than God's instruction to them.

Then as now, if human beings deny that we should weigh our choices against the difference between good and evil, havoc results. Why is this? This is because autonomy is not an end unto itself.

This should be obvious even to someone who is not Catholic. Even though we may realize that every action we take will have a result, it does not automatically follow that we will always make good choices. We have to have some sort of guideline that exists outside of our personal opinions on such matters. But if that guideline is muddied, ignored, or denied, then anything goes—even among those who know better, such as Catholic theologians, priests, and bishops.

This is so because, for the believing Catholic, we understand as a fundamental part of our Catholic identity that we should examine our autonomy in the context of Catholic teaching and the magisterium. This is what distinguishes the Catholic Church and its teaching and what defines us as Catholics. The Church gives us guidance, but first we have to be taught by those who know and understand what the Church has to say on this subject.

If those to whom the teaching of the faithful is entrusted fail to deliver the Catholic teaching in a clear and unequivocal manner, the result is chaotic. The very people who are depending on that instruction to be formed in Catholic thought are misled and subsequently can mislead others. It is a train wreck waiting to happen when Catholic teaching is perverted, denied, or ignored by those who know better.

Pope John Paul II and autonomy

There is no doubt that this is part of the reason why Pope John Paul II wrote about autonomy in one of his encyclicals. It is fair to suggest that he did so in a renewed effort to clear away the fog, dig out the problems that are created in the vacuum of failed teaching, and expose truth once again in all its beauty and clarity. In his 1993 encyclical, *Veritatis Splendor,* Pope John Paul II taught:[9]

God's law does not reduce, much less do away with human freedom; rather, it protects and promotes that freedom. In contrast, however, some present-day cultural tendencies have given rise to several currents of thought in ethics which centre upon "an alleged conflict between freedom and law." These doctrines would grant to individuals or social groups the right "to determine what is good or evil." Human freedom would thus be able to "create values" and would enjoy a primacy over truth, to the point that truth itself would be considered a creation of freedom. Freedom would thus lay claim to a "moral autonomy" which would actually amount to an "absolute sovereignty.". . .

. . . These trends of thought have led to a denial, in opposition to sacred Scripture (cf. Mt 15:3-6) and the Church's constant teaching, of the fact that the natural moral law has God as its author, and that man, by the use of reason, participates in the eternal law, which it is not for him to establish.

The key phrase in this eloquent statement is "not for him to establish." Yet this is precisely what is happening in the Catholic Church in America today. There are individuals in high places who believe that the natural moral law and consistent teachings of the Church are subject to refining, clarification, personal perspective, and revision.

To that twisted concept, Pope John Paul II says "NO!"

Pope John Paul II's analysis of the clash between divinely inspired teaching and human autonomy run amuck is an eye-opener and further affirmation of all that Pope Leo XIII warned about at the end of the nineteenth century. Today there is no question that an erroneous concept of personal autonomy has led some within the Catholic Church to view their opinions—which are contrary to Catholic teaching—as compatible with them. Yet there are still others who, whether with intent to do so, or simply out of pure arrogance, have chosen to characterize certain Church teachings—each of which are based on scriptural and Catholic truths—as being fungible.

The tragic result of these manipulations and machinations perpetrated by ordained priests, as well as some bishops, is that Catholics and, to a large extent, the public are left in a state of confused ignorance.

Into this stifling vacuum of error steps the media which, in all too many cases, is willing to further misinterpret Catholic teaching. This occurs because those with the God-given power to clearly define and teach fundamental truth are not doing so with consistency, conviction, and commitment.

Let's face it. The Catholic Church leadership in America should have recognized long ago that this nation is locked in a culture war. Some might suggest that this cultural conflict is a struggle between liberals and conservatives, but that is really not at all what this is about. This is, quite simply, a battle that pits good against evil. It pits those who love God against those who deny that God exists. In other words, it is a real life war between those who want to put God in a box and those who believe in a powerful and omnipotent God.

This is not a battle for sissies. It certainly is not a battle that can be waged using compromise, political politeness, and hubris. It is the age-old conflict that started in the garden with our first parents. It is a struggle between God and Satan. Nothing new, really, but the struggle has taken on an extraordinarily distinct meaning in recent times.

Judie Brown with Pope John Paul II in 2001

Catholic bishops aren't even in the game

As most bishops of the Catholic Church and their bureaucrats have backed away from standing up for Christ and carefully teaching truth to those who are Catholic, a sort of secularism has crept into the Church.[10] I sometimes wonder if most bishops have even noticed the snake in the Church—and believe me, it is there.

There is little doubt in this age of Internet, Tweeting, and Facebooking that the Church has been debilitated and its moral authority undermined not by those who detest the Church, but rather by those who have failed to teach truth and defend the Church in the first place.

The history is evident. What is not clear is why so many priests, bishops, and theologians have opted to dissent from Catholic teaching and have not been chastised. These individuals remain entrenched in the Church without correction of any kind. What is equally mysterious is how we got to this stage when the Church has such a vivid history of fighting against all odds to maintain and defend truth, even at the cost of lives. I cannot think of one martyr, for example, who would have preferred to agree to discard a little bit of truth for the sake of popularity, financial support, or political entrée. The true heroes of the faith would rather die before turning their backs on Christ—and many of them did.

That's not to suggest that, through the centuries, the Catholic Church has not had its share of charlatans, but never before has there been such a defining moment as the one we are facing today. That is because there is more attention being paid today, more opportunities to take a wrong turn, and more anti-Catholic eyes watching for the opportunity to record a misstep, blow it out of proportion, and create a headline out of nothing.

When St. Thomas Aquinas walked the earth and wrote all those volumes of remarkable teaching, NBC News was not around to record a single word he had to say. Perhaps we should be thankful for that. Though we cannot go back, we can certainly continue to teach the very same truths that St. Thomas elaborated on with such eminent brilliance.

Today's Church must meet the challenge

While never diluting what makes the Church the bride of Christ, it must move forward because it has always been relevant to current times.

What the Church needs today is strong leaders with a single-minded focus to carry on its legacy and instruct with integrity and purpose.

The Church needs heroic, holy, ordained men who are willing to stand against the pressure brought upon them by those who detest all that it means to be Catholic.

Where are those today who are willing to die for Christ instead of sitting with the devil? What has made it so difficult for Catholic bishops to act decisively? Is it a crisis in faith? Is it Americanism? Or could it be something else?

Most importantly, what can you do about this?

In the coming chapters, we will discuss the challenges and duties we each face as members of the Holy Roman Catholic Church. We are all responsible for the care of the Church and the Word. Paul tells us in 2 Tim. 4:2-5, "Proclaim the word; be persistent whether it is convenient or inconvenient; convince, reprimand, encourage through all patience and teaching. For the time will come when people will not tolerate sound doctrine but, following their own desires and insatiable curiosity, will accumulate teachers and will stop listening to the truth and will be diverted to myths. But you, be self-possessed in all circumstances; put up with hardship; perform the work of an evangelist; fulfill your ministry."[11]

Our Church is not an inanimate building. Nor is it defined by the actions or inactions of a particular leader. Through Christ and His grace each of us is an irreplaceable living stone that builds and sustains the Church upon the rock of Peter. Each stone—each of us—is equally important in the eyes of God and the eyes of the Church, but we must all take action. You will be utterly amazed at what one everyday faithful Christian can do when, in faith, he just steps out on the water!

2

CHAPTER TWO:
A Diseased Body

We must obey God rather than men.

– Acts 5:29

Individual Catholic bishops can only address the challenges that currently confront them if they realize, first and foremost, that something rather toxic has been infecting the Church for many years. We have heard various opinions about the current state of the Church, and some of them are quite interesting. There are those who say the venom comes from those pesky "pre-Vatican II Catholics"—Catholics who want things done the old-fashioned way. Others suggest that the source of the problem is a lack of compassion for sinners. Still others opine that the problems stem from the "old men in Rome" who think they can control everybody. Nearly everyone who has noticed the dilemma has an opinion.

Yet we really only need to ask one question: Why is the Catholic Church today shrinking in size and closing down parishes, schools, and other services once taken for granted?

I don't blame any particular segment of the Catholic population for the current morass. Yet, what is obvious is that a fundamental cause for the crisis—the great divide among today's Catholics between the calling of

Christ and the expectations of the society around us in America—is being ignored.

In plain English, this disease was born from a clash between the world and God Himself.

The 18th century and agnosticism

It all started during the period of Enlightenment. During that time of heightened awareness regarding man's perceived power to manage his own fate without the help of the good Lord, atheists and agnostics began making inroads in education, politics, and even religion. You might think that is a bit odd, as such people were and are anti-Christian in the first place. But such folks are clever, and the best place to start wreaking havoc is always in the place you most detest. This is how they began getting a foothold in the culture and in religious bodies including the Catholic Church.

Now don't get me wrong. There weren't thousands of them pursuing a destructive agenda, but rather a few who were in positions of influence and who used their power effectively. Many wise scholars and churchmen took note almost immediately of the deleterious effect these people and their views were having on Christianity. In fact, it was said that the rise to positions of prominence among those who were bent on denying Catholic truth or twisting it to suit an agenda created an atmosphere of uncertainty among the masses. Far too many became skeptics—questioning religious faith, its value, and its credibility.

Many so-called experts preferred to label faith as "superstition," to plant seeds of doubt among the faithful, and to publicly proclaim that faith was really nothing more than one's personal opinion about God, His power, or His involvement in life itself. This predisposition to disbelief began affecting how certain members of the Catholic hierarchy viewed Catholicism and its value in the context of public life. As the years have progressed, it has become painfully obvious that the situation is not improving.

That is not to say that atheism is so prevalent today that clergy are working overtime to redefine Catholic thought in terms of secular ideology, but rather that in many sectors of the Church Catholic teaching suffers at the hands of those within the Church who wish to mollify the anti-God cultural currents by softening the truth.

David Carlin, a professor of sociology and philosophy best known for his book, *The Decline and Fall of the Catholic Church in America*, has effectively argued that while some of our current "conservative" leadership like to think of America as a Christian nation, such a notion is becoming more and more improbable. Carlin writes, "There are now too many atheists in America for the U.S. to return to that old self-definition of itself. Though still relatively small in number, atheists are disproportionately represented in what may be called the 'command posts' of American culture referring to elite universities (including law schools), the national press, and the entertainment industry."[1]

Atheism is a direct contradiction to Christianity's premise that Christ is fully God and fully man. The atheist's intellectual argument is that if one cannot prove a certain statement scientifically, then there is every reason to doubt its validity. For example, the question, "Who really knows for sure?" can create suspicion even in the heart of a believer.

Ageless Gnosticism

The current crisis in the Church could also be attributed to Gnosticism—a philosophy that is opposed to all that is of Christ. Yet, to the dismay of the Church, there are many who can be found within the faith who practice these beliefs. Imagining a chameleon will give you a pretty good idea of how the Gnostic thinks and acts. What appears to be Catholic is never really Catholic and, when such behavior is attributed to theologians and others within the Church, bad things happen.

Gnosticism is fundamentally paganism. It is a denial in the supremacy of God, in the existence of Jesus Christ as the Son of God, and a rejection of the Holy Spirit. It is a belief system centered on the idea that the intellect is supreme. Gnostics believe that man can achieve salvation by human intelligence alone. While this may sound like a position that could never be associated with anything or anyone claiming to be Catholic, it is not going to surprise you, by the time you finish this book, to learn that there are many priests and nuns who are teaching this false doctrine. It has already infiltrated the Church in areas where one would not expect to find it.

As Catholic journalist, Mary Jo Anderson, explains, [2]

The strategy to empty the Catholic Church of its doctrine and to supplant it with a false religion is advanced by several tactics. Primary among them is to amalgamate error and truth under one teaching. Thus "human rights," a truth, is in fact used to ensure universal abortion "rights," a perversion of truth and life. By such methods any number of false teachings can be hidden in warm and fuzzy sounding slogans. When the teaching Church opposes the deception, some with "itchy ears" then turn on the Church with a vengeance.

The curse of the Arian heresy

As if atheism and Gnosticism weren't bad enough, we have also seen a rise in Arianism, a false philosophy first identified within the Catholic Church in the fourth century. Arianism is defined by the Catholic Church as a heresy. A heresy is a public position taken by individuals within the Church that requires a public condemnation by the magisterium of the Church lest the Church suffer damage from within.

Such was the case with the Arian heresy and its proponents. These individuals were spreading grave error upon the Church and its people until the heroic bishop, St. Athanasius, stepped in to expose it. In retired Catholic bishop Rene Gracida's eloquent article, "The Arian Heresy Revisited," he writes,[3]

The heresy of Arianism propounded by the priest Arius in Alexandria, Egypt, denied the divinity of Jesus Christ. According to Arianism, there are not three distinct persons in God, co-eternal and coequal. This heresy held that there is only one person in God, the Father. Arians believed that the Son is only a creature, made from nothing, *ex nihilo*, like all other created beings. The great danger of Arianism was that it reduced the Incarnation of Jesus to a mere figure of speech. It robbed the redemptive act of Jesus' dying on the cross of its efficacy, since only God could redeem fallen man. Man could not be redeemed by a mere man.

If this heresy sounds similar to Gnosticism to you, then you have already seen the parallel we are drawing here. For while the Gnostic cult penetrated all walks of life during the pagan experiences of various cultures before Christ and the prophets, the Arian heresy, a manifestation of Gnosticism, was particular to the Catholic Church. And while it is a boon to Catholicism that St. Athanasius drove it out, it really never left. For, as Bishop Gracida tells his readers,[4]

In the Catholic Church, the heresy of the rejection of belief in the sacredness of human life really began to manifest itself in the dissent which followed the publication by Pope Paul VI of his encyclical *Humanae Vitae* [in 1968]. That dissent has grown in the acceptance of one after another of the violations of the sacredness of human life. . . . This heresy has grown exponentially during the past three decades and has now assumed a status analogous to the great heresy of the fourth century: Arianism.

Arianism, which is a combination of Gnosticism and atheism, could be the root cause of the tragic condition that is eating away at the heart of the Catholic Church in America today.

Americanism—the real disease?

It is this concern that was at the core of Pope Leo XIII's expression of concern when he wrote to the American bishops in 1899 and addressed what he called Americanism. Americanism is today's Arianism. Seen in the context of the current political climate in America are the threads that weave a seamless garment of disregard for genuine Catholic teaching in deference to specifically American expectations of the Church and its teaching.

American Catholic priest Anthony Brankin, an expert on Americanism, has spoken extensively on this topic. In one of his 2007 speeches he told a stunned audience of Catholics the following:[5]

> Let me give an example of Americanism in action. Only two months ago 18 Catholic politicians—all liberal—all pro-abortion—and sadly representative of hundreds of punier pro-abortion Catholic politicians were offended that His Holiness Benedict XVI had proclaimed that they—by virtue of their promotion of killing children in the womb—had excommunicated themselves.

> In typical high-dudgeon these erstwhile Catholics and loyal secularists criticized the Successor of Christ for daring to think the killing of babies might be a public issue, a human issue. They were appalled that he dared to hold them to the moral demands of the faith.

> They felt they had to correct the pope for his violation of the American system. Doesn't he know? We are Americans! We don't need revelation or a Church! We vote on what is moral or immoral in this country. This is the will of the people, the consent of the governed. It is if we say it is; and no foreign power can contradict us.

The very idea that any group, or individual, could "correct the pope" with impunity is not only ridiculous, but pure Americanism in action.

Recall, if you will, that the pope is the vicar of Christ on earth, and that in matters of faith and morals his teachings are infallible! What this means is that a Catholic in good standing accepts Catholic teaching and assents to it, though he may question or be grappling with a particular teaching. Questioning a teaching is a perfectly human reaction; denying that it is true is profoundly wrong. The last thing a Catholic who is struggling with faith would do is publicly argue that the Holy Father is simply wrong!

But these elected officials to whom Father Brankin is referring claim to be Catholic, while at the same time defying infallible Catholic teaching. As Americans, these individuals obviously believe that the revelation of the Church is secondary to their own interpretation. Such public figures take the position that their primary role in government is to be supreme in the judgments they make about what is good and what is bad for America.

You may ask the question: Were these 18 Catholics reprimanded and instructed that they, due to their propounding of false doctrine, must not define themselves as Catholic until they repented of their disrespectful comments?

The answer is **No!** The USCCB issued a statement, and that was the end of the matter. There was no public reprimand; there was no type of corrective action taken by either a single bishop or their collective voice—the USCCB.

Clearly this single event represents a recent example of how the Americanism cancer spreads in the Church. Father Brankin gets to the heart of it in a 2009 address called "Americanism and the Culture of Death." His words make the case far better than anything I have read or heard.[6]

> I think most of us can agree that we American Catholics can sometimes be so intent on being good Americans that we might neglect being good Catholics. In other words, often enough it has been more important for us as Americans to profess and proclaim our loyalty to America—no matter what America did—even if it conflicted with our faith— than to stand apart and say, "No. We cannot do that—we shouldn't have done that."
>
> Did we ever consider some of our history from the viewpoint of the Indians or of the Mexicans?
>
> When our hearts thrill to hear of the heroics of the Alamo, do we not remember how Texas gained its independence?

Are we not allowed to ask about the morality of the fire-bombing of Europe or the atom bombing of Japan in WWII?

And even if we couldn't find ourselves going along 100 percent on every issue, I bet most of us can find a way to twist the morality of a particular policy to fit our consciences.

But you see, that is the heart of Americanism—that the standard of moral reference for America is what the politicians and pundits say are the needs of the nation. We need not look to the tradition of the Church and the teaching of the pope for our moral guidance—but merely to our needs.

And it is my contention that it is a very slippery slope from Americanism to the culture of death.

Now, "Americanism" in this sense was actually a word coined by Pope Leo XIII in his encyclical *Testem Benevolentiae.*

Leo, from his throne in Italy, was watching the great struggle going on in America between the Protestants and the Catholics—and that struggle was being played out between those bishops and clergy who said we needed to tailor and customize our Catholic beliefs and practices in order to fit in more amicably and smoothly with the Protestant Americans, and those bishops who, understanding the connection between faith and culture, warned that the Catholic people must not surrender to American pluralism, Congregationalism, or practical atheism or they would lose their faith.

Americanism was a heresy like modernism—it was more of a way of life—a way of looking at things. Americanism—was (and is) an attitude—a lens, a filter through which everything is interpreted. And you never notice until someone points it out that you may very well be infected by Americanism. . . .

. . . [A]s Catholic immigrants throughout the 19th century were streaming in from Europe—Ireland and Germany in particular—it was growing clear to Catholic . . . bishops that, when the faith of these immigrants would inevitably clash with the faith of the host, something was going to have to give.

We all know of the riots and church burnings that took place in Boston, New York, and Philadelphia. The reaction of the American population to Catholics coming to America was violent: "You are not true Americans—you are loyal to the pope in Rome," was their cry. And Catholics suffered mightily for their faith.

Now it dawned on some of the bishops—particularly the Irish ones—that the solution might be to go easy or ignore certain features or teachings of the Catholic faith. In other words, if Catholics could prove to the Americans that they didn't really believe all that popish mummery—at least not enough to let it jeopardize their relationship to the Americans, then maybe they could finally be accepted by their host.

And the way they figured they could do that without doing too much violence to their faith and the faith of their fathers was to do what the Americans did when confronting the world—define themselves as American before anything else and therefore unique and exceptional and unassailable.

What they said in effect was this, "We American Catholics are different than the rest of [the] Catholics in the world precisely because we are Americans. Nothing applies to us as it might to Europe's or Latin America's Catholics because we are in a different situation with different problems."

The Americanism phenomena resulted from what is, in retrospect, the misguided perception of American bishops, led by America's first Catholic bishop, John Carroll.[7] Even though there was debate among them, history makes it clear that the majority of Catholic bishops wanted to rearrange the Catholic Church in America in a way that would make it more palatable to their Protestant counterparts. Whether they thought they could convert their fellow Americans or not, the approach they took was disastrous.

Bishop Carroll in particular wanted freedom from the Vatican as indicated by his statement, "Bishops may be elected, at this distance from Rome, by a select body of clergy constituting as it were a Cathedral Chapter. Otherwise we shall never be viewed kindly by our government here, and discontent, even amongst our own clergy, will break out."[8]

In other words, in order for American members of the hierarchy, and thus Catholics as a whole, to be acceptable to the government and the culture, the structure of the Church in America had to be drastically altered. Thank heavens that did not happen, though some would argue that what flowed from it is even worse than creating a separate electoral college for American bishops.

Historians have hotly debated the extent to which these first American Catholic leaders fostered the attitude that has become quintessential Americanism. Be that as it may, it is to this day what plagues Catholicism in America. Anyone who studies the situation in those early days realizes that the Catholic hierarchy really believed that, to be a Catholic in America, a person must first be an American.

Brankin opines,[9]

> Many of the bishops actually thought that if we played it carefully—and didn't push our religion too much—we might even convert the country to Catholicism—never mind that we had just emptied it of any content.
>
> This is where Leo XIII comes in because in his encyclical [*Testem Benevolentiae*]—which is actually

very peaceful in tone—he sees this attitude as a dangerous heresy that he calls "Americanism." He defines it as the misbegotten hope that Catholics could shape Church teachings in accord with the spirit of the age and the nation. He warns that making concessions to the reigning culture and remaining silent on contentious points for the sake of patriotism is dishonest.

He was convinced that the American bishops were doing just that—and he forbade them "to suppress for any reason any doctrine that has been handed down."

Leo highlights the particularly Americanist habits of . . . "confounding . . . license with liberty, the passion for discussing and pouring contempt upon any possible subject, the assumed right to hold whatever opinions one pleases upon any subject and to set them forth in print to the world."

Pope Leo warns the bishops that these habits wrap our minds in a sort of darkness and convince us that our free speech is somehow consecrated by the Holy Spirit who is now pouring richer and more abundant graces into our American souls than into anyone else.

It wouldn't be long before Americans would begin to believe that with this superabundance of grace, American opinions and decisions—and very lives—would be truer and more authentic than those of the rest of humanity.

Leo worries that such a super-inspired citizenry puffed up by its exalted opinion of itself would eschew the need for the guidance either of history or the Church—being eminently capable of discussing its way to truth.

They would no longer see the need for supernatural virtues and counsels of "poverty, chastity and obedience" because those are passive virtues while what they would claim . . . the world really needs is the dynamism of active virtues—and those, of course, are so abundant in America.

Leo did not mystically intuit his concerns about what was going on in the minds of the American hierarchy. He probably read it from the American bishops own words. . . .

This is the monster of treachery and false patriotism that Leo had to confront in *Testem Benevolentiae* and before which it was clear, many American bishops were groveling.

With no small amount of irony in his tone, Pope Leo assures the bishops that he knows that they would be the first to repudiate any hint of such attitudes. Confident that they would never teach doctrines or hold beliefs that America was superior to other nations or that she was specially chosen by God to lead the world or that the American Church exists differently from the Church in the rest of the world, he closes with the salutation of a loving father.

Leo notes very generously that God loves all his children, recognizes that each has certain gifts, but that they are all equal in His eyes, and that special treatment has no place in the home called Church.

Testem Benevolentiae was addressed to the head of the American Catholic Church at the time, Cardinal James Gibbons. Upon receipt of that papal letter, the cardinal responded on March 17, 1899, extending his gratitude for the encyclical and reassuring the pontiff that he was positive Americanism could never be found in any corner of the Catholic Church in America![10]

Gibbons' letter reflects the sad fact that he was blinded by his love of America—so much so that he put America first and the Church second. And as one homilist told his congregation not too long ago,[11]

At the time Cardinal Gibbons received these words from the pope, no one dreamed that American Catholics would ever feel pressured by their fellow Americans to compromise their belief on the right to life or the sanctity of marriage. The pope maintained that the threat was not to Catholic morals, but to the faith. His fear was that American Catholics were beginning to dilute their faith in order to blend in with their Protestant neighbors, and that they were doing so with an ever increasing spirit of independence from Rome. He feared that the Catholic Church in America was becoming the American Catholic Church. And if Catholics were ready to compromise their faith today, they would be ready to compromise their morals tomorrow.

In hindsight, we can see with clear vision that Pope Leo XIII knew exactly what was at stake, and today he would be heartsick at what has come to pass. This is precisely why it is a good idea to pose the same questions now that Father Brankin posed to his audience in 2009,[12]

[I]s tonight's talk a history lesson or more of an examination of conscience? We as modern Americans must ask ourselves: In our bid to remain faithful Americans, have we forgotten what it means to be faithful Catholics?

Have we ever felt that because we are Americans, then that which we do—whether it be political or philosophical or moral is by definition right and good?

There is always a certain ambivalence or tension between the demands of faith and the demands of citizenship; but the Church calls us to account if we find ourselves going along to get along.

And it would seem that this attitude has perhaps resulted in the near triumph of the culture of death.

How else could we understand the almost total silence from the American episcopate when the pope a few years ago told Mexican politicians they would be automatically excommunicated if they promoted abortions; yet we heard no great American ecclesial from the bishops other than that they were uncomfortable with mixing politics and religion.

And what does that silent portion of our episcopate gain by saying nothing of substance to those who promote killing babies? Are they hoping for greetings of respect in the marketplace, or that they will be asked to sit at more head tables and at better banquets? Are they in breathless hope that they will finally be liked by the American establishment—if they would just be reasonable and peaceful about such enormities as abortion, mercy-killing and same sex marriage? . . .

. . . I wonder if we are losing the culture war because of the long-ago pact we made with our Protestant—and now secularist—masters—the Americanist pact where we promised we would not let our Catholic faith influence or contradict our citizenship. And it is clear we do not let our faith call our country to task.

We see the shameful spectacle every four years where the Catholic states in our country are also the most relentlessly pro-death and anti-love. I don't have to remind anyone here that it was Catholics—practicing and non-practicing—who helped elect the most pro-abortion president in our history.

Is it not clear from this last campaign and election that the bulk of the Catholic population doesn't really care anymore about these issues?

We talk always of the culture of life, but it is pretty evident we could not create a Catholic culture of life—even a Catholic party if we wanted to—because we really don't want to. It is more important for us as Americanists to be quiet and be accepted rather than to stand out and stand against the culture of death.

Who does not foresee the universal legalization of homosexual marriage in this country? And euthanasia—mercy-killing is making its dark way across this continent. Does anyone doubt that it will be the law of this land before too long?

And how did it get to this point? How is it that we as Catholics have lived in this country for more than 200 years and are now paralyzed, unable [to] put up more than token resistance to the modern nightmare? How is it that we who have had the benefit of the Church and her teachings—unchanged in 2000 years—and the incalculable grace of the sacraments—have not been able to change or mold or even tweak this culture into something resembling a culture of life—or a Catholic culture?

Plainly and simply we can blame Americanism—and the accumulated consequences of two hundred years' worth of believing that it was better to be a little more American and a little less Catholic.

Now, Americanism actually has very little to do with America and everything to do with what we believe about the relationship of the Church to America. The Americanist has no trouble seeing the Church as being subservient to the needs of the government.

Was it not only a month or so ago that about 15 to 20 Catholic politicians—including the vaunted pro-life Democrat Robert Casey—voted to start funding the killing of babies in poor countries? Why not! Public policy trumps private belief anytime they clash. Besides, what consequences could their bishops make them face that would outweigh the joy of being part of the American team?

We are Americans! We don't need revelation! We don't need a Church! We take a vote on what we think is moral or immoral in this country. This is the will of the people, the consent of the governed. It is if we say it is; and no foreign power like a pope or Church can contradict us. And make no mistake, we now hear that from Catholics.

Americanism has left us impotent as a Church—first its bishops and then us. And don't worry about the bishops: How did we answer as Catholics or as Americans—when moral questions were asked of us?

What did we do with the most fundamental moral principle—that we may not do evil even if good may come of it—when we heard of the firebombing of German cities—or the incineration of Hiroshima and Nagasaki—or when we shelled Belgrade or condoned torture in Iraq?

What did we say the first time we heard that we were stockpiling "weapons of mass destruction" which we would then sell to other nations?

We can rail against the nightmare of abortions and fetal farms and human-animal hybrid factories but not if we said nothing when the same cast of characters gave the world nuclear bombs and nerve gas, chemical and biological warfare.

Often enough we will hear it was moral to drop the bomb on Hiroshima and Nagasaki and kill 300,000 people . . . because it stopped the war and saved what they told us would be a million American lives.

And many American Catholics believed this was a just and moral action because it saved American lives. Well in that bombing did we not . . . forfeit the lives of a whole class of human beings simply because they were an obstacle to the rest of us?

And is this not the rationale for 50 million abortions—that for the sake of some of us others may die? And as loyal Americans if we defend such an attitude when it comes to war—how can we object to abortion?

This is how we go from Americanism to the culture of death—if we do it—and it is good for America—then who can complain? . . .

The love of the land and of our people is a healthy patriotism—and we must all be patriots. But there is a difference between being grateful for the blessings which God has granted us and concluding that America is chosen from among all other nations to lead the world.

Americanism creates a huge disconnect in our minds and hearts—between what we believe and how we act on those beliefs. In other words, if our beliefs make America uncomfortable, then we will not act on them.

Eventually, unwilling to act on those beliefs, we will no longer be capable of being shaped or formed or molded by them.

But we will certainly be shaped by other things—Hollywood, television, newspapers, Internet—popularity polls but not the Church.

This is how we have gotten to the point [that] American Catholics' morality is no different than that of the rest of the country. We do not want to be different.

We want contraception and abortion and embryo creation and destruction in equal measure to everyone else. And the Church is terrible and strident and unyielding if she should say no.

No! We are Americans! No one tells us no! When the Russian president has to comment on the lack of American morals, we know we have reached a special moment in history.

But we don't care what the Russian says. We don't care what the Holy Father says: we are free—we are not encumbered by anything.

Americanism as our own little heresy has become the essential element of the modern Catholic life and it still burrows its way into our hearts.

It has destroyed Catholic education and stalled the pro-life movement. It has overseen the universal sterilization of our families. It has dulled the minds of our adults and coarsened the lives of our youth.

Americanism as a habit of mind and attitude of life makes us ignore the worst excesses of globalism, capitalism, and secularism. We accept and defend free trade, unjust wars and blockades—and uncritically—and even when the pope preaches peace.

Sometimes we can look at such a lineup of social and moral disasters and try to convince ourselves that these evils are being done by aliens—this must be some other country doing such evil things. We don't do such things.

But we do do such things. It is our nation that has given birth to the global culture of death under which we groan and which we try to ignore.

Every time we American Catholics play nice—every time we say nothing for fear of being divisive or judgmental—every time we vote for the lesser of two evils, we are co-operating with our sworn enemy.

We can boast, as did Archbishop Ireland and Msgr. O'Connell, about how we are spreading liberty and freedom and American values to the world—democracy and fair-play—but we forget that we are actually at the service of other Americans—the ones who are really in charge of this country—who are spreading other values like abortion, contraception, pornography, sexual license, feminism, and homosexualism. And they also claim to be American.

It was our Constitution and our judges and our politicians and our media with the consent of our people that have made every perverse and deadly desire a basic human right. We can pretend all we want that this is Norman Rockwell's America—or *Little House on the Prairie*—but it isn't. And maybe it never was because the very sources, structures, and foundations of this country never included the Church of Christ.

And the day we—just regular ol' Catholics—bought into the notion that America was uniquely good and thankfully free of Catholic constraints was the day our Church's voice was stilled.

It is clear that Father Brankin exposes the soft underbelly of erosion that is occurring even now within the heart of the Catholic Church in America. Far too many Catholics have fallen prey to Americanism and are willingly leading others down the same error-filled path.

Today's American Catholic Church is grievously infected with Americanism. As we have seen, Americanism is an amalgamation of pluralism, modernism, atheism, Gnosticism, and Arianism. It is a terminal illness running rampant through the bloodstream of the Church. It must be taken seriously before it is beyond treatment.

While radiation therapy, chemotherapy, or surgery can sometimes alleviate cancer from the human body, the disease festering in the Catholic Church is far more lethal, for it is a condition of the soul—the very core of the Catholic Church in America.

The good news is that the healing process begins with you and your efforts to be a healing salve for your bishop, your priests, your fellow Catholics, and those you love. We should not fear exposing what is hurting our fellow Catholics—helping them see that the Church is not about politics but rather about witnessing to truth. Each of us can be a light shining the way to Christ, who loves us unconditionally.

As you will see in the next chapter, many ordained priests, not to mention the Catholic priesthood itself, are in need of divine intervention. This is why your prayers, your efforts, and your love for Christ can and will make a difference.

3

CHAPTER THREE:
The Catholic Priesthood in Chaos

Some American bishops have made a travesty of canon law and have sacrificed their priests' reputations to quell a crisis basically of their own making. In doing so, they jeopardize the souls entrusted to their care as well as their own. If they are so willing to sacrifice their own sons how can anyone take them seriously when they call for justice in society and preach the dignity of persons as a basic moral principle?

– Fr. Michael Orsi, "Abusive Bishops and the
   Destruction of Priests' Reputations"

More than three billion dollars later, the sex abuse scandals among members of the Catholic clergy still loom large, even though the cases date back many years. Because the media has enjoyed creating the feeding frenzy in an effort to further alienate Catholics and the public at large from the Church, many Americans have grown accustomed to lashing out at any Catholic priest heroic enough to wear his collar in public. Several priests have told me that people have made cruel comments such as, "You are a Catholic priest? You must be molesting children!"

As hurtful as this is to the priest who is profoundly committed to his vocation, it is occurring with increasing frequency. While such comments are oftentimes made in ignorance, they are uttered primarily because the media has made it a habit to repeatedly focus on sex abuse cases, the perpetrators, and the bishops involved without ever dealing frankly and honestly with all the facts. It's a circus one can attend on a nearly ongoing basis.

Silence and the sex abuse scandal

I am not suggesting, of course, that every bishop is free from blame. Far from it! But I am suggesting, as have many excellent Catholic apologists, that the media—being no lover of the Catholic Church in general—has found the salacious subject of sex abuse too tasty to be avoided. The reasons this is so are not pretty.

Monsignor Charles Pope's analysis of a 2010 *Washington Post* story, written for no apparent reason other than poking a finger in the eye of the Church, makes it clear why so many people are so ill-informed about the crisis—a crisis that is real, but that is rarely presented objectively.[1]

Pope tells his readers that the *Post* article[2]

> doesn't discuss the breadth of what the Church has done to protect kids nor does it show how much has been developed, including criminal background checks of all priests and lay staff who have any contact with youth. No mention is made of the reporting and accountability to third parties, that all abuse prevention training is up to date and that all requirements are met yearly in terms of legally recognized abuse prevention programs. Neither does the *Post* article make clear that historical data and names of all accused priests have been made public. All the men mentioned in the article have been named publicly before by the Church. Further, it is the policy of the archdiocese [of Washington D.C.] to immediately inform the local police of any charges of abuse, past or present. None of this is mentioned and the impression is allowed by the article that the archdiocese is somewhat cavalier about men who are barred from ministry and child safety, which is not true.

Clearly such bias, which borders on bigotry, does not sit well with faithful priests, but the *Post* and media like it couldn't care less about facts when it comes to Catholic bashing. The media gravitates toward organizations like Voice of the Faithful[3] and SNAP.[4]

Msgr. Pope, like the majority of orthodox Catholic priests who are faithful to their vocation and who do not abuse children—or anyone for that matter—cannot combat the type of railing that persists in the media. The reason that this is so leaves me wondering about Catholic bishops.

Rather than hosting press conferences and airing the truth about Catholic doctrine, sex abuser priests, and what the Church is doing and has done about it, bishops have, for the most part, remained silent. They have sent their spokespeople out to talk about particular problems, but only when the media is asking questions. The entire concept of going on the offense instead of playing defense has not occurred to most bishops.

By hiding in the rectory and failing to demand accuracy from the news reporting community, the bishops are failing their priests. The exaggerations being enunciated go unaddressed by the very people with the moral authority to set the record straight. This is why even the pope himself has come under fire.

As recently as April of 2011, the famously liberal American Catholic newspaper, the *National Catholic Reporter*, editorialized on Pope Benedict XVI, giving credence to the rumor that the pope had participated in a cover-up of priests accused of sexual abuse.[5] The paper "demanded" that the pope answer its questions. Such flippancy from the *Reporter* is not shocking considering the fact that the *Reporter* is friendly to those within the Church who are immersed in Catholic deconstruction. Facts have no place in such circles. This is part of the reason why even the pope is not exempt from scandalous accusations.

But it should also be a motivational factor inspiring bishops to defend the vicar of Christ! However, no such action has been reported because no such action has been taken.

This is part of the reason why even the average Catholic is not immune from the harm caused when the media is dishing dirt that goes unaddressed by the bishops. If the local pulpit is silent and the hierarchy is not speaking out as a united body of shepherds, falsehood goes unaddressed and mayhem ensues.

Sexual abuse and homosexuality in the priesthood

The media has not been honest or fair about many things, including the fact that a direct connection between homosexuals in the priesthood and the sexual abuse of minors has been made. Even though the Vatican has issued, and subsequently renewed, its instruction that there must not be admission of homosexuals into the priesthood—including the seminaries—there is evidence everywhere that few are listening. As Father Paul Shaughnessy, SJ, wrote a decade ago, the problem is "quite simply, those entrusted to fix what is broken are broken themselves."[6] While he was referring to the Jesuit order[7] in particular, the same can be said for the priesthood at large.

The USCCB's National Review Board report of 2004 issued a finding that stated, "That 81 percent of the reported victims of child sexual abuse by Catholic clergy were boys shows that the crisis was characterized by homosexual behavior."[8] This finding was confirmed in 2009 by Archbishop Silvano Tomasi, the Vatican's representative at the UN, who said, "Of all priests involved in the abuses, 80 to 90 percent belong to this sexual orientation minority which is sexually engaged with adolescent boys between the ages of 11 and 17."[9] The report continues, "His [Tomasi's] statement is backed up by a report commissioned by the U.S. bishops that found that in the overwhelming majority of cases the clergy involved were homosexuals, with 81 percent of victims being adolescent males."

Even though this connection has been made, there is evidence that the actual problematic nature of homosexuals in the priesthood has not been dealt with definitively by many U.S. Catholic bishops. In addition, many good priests who might otherwise have had the ability to clear their good names have been railroaded for what can only be described as suspicious reasons. Father Orsi writes,[10]

> This violates justice. It can be said that when a bishop allows this to happen he has been negligent in his duties since he is the chief magistrate and shepherd of his diocese. As one bishop caustically said to me regarding his power in the diocese, "I hold all the marbles here." And, unfortunately this is true. He then proclaimed, "We have less than zero tolerance here!" Less than justice? It may be that he stands condemned by his own words.

Speaking of justice, addressing the questionable allegations made by a disgruntled employee against Father John Corapi, SOLT, retired bishop Rene Gracida wrote,[11]

> It is a matter of justice, the disciplining of priests accused of sexual misconduct with an adult, but unfortunately grave injustice is frequently done to individual priests and to the Catholic priesthood by individual bishops and religious superiors.
>
> The public controversy over the announcement of the accusations against Father John Corapi, SOLT, and his suspension from exercising his priestly ministry offers an opportunity to reflect on the flawed procedure apparently being followed in too many dioceses of the United States these days in the case of a priest accused of sexual misconduct not involving minors.[12] The procedure is flawed because it inflicts grave injustice on the priest and serves as a deterrent to young men thinking of offering themselves as candidates for the priesthood.
>
> The procedure operates something like this. A person accuses a priest of sexual misconduct (again, not involving a minor). The priest is

immediately suspended from active exercise of his priestly ministry while an investigation is launched into the truth or falsity of the accusations.

There is no need for a public announcement to be made that gives the name of the priest and the fact of the accusation and the suspension, and yet, all too often such a public announcement is made. Such public announcement by a diocese almost always results in media exploitation of the news in a sensational manner to the detriment of the Catholic Church and its priesthood. It seems that rarely, if ever, is mention made in the announcement of the name of the accuser.

The investigation may take days or months or years to complete. In the meantime the priest's reputation is effectively destroyed and perhaps he is "thrown out on the street" with no means of support. The accuser, on the other hand, enjoys anonymity and suffers no loss of reputation or negative material consequences and, in the case of an accusation later proven to have been false, the injustice to [the] priest is great.

In cases where the priest is accused of having used force (rape or some other form of involuntary abuse) there is some justification for not publishing the name of the accuser. But, where there is reason to believe that the alleged sexual misconduct was effected through mutual consent there is no justification for not publishing the name of the accuser.

Under the present procedure it is too easy for a person to allege sexual misconduct (again not involving minors) for a variety of possible unworthy motives: revenge, hope for monetary gain, hostility to the Catholic faith, etc. Such is reported to have been the case of the accusation against Father Corapi. The only safe way to guard against damaging the reputation of individual priests and the Catholic priesthood in general is to not publish the name of an accused priest until an investigation has proved beyond doubt the guilt of the priest.

Father Corapi is not the first man to be placed in such a position. Because Corapi made a public statement, many Catholics are disappointed and some have even suggested that he acted arrogantly. I cannot know whether such opinions are justified or not, but as was the case with the original accusations, it's all speculation and innuendo. Two things are certain.

The first is that anyone who was aware of his strong voice in defense of Catholic doctrine can pray for Father Corapi; pray earnestly, relying always on the Lord's justice.

The second is that the Father Corapi example ought to give every bishop pause, not because of his yet unproven guilt or innocence, but because his status as a priest once the allegations were made was immediately the brunt of criticism. In fact, the statements of his accuser appeared to receive more attention than the 20-year record of this Society of Our Lady of the Most Holy Trinity priest.[13]

"Innocent until proven guilty" should be the position taken by any bishop or religious superior until the facts are well-known, investigated, and privately evaluated.

So why aren't the bishops, as a unified body, issuing a statement similar to Bishop Gracida's on the broader question of dealing with allegations of sexual improprieties against priests? What could there be to stop them from demanding justice for their priests and fairness in the media?

Catholic confusion

All of this lack of continuity is magnified among Catholics in general who either do not know what the Church teaches about homosexuality or arrogantly deny that the truth exists on this subject. Msgr. Pope suggests that the confusion among Catholics in things as fundamental as the fact that the practice of homosexuality is sinful is "likely due to confusion brought on by a loud culture and a quiet pulpit."[14]

When suspicions abound regarding the moral high ground previously assumed to be occupied by priests, and the media is painting them all as potential sexual abusers, the climate is hostile to the priest who sets forth the truth about the practice of homosexuality, abortion, contraception, or any of the other "issues" that the media loves to characterize as part and parcel of the Church's "insensitivity." Such heroic priests have to contend with not only the refusal of their parishioners to learn the truth, but the blatant examples the media provides of those who choose not to live up to what is expected of them as ordained priests and bishops.

In the Archdiocese of San Francisco, for example, Archbishop George Niederauer is a master confusion creator. When gay activists known as the Sisters of Perpetual Indulgence—fully dressed in their bizarre garb—approached Niederauer for Holy Communion, he gave it to them. Once the story became public and Catholics who were up in arms about this scandal made their voices heard, the archbishop was forced to apologize for what he had done, but claimed he did not recognize the activists.[15]

Niederauer might have received a pass on this had there not been other instances that raised red flags as well. He is reported to have liked and been "deeply moved" by the homosexually-oriented movie, *Brokeback Mountain*,[16] and he approved a compromise measure in his archdiocese that permits Catholic Charities adoption workers to work with Family Builders by Adoption—an agency that places children with homosexual couples.[17]

In this latter case, he apparently thought that by making this arrangement he could absolve the diocese from being directly involved in arranging adoptions for homosexual couples. However, the taint of collaboration is obvious.

In another example, Bishop Terry Steib, of the Diocese of Memphis, Tennessee, allowed a priest who was credibly accused of child sexual abuse to minister on a trip to Mexico.[18] Steib sent a letter of good standing to Church officials in Mexico and later said that his letter of recommendation had been a "mistake." But whether he really thinks he made a mistake is unclear since Bishop Steib said that the priest in question was falsely accused.

Steib did eventually send the priest for counseling, but the priest remains pastor of a parish and, to this day, the record has not been clarified.[19] Whether or not the "falsely accused" priest was an offender may never be known even though the bishop could have clarified the matter one way or the other.

The pattern that emerges from such incidents is but another example of the baffling signals being transmitted by bishops. The end result is that a shepherd's moral authority is being spent foolishly because he chooses to act out of a distorted type of tolerance based on what is perceived to be culturally acceptable. Why else would we see flexibility in lieu of hard and fast teachings when addressing something such as the practice of homosexuality and its progeny?

The bright side

The good news for the Church is that the current crop of seminarians appears to be pregnant with men who truly want to serve God instead of the fashionably American concept of what it means to be a priest. According to a recent survey, 50 percent were actually discouraged by their parents from becoming priests and yet discerned a vocation and followed it into the seminary anyway.[20] In today's climate, one can understand the sincere concern parents would have about the verbal abuse and discrimination their sons would suffer if indeed the priesthood were chosen; yet in order to turn the tide and restore the Church in this country, strong, dedicated priests are a necessity.

Examining the United States' upward trend when it comes to young men who are responding positively to the priestly vocation, it is realistic to say that, where inspiring bishops and holy vocation directors are found, a dramatic increase in vocations will also be found. *Catholic World Report* made this evident in a recent report,[21]

> Typical among these "great men" is Father Thomas Richter, vocation director of the Diocese of Bismarck, the second most vocation-rich diocese in the nation in 2005 (up from 24th in 2003 and 12th in 2004). Bismarck bishop Paul Zipfel told *CWR* last year that Father Richter's plan has been "to visit each parish and mission and to preside at all the Sunday Masses and speak about vocations to the priesthood." In doing so, according to the diocesan website, Father Richter is seeking—and finding—men with a . . .
>
> . . . deep love for the Eucharist, for the Mass and for the Church. They are men of fidelity; they want an undivided heart for Christ. Their heroes are Pope John Paul II and Mother Teresa of Calcutta. They are not interested in fluff or watered down teaching; they loathe mediocrity. . . . They are prayerful. Along with daily Mass, daily rosary, praying the breviary, they spend an hour each day in quiet prayer. They want to teach the truths of the Catholic faith. They love to explain and help people understand the faith. Most of them went through a religious education system that left much to be desired, but at some point they were taught the reasons behind our faith and it changed them. . . . They are men in Christ, men of the Church, and men for others.

Clearly there is hope for the future within the context of the Catholic priesthood. There was a time when the Catholic priest was one of the most respected vocations on Earth. It's time to get back to that state of respect—in fact, it is time to demand it. If it is a matter of supply and demand, then we must encourage the young to consider this calling and we must ensure that those responsible for the selection process respect it. Political correctness has no place in a shepherd's moral authority. Prayers are in great need, but so is direct action.

Catholics are called to faith and reason. One place to start is by supporting seminarians of character and seminaries of good repute in the spiritual formation of our future spiritual leaders. Likewise, we must call to task, withhold financial support, and proactively resist orders and seminaries that diminish and dilute Catholic precepts.

The next thing that is needed is a renewal among bishops—a renewal that must begin with a commitment to be men of the Eucharist rather than cultural kingpins.

4

CHAPTER FOUR:
Kingpins

Christ said to his disciples: "[T]he Son of Man did not come to be served but to serve and to give his life as a ransom for many."

– Matthew 20:28

A kingpin is someone who is perceived to be the chief individual or, in layman's terms, the boss. In a Catholic sense, that is one way of approaching the authority a Catholic bishop possesses. He is the moral kingpin, or leader, of his priests and the Catholic lay people in his diocese. He is responsible for nurturing and feeding their spiritual hunger. At least that is how it should be. In this chapter I will provide examples of how that role can be a blessing or a curse depending on how the bishop presents Catholic teaching by example and in word. The bishop who stumbles when it comes to Catholic doctrine can create problems for those who should be able to look to him for guidance, inspiration, and education.

Bishops who fall prey to worldly expectations rather than the call to holiness that is foundational to their vocation can set examples that confuse and alienate Catholics. Such a prelate seems to ignore his role as spiritual minister to God's people in deference to other agendas. Below are a few concrete examples from the archives of American Catholic history.

Bishop Gerald Kicanas

Let's start with Bishop Gerald Kicanas, known for many things throughout his term of power in Arizona. A July 2008 Matt Abbott column quotes commentator Tom Roeser:[1]

> "Last month Kicanas received an award named for . . . who else? . . . the late Joseph Cardinal Bernardin whose departure from this world was serenaded by the Gay Men's Chorus at Mass . . . for 'efforts in handling the sexual abuse both locally and nationally.' The Common Ground initiative formed by Bernardin which selects recipients for the honor described Kicanas as 'a champion of dialogue on contentious issues.'"

Further, Bishop Kicanas attended a pro-life prayer service in February of 2008. He extended his thanks to those in attendance, telling them how much he appreciated their staunch opposition to abortion and, yes, racism! Shocked into speechlessness, one of the attendees wrote to me expressing concern. Apparently Bishop Kicanas, reflecting sentiments from a recent USCCB document, views abortion and racism as equally offensive.[2] Yet the difference between the two is clear—or at least it should be clear. While it is true that racism is an example of extremely bad behavior that should never be condoned, abortion is an act of killing. The two should not be equated as having the same moral gravity. A pro-life prayer gathering for the souls of mothers who have aborted their own children is not the proper place to bring in other social concerns. The people in attendance are there to mourn the deaths of babies and the sadness that accompanies this, not to contemplate the problematic nature of racism.

However, a bishop or group of Catholic leaders that is focused on current cultural questions involving tolerance and the like will not be as concerned about guiding his people along the path to holiness as much as he will in mouthing platitudes that have little to do with Catholic doctrine. Kicanas is one such bishop.

Bishop Blase Cupich

Another bishop who focused on racism prior to the 2008 election was Rapid City, South Dakota's bishop, Blase Cupich, who wrote in *America* magazine,[3]

> In any election people have many reasons to support one candidate or to oppose another. Some of these reasons may be wise and good, some not so good, and others simply wrong. . . . Voting for a candidate solely because of that candidate's support for abortion or against him or her solely on the basis of his or her race is to promote an intrinsic evil. To do so consciously is indeed sinful. That is behavior incompatible with being a Christian. To allow racism to reign in our hearts and to determine our choice in this solemn moment for our nation is to cooperate with one of the great evils that has afflicted our society. In the words of *Brothers and Sisters to Us*, "It mocks the words of Jesus, 'Treat others the way you would have them treat you.'"

Bishop Cupich makes my point for me when he writes that if a person allows racism to reign in his heart, then we are cooperating with one of the great evils of our time. However, the heart blackened by commitment to racist tendencies is not obvious to anyone; we cannot meet someone on the street and see his racist attitudes.

On the other hand, we can see with both eyes the tragedy of killing the preborn and the devastation such an act wreaks on the survivors.

Racism and abortion are NOT the same.

The problem of using racism as the equivalent to abortion is obvious. As we have said, the act of abortion is an intrinsic evil, but the *Catechism of the Catholic Church* does not define racism in those terms; in fact, the word racism is not in the *Catechism*. This is not to say that racism is not a sin against the principle of justice; of course it is. But it is a private sin. It is not in any way, shape, or form the same as killing an innocent baby prior to birth or, for that matter, after birth—even though the United States Conference of Catholic Bishops said it is in its 2008 pronouncement made after the election.[4]

Bishop Howard Hubbard

In January of 2010 we learned that, "Bishop Howard Hubbard of Albany, who serves as chairman of the United States Conference of Catholic Bishops' Committee on International Justice and Peace, has approved a proposal by diocesan Catholic Charities to distribute free needles to drug abusers in the hope of preventing the spread of AIDS."[5]

The report went on to say that an $83,000 van filled with syringes was to be parked in two different neighborhoods and that Catholic Charities would assist in the distribution. This flies in the face of the official statement the American bishops affirmed in a 1987 statement, "The Many Faces of AIDS": "[A]bstinence outside of marriage and fidelity within marriage as well as the avoidance of intravenous drug abuse are the only morally correct and medically sure ways to prevent the spread of AIDS."[6]

Sometimes audacity is simply too much to bear! Coming from a Catholic bishop, this sends all the wrong messages.

Bishop Lori and the Connecticut Catholic Conference

Our next example of muddled thinking concerns a situation that erupted in the state of Connecticut a few years ago involving not one, but all, of the bishops in that state. The Connecticut Catholic Conference of Bishops jointly discussed the question of using the morning-after pill as "treatment" in cases of criminal rape. To quote Bishop Lori's October 2007 blog,[7]

> There is uncertainty about how Plan B works. Its effect is to prevent fertilization of the ovum. Some

believe, however, that in rare instances Plan B can render the lining of the uterus inhospitable to the fertilized ovum which must implant in it in order to survive and grow; many other experts dispute this. For their part, the bishops of Connecticut felt it was best not only to administer the standard FDA-approved pregnancy test, but also an ovulation test. However, this course of action was only a prudential judgment, not a matter of settled Church teaching and practice. Other bishops and moral theologians hold that a pregnancy test alone suffices. Indeed, the Church does not teach that it is intrinsically evil to administer Plan B without first giving an ovulation test or that those who do so are committing an abortion.

The problem with this position is two-fold. First and perhaps most important is that if there truly is a concern that the Plan B morning-after pill can abort a baby, then the best Catholic position is to pronounce that, when doubt is involved, the Church opts to defend life. Therefore, there is no circumstance under which a potentially abortive chemical can be used. Further, in October 2000 (seven years before the Connecticut statement), the Vatican's Pontifical Academy for Life made it perfectly clear that Catholics must object to the use of this pill in any circumstance due to the potential for abortion by chemical means.[8]

Why weren't the Connecticut bishops aware of this Vatican pronouncement? Why didn't they take the Catholic position instead of what was clearly the politically motivated position taken just days before a new state law went into effect?[9] At the time there was pressure from the state to bring Catholic hospitals in line with state policy regarding morning-after pills and their use as treatment for rape. The Connecticut bishops could have mounted a legal challenge to this discriminatory law since it was used as a hammer to thwart Catholic medical ethics. Making excuses for approving a clearly abortive drug—a drug that is not proven to be safe for patients—is ludicrous. Plan B and other pills like it do nothing to serve the best interests of the women who may ingest it, or the preborn children who may die. The Connecticut bishops' approval of the drug defies logic and contradicts Catholic teaching—which is what bishops are called to teach.

As of the writing of this book, no changes have been made in the Connecticut Catholic Conference policy. The state won; Catholics lost.

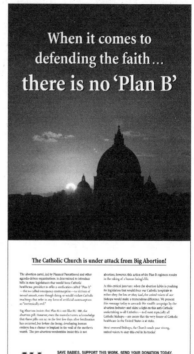

ALL shone a light on the pro-abortion lie that Plan B is not abortion in its 2007 "Plan B" ad.

Bishop Robert Morlino

Bishop Robert Morlino, on the other hand, took a completely different approach when the Wisconsin Conference of Catholic Bishops adopted a position of "neutrality" on the new state law requiring hospitals to provide the abortive morning-after pill to victims of sexual assault. In a letter dated December 17, 2007, he told state lawmakers to oppose the law in question, stating,[10]

"The hoped-for effect of the Wisconsin Catholic Conference's earlier stance of neutrality on this bill was to protect women who are the victims of rape, while also protecting the possible preborn human being, by affirming the necessary conscience exemption for institutions and individuals with regard to the appropriate testing, so as to avoid abortifacient [chemical abortion-causing] emergency contraception."

He adds: "It is my judgment as bishop of Madison that the earlier position of neutrality did not have its hoped-for effect, and so it is now moot, and this neutrality position has now expired. . . .

Our conference's neutrality stance has also unintentionally provoked scandal among Catholics who have been persuaded by statements in the media that we are becoming less fervent in our defense of the dignity of preborn human life."

Bishop Jerome Listecki

A few days later, Bishop Jerome Listecki of the Diocese of Lacrosse, Wisconsin, followed suit, suggesting to us that bishops can stand up for truth rather than pander to what is politically expected.[11]

Bishops Robert Morlino and Jerome Listecki stand as exemplars of true shepherds.

Cardinal Francis George

But as we have seen, not all bishops have such strength of conviction when the rubber hits the road. For example, the Archdiocese of Chicago has a different problem, or should I say, set of problems, brought about by confusing leadership at the top. One of the most powerful cardinals in the Catholic Church is Cardinal Francis George of Chicago. But the cardinal has done things that are mind-numbing. For example, he looked the other way when Hillary Rodham

Clinton visited Chicago to keynote a luncheon hosted to benefit the Mercy Home for Boys and Girls. The home, "an organization run by Catholic priests, invited Mrs. Clinton despite the Church's prohibition of giving pro-abortion political figures a public forum to speak."[12]

The Clinton debacle sent mixed messages to the faithful. It was clear that the cardinal, for whatever reason, either avoided addressing the situation or ignored it. As a result, seeds of uncertainty were sown; these seeds contribute to doubt among Catholic people. Catholics who observe such events wonder how serious the Church really is when it comes to protecting the souls of its people and exposing evil when it arises. The evil we address here is not Hillary herself, but her pro-abortion philosophy which generates death for preborn babies.

Another dilemma in Chicago involves a particular pastor. We asked the cardinal on numerous occasions why the pastor of St. Sabina's Parish, Father Michael Pfleger, who was consistently inviting pro-abortion leaders to speak in his parish, was not disciplined. For example, when we learned that Al Sharpton was going to speak at the parish we immediately wrote to both Pfleger and Cardinal George, begging both of them to assure us that Sharpton would be cancelled. No response to our request was received and Sharpton spoke.[13]

In 2010, just prior to the elections, Fox News' Bill O'Reilly got into the thick of the Pfleger circus when he found that Pfleger was to be honored as a "living legend" alongside Louis Farrakhan and Jeremiah Wright. O'Reilly stated, "[W]hat is a Catholic priest doing standing with Farrakhan and Wright? Catholics follow Jesus, a man who preached peace and love for all men. My staff called the archbishop of Chicago, Cardinal Francis George, for comment. But he doesn't have a comment. Are you kidding me? I'm a Catholic—I'd like to know what's going on!"[14]

In March 2011, Cardinal George appeared to finally have had enough and he requested that Pfleger move from St. Sabina Parish to the position of principal at Leo Catholic

High School; Pfleger said he would leave the Church rather than accept the appointment![15] This brings up two questions.

Why would the cardinal take an intransigently antagonistic priest and place him in the position of principal in any Catholic high school? And, further, why hasn't Pfleger been, at the very least, moved out of any position of influence due to the ongoing scandals he has created? It is no secret that Pfleger unabashedly provided ringing endorsements to President Barack Obama and made numerous national television appearances on the subject.

And the Church's response to this is promoting the priest to the position of principal of a Catholic high school?

In late April 2011, Pfleger finally drove Cardinal George to the brink and the cardinal suspended the priest, saying in a letter to Pfleger, "If that is your attitude, you have already left the Catholic Church and are therefore not able to pastor a Catholic parish."[16] Two days after the suspension, the cardinal explained to the media that he was hoping to meet with Pfleger in the near future.[17] And lo and behold, as if by some sort of nefarious magic, Cardinal George has since reinstated Pfleger to his post as pastor of St. Sabina's Parish in Chicago.[18] And that's that!

Cardinal Roger Mahony (retired)

There's also the case of recently retired Cardinal Roger Mahony who spoke with the media in 2009 about whether or not he thought abortion should be funded under Obama's health care law. Rather than setting forth an absolute no, he told the interviewer that the "issue" of abortion was "way beyond my field." He went on to explain that his area of expertise is immigration.[19]

Such senseless comments from a prince of the Church send a message to the public that Catholic leaders differ on a teaching as crucial as abortion. By extension, this sort of message breeds ambivalence among Catholics who often come to the conclusion that if the bishops don't agree on abortion—or know that it should not be funded by the government—why should they care? Is this why Catholics abort their children along the same percentage lines as the general population?

Bishop Tod Brown

Further, there is the example of the things that occur right under the noses of Catholic bishops and apparently without their opposition. In Bishop Tod Brown's diocese in Orange, California, a very questionable speaker was invited into St. Simon and Jude Parish in September of 2010. Mary Ann Kreitzer, editor of *Les Femmes* newsletter, wrote,[20]

> St. Simon and Jude Catholic Parish in Huntington Beach (Diocese of Orange under Bishop Tod Brown) is hosting the infamous Fr. Richard Sparks on September 17 (they're advertising him on their website). For those unfamiliar with this disgraceful excuse for a priest, you can read some of his blasphemies by visiting the websites linked at the end. These outrages include suggesting that Mary and Joseph may have "fondled" each other and Jesus may have necked with Mary Magdalene. He also tells audiences he likes women's breasts and he's got a bigger thing than Mel Gibson. He says, "I'm not anti-choice," which in my interpretation of the English language means he's pro-choice! He calls the Catholic Church a "denomination" and idolizes dissenters Fr. Charlie Curran and Fr. Richard McBrien.
>
> Even worse than his blasphemous talks to adults is his sex ed series, *Growing in Love*, which is aimed at children. It includes teaching third graders about mutual masturbation, fourth graders about oral sex, and seventh graders about sado-masochism, sex toys, anal sex, and bestiality. Fr. Sparks' fixation on sex and his desire to teach children about its most depraved practices is chillingly reminiscent of the actions of priests engaged in child abuse. If a dirty old man in a raincoat gave children the information in Fr. Sparks' books, [he] could be arrested for abuse.

Perhaps, you might ask, there was a mistake and Sparks was cancelled? Not at all. Sparks came and poisoned the minds of "seminar" attendees. Did Bishop Brown not realize that Sparks would be speaking from a perspective at odds with Catholic teaching? Did he care? We do not know; all we do know is that once again that virus of dissent was spread around a vineyard that should be cultivated rather than denied the irrigation of truth and proper teaching.

Bishop Matthew Clark

Bishop Matthew Clark of Rochester, New York—described in some circles as a moderate—gave an interview to his local newspaper in which the subject of his "welcoming" attitude toward homosexuals was discussed. Specifically, there was a question about homosexuals in the priesthood. Having been asked for his opinion, Clark opined,[21]

> I know some magnificent gay priests. If they are openly gay in terms of living a lifestyle that is incompatible with their basic commitments, we have to intervene.
>
> But I have always tried to be open to such candidates. There was, as you know, a lot of attention given to that by the Holy See [the Vatican] over the years, and one of their statements left the impression that under no circumstances could a person of gay orientation be ordained a priest. And that's not so.
>
> If a person's sense of himself as a gay individual inevitably leads him to campaign against the Church's formal teachings or live a lifestyle that is upsetting to the community or scandalous, such a person would not be an apt candidate for the priesthood.

Clark misrepresents the Vatican's position on homosexuals in the priesthood, apparently thinking that to repeat sound Catholic teaching might appear too harsh to the secular media. The facts are clear and Clark should have repeated what the Vatican sets forth, namely, referring back to earlier Church teaching that maintains that it is necessary to clearly state "that the Church, while profoundly respecting the persons in question cannot admit to the seminary or to holy orders those who practice homosexuality, present deep-seated homosexual tendencies or support the so-called 'gay culture.'"[22]

Had Clark simply provided that statement in addition to the Vatican warning that if a candidate for the seminary has any type of homosexual tendencies, "such tendencies must be clearly overcome at least three years before ordination to the diaconate," the Vatican's position would have been clarified for the interviewer.[23]

Obviously had Clark used the Vatican's precise words, his interview might have been a bit less conciliatory to the homosexual community, but it also would have been straightforward. Such clarity is always helpful. But one must recall that Clark was voted one of the most "gay friendly" bishops in 2004.[24]

Archbishop Favalora

In the Archdiocese of Miami, the University of St. Thomas featured a program of spiritual exercises given by Franciscan homosexual-activist priest, Father Richard Rohr. When Catholics protested the presence of this priest with letters and phone calls to Archbishop Favalora and the president of the university, there was silence. But LifeSiteNews reporter Eric Giunta provided details on a pattern that suggests why there was "no comment" from the archbishop:[25]

> [T]he Miami Archdiocese is not new to sponsoring such events. In February 2009, the Miami Gay Men's Chorus held their season premier concert at a Miami Beach Catholic Church. Earlier that same month, Saint Thomas University's School of Theology Ministry featured a guest lecture by "ecospiritualist" Sr. Miriam Therese MacGillis, a Dominican nun who promotes goddess-worship. In 2007, LSN reported Barry University's granting

a theology award to another notorious goddess-worshipping feminist Dominican nun, Sr. Elizabeth Johnson.

Two of the archdiocese's parishes, Saint Anthony and Saint Maurice, are listed as "gay friendly" in a directory published by the Conference of Catholic Lesbians. Both of the archdiocese's universities, Barry and St. Thomas are also categorized as "gay friendly" by the conference.

There are many sad stories of how disastrous the silence and/or denial of the bishops can be to the people of the Church. A couple of examples may help the reader see why it is sometimes difficult to know who is really on the side of teaching right and wrong.

The fruits of flawed leadership

One personal story came to me in 2007 from a woman I will call Jane. Her firsthand experience makes my point:

Dear Judie,

While I understand the need to not offend can come from a genuine desire to be pastoral, it is not helping those of us who are or were suffering in silence in the pews. I am a post-abortive woman of 30 years and a Catholic for 28 of those years. The first time I walked into the Catholic Church as an unbaptized woman of 19, the priest very firmly spoke of the sin of abortion. He was direct, unambiguous, kind, and respectful. I looked at my Catholic friend (and future husband) and wondered aloud . . . *Could the priest read my heart? How did he know I was post abortive?*

The following week, **at the edict of the local bishop, he was ordered to apologize for his homily and told never to mention abortion again**! I was very confused. But it was too late because the priest had told me something that in my heart I already knew—that abortion was a sin.

No taking back a word already spoken, a spent arrow. . . . What happened after that was the beginning of my many years of recovery from the abortion I had when I was 18.

It is flabbergasting that a bishop of the Church would use his authority and his credibility to thwart any future words of truth spoken by a priest to his flock. What is it about valid Catholic teaching that drives some of these bishops crazy? The answer is, at least in part, that there are bishops who are consistently presenting a paradox by what they say versus what they permit. In the process, the good priest who understands what he is called to do as part of his vocation to the priesthood is left reprimanded for doing good.

In case this isn't clear, examine the case of a pro-abortion Dominican nun in the Archdiocese of Chicago. When Sister Donna Quinn was reprimanded by her order for her role as an escort who would take pregnant women into an abortion clinic, her retort was not unexpected. First, she celebrated the defeat of a so-called pro-life amendment to the Obama health care reform bill, then she proceeded to write her supporters stating that "faithful and respectful dissent is vital to the life of the Church."[26]

In addition, Quinn, who also publicly supports homosexual rights, was observed at a Catholic Mass receiving Communion, taking a portion of the Eucharist she received in her hand, and giving it to a Rainbow Sash member who had been refused Communion by the priest celebrating the Mass. Father John Malloy says that the fact that Quinn "is still allowed to call herself a Dominican is a scandal, and an insult to the true followers of St. Dominic."[27]

Indeed! After behaving in a manner so contrary to Catholic Church teaching, this nun was not excommunicated, nor was she was instructed to make a public apology for her actions. To this day she remains a full-fledged member of a religious order.

Where's the justice?

True heroes

Lest the reader be left with the impression that all kingpins are at odds with the Church from one perspective or another, there is plenty of good news and solid Catholic commitment among bishops who love their vocation, their flock, and the Lord's truth.

Baker, Oregon, shepherd Robert Vasa delivered a stirring homily to Catholic physicians, focusing on their role as Catholics first and doctors second, saying,[28]

> In our subjectivist, relativistic age which often masquerades as an age of pure reason it is tempting to put a lot more faith in science and reason than it is to put faith in God. . . . Yet, both are acts of faith and both are directed toward a perceived god. For much of our society that god is science or government or technology. For us there is a greater God and a greater good.

By reminding doctors of their obligation as ministers to God and the people they serve, Bishop Vasa inspired appreciation for the faith rather than doubt and confusion.

Lincoln, Nebraska's bishop, Fabian Bruskewitz, is another example of inspiration, as noted in an interview regarding the reasons why Catholic priests must speak clearly on the subject of homosexuality.[29]

> "Caution and prudence are important, but I don't think they should be excuses for not properly speaking when speaking is necessary or extremely important pastorally," the bishop told LifeSite-News. . . .
>
> He said priests may be reluctant to address homosexuality because "there's a lot of intimidation in various places," but he stressed that the wide promotion of openness to homosexuality in our culture demands that they present the Catholic Church's teachings clearly. "In a culture in which this kind of activity is broadcast all over,

I think it's important that the teaching of the Church be clear and precise," he said.

"Homosexual acts are intrinsically evil, and if one does them with full knowledge and consent, they're mortal sins and place one's eternal salvation in the gravest of jeopardy," he added.

Delaware's bishop, Francis Malooly, courageously castigated vice president Joe Biden when he was a candidate for vice president, saying publicly,[30]

"Sen. Joe Biden presents a seriously erroneous picture of Catholic teaching on abortion. He said, 'I know that my Church has wrestled with this for 2,000 years,' and claimed repeatedly that the Church has a nuanced view of the subject that leaves a great deal of room for uncertainty and debate. This is simply incorrect. The teaching of the Church is clear and not open to debate. Abortion is a grave sin because it is the wrongful taking of an innocent human life."

In 2010, Charles Chaput, then archbishop of Denver, inspired Catholic cadets at the U.S. Air Force Academy when he challenged them with a vision of whom they must aspire to be,[31]

Knighthood is an institution with very deep roots in the memory of the Church. Nearly 900 years ago, one of the great monastic reformers of the Church, St. Bernard of Clairvaux, described the ideal Christian knights as Godly men who *shun every excess in clothing and food. They live as brothers in joyful and sober company (with) one heart and one soul. . . . There is no distinction of persons among them, and deference is shown to merit rather than to noble blood. They rival one another in mutual consideration, and they carry one another's burdens, thus fulfilling the law of Christ."* . . .

The Church needs men and women of courage and Godliness today more than at any time in her history. So does this extraordinary country we call home in this world; a nation that still has an immense reservoir of virtue, decency, and people of good will. This is why the Catholic ideal of knighthood, with its demands of radical discipleship, is still alive and still needed. The essence of Christian knighthood remains the same: *sacrificial service rooted in a living Catholic faith.*

A new "spirit of knighthood" is what we need now—unselfish, tireless, devoted disciples willing to face derision and persecution for Jesus Christ. We serve our nation best by serving God first, and by proving our faith with the example of our lives.

Other inspiring kingpins include Cardinal Raymond Burke, who is now serving the Church in the Vatican; Bishop Robert W. Finn; Archbishop Joseph Naumann; and so many more. There are remarkable bishops who always place themselves at the service of truth and the souls of their people. For that we are most particularly grateful and we applaud their heroic virtue.

In summary

The inconsistencies, however, among those we have noted and others not mentioned do great damage to the Church. Folks often question why Catholic churches appear so much emptier, Catholic schools are being closed, and the teachings seem to be bandied about in the media like they were nothing more than political topics. But frankly, Catholic teaching is addressed by the press more than it is from the pulpit—and that has to change. With vocations barely maintaining themselves, it is time for every Catholic to do his part by figuring out why this is happening, recommending positive actions to our good bishops, and praying that every bishop will be a kingpin in the image of Christ whose power is indeed the only power that matters.

In a Church that stands in the very same place today on the question of doctrine as it did more than 2000 years ago, there should be strength and cohesiveness, not disparity and despair.

Yet as we consider those bishops who appear to be confusing the public by what they say and what they do, you have to wonder if maybe they have bureaucrats advising them in ways that are not at all helpful to a bishop's understanding of the situations at hand. We will address that in the next chapter.

How to make a difference

But right now, let's consider this quote by Sir Edmund Burke: "When bad men combine, the good must associate; else they will fall one by one, an unpitied sacrifice in a contemptible struggle."[32]

There is no better way to steer the American Catholic Church back onto a righteous path than to visibly and vocally advocate for those leaders who stand for a righteous Church. Has your priest, deacon, bishop, or another taken a bold public stand on a matter of Catholic teaching regardless of its popularity?

Of course they need your prayers, but since they are only human too, they also need encouragement and positive reinforcement. Show your support publicly by telling family and friends about the good work they have done, by contacting them directly to express your appreciation, or by sending a kind note to let them know you are grateful for their strong Catholic leadership.

Likewise, do not believe bishops and ordained are impervious to your petitions, perturbations, and prayers when the situation is not so positive. A quiet word to your priest, a respectful letter to your bishop, a post on the diocese blog, or a call to your local Catholic media can have a dramatic effect.

In either case, show you are listening and you care!

5

CHAPTER FIVE:
Bureaucrats Speaking for Bishops?

I am the good shepherd; I know my own and my own know me,
just as the Father knows me and I know the Father; and I lay
down my life for my sheep.

– John 10:14-15

Over the years there has been an increasing tendency among Catholics to think of the operations at the offices of the United States Conference of Catholic Bishops, and the various bishops' conferences in the 50 states, in terms of representing the bishops throughout the country and speaking on behalf of these bishops. Some say that these conferences are helpful to the bishops because they are empowered to do things in the name of bishops. Such bureaucrats presume, in many cases, to be the actual voice of the various bishops. While this has never been the role of bishops' conferences, perception can be reality.

It is now time to take a look at the USCCB and examine how much authority it really has.

A question of authority

The primary question is this: Does the USCCB have authority in the Church over individual bishops?

The answer, published in the *South Nebraska Register,* is,[1]

No, the United States Conference of Catholic Bishops does not have any authority over individual bishops. Only the bishop of Rome, the pope, has such authority. Bishops' conferences are [neither] law-making nor law enforcement authorities in the Catholic Church. There are, however, a small and limited number of matters about which such conferences have authority in Church law (such as the vernacular translations of the language of the sacred liturgy), but even in those matters the conferences' actions have no effect without the subsequent approval ("recognitio") of the Holy See, and the conferences must carry out their work in accordance with the directives of the Holy See. Conferences were erected by bishops throughout the world after the decree on bishops of the Second Vatican Council ("Christus Dominus" n.37). They are regulated by the "Motu Proprio" encyclical of Pope John Paul II, entitled *Apostolos Suos,* by the *Code of Canon Law,* and by their own internal statutes, which have to be approved by the Holy See to be in force. The conferences mainly provide occasions for the bishops to exchange experiences, receive advice and help from each other, to obtain information that might be difficult or impossible for an individual bishop to gather, and to address matters of mutual concern, especially those on a national or regional level. Pope Benedict XVI has said very clearly that "episcopal conferences have no theological basis; they do not belong to the structure of the Church as willed by Christ. . . ." They are man-made constructs that might be useful but, if not, could be discarded. See the "Ratzinger Report" (Ignatius Press), pages 58-69, and see the *Catechism of the Catholic Church,* numbers 877-887 and 1577.

Pope Benedict XVI reiterated this several times including a 2010 statement in which he pointed out, "[The Bishops

Conference] must 'avoid placing itself as a parallel or substitute of the ministry of each of the bishops,' or 'constitute itself as an intermediary between the bishop and the See of Peter.'"[2]

And it is not only the Vatican that has made this point, but Catholic organizations such as the St. Joseph Foundation as well. The foundation is composed of specialists in Catholic law known as canon law. In an article entitled "Domus Dei: A House Built on a Weak Foundation," Charles Wilson, director of the St. Joseph Foundation, makes the point that the Church got along very well without these bureaucratic structures for hundreds of years.[3]

But during the past 40 years or so, when these conferences began to take on more and more authority, some detrimental things began to occur—endeavors harmful to the bishops, their credibility, and their authority.

Call To Action

Let's start with The Call To Action (CTA) of 1976.[4] CTA comes to mind as perhaps the beginning of a problem involving the unraveling of Catholic doctrine by people whose goal is to reshape the Church along political lines.

Sponsored by the then National Conference of Catholic Bishops (NCCB), the CTA wrought a havoc which reporter Stephanie Block best describes as "a syndrome of internal heresies."[5] In other words, the CTA became a gathering point for Catholic groups and theologians who take issue with Catholic teaching and are committed to misrepresenting the essence of Catholicism whenever the opportunity presents itself.

At one point Bishop Fabian Bruskewitz, having become quite familiar with CTA's agenda, warned the people in his diocese that membership in Call To Action was grounds for immediate excommunication.[6] Sadly, Bruskewitz was the only bishop with the valor to act definitively in this manner. And though it took 10 years, the Vatican spoke in support of the action Bishop Bruskewitz had taken.[7]

This event is an excellent example of the difference between the shepherd who is constantly caring for his sheep and a shepherd who delegates to other folks who may not necessarily care a hoot about defending the truth. But this is only the tip of the iceberg.

The merger

The USCCB, which is the name that came as a result of the 2001 merger of the NCCB with the United States Catholic Conference (USCC), has many more problems.[8] For example, while it is constantly issuing "teaching documents" whenever there is a major crisis, an election, or some reason to make a political statement of some sort, such documents are not necessarily as sound as the doctrine they claim to be teaching.

Such statements have included the 1978 *Environment and Art in Catholic Worship* (*EACW*). According to the St. Joseph Foundation, "Like the statements, 'The Many Faces of AIDS: A Gospel Response' (1987) and 'Always Our Children' (1997), *EACW* was never brought before the plenary session of the NCCB. Yet, all are held out to the trusting and uninformed faithful as legally binding pronouncements of our bishops. Unfortunately, the [USCCB] as a whole has never repudiated these illusory practices."[9]

And as a matter of fact, even more such misguided projects have been pursued.

Catholic Charities

Among the most insidious of these is the USCCB's Catholic Charities—an organization that was founded more than 280 years ago for the express purpose of serving the poor, the needy, and the disenfranchised. Fast-forward to today and we learn that Catholic Charities has a nationwide network of volunteer-based service agencies and "touches the lives of more than 7.8 million people of all faiths [each] year." It reports that 90 cents of each dollar donated to the organization goes directly to programs and services.[10]

Note that 67 percent of its $4.2 million budget comes from taxpayer dollars (federal government money). Based on this fact, we can say that two-thirds of its "donations" is really government dole money. Perhaps this is why odd things happen at the Catholic Charities home office.

Catholic Charities pandered to the Obama administration during the health care reform struggle doing all it could—including sending out e-mail action alerts to its lists. Shortly after these activities were completed, a strange thing happened. The government awarded Catholic Charities a $100 million disaster relief grant.[11]

Some said it was just a coincidence that this grant was given after Catholic Charities bent over backward supporting Obamacare. We don't think so.

In the state of California, another strange political alliance occurred. During the election campaign cycles, one of the Mobilize the Immigrant Vote collaborators was Catholic Charities.[12] While we cannot say there is anything wrong with political organizations doing what they can to mobilize voters to support their candidate or their ballot measures, we can say that it is quite strange for Catholic Charities to be aligning itself with any political group— particularly one that publishes a voter guide promoting homosexual rights and abortion.[13]

It is difficult to comprehend the connection between the political activities we have presented here and serving the poor by using the donations given to them to feed, clothe, and house the needy. We have just briefly scratched the surface of the challenges Catholic Charities has created by its flagrant brand of partisan politics, but clearly the bureaucrats in charge are spending too much time on political activity rather than acting out the beatitudes among the poor.

As if this were not bad enough, there was the case of an abortion involving Catholic Charities in Virginia. In 2008, a Catholic Charities staff member from the Diocese of Richmond, Virginia, encouraged a sixteen-year-old Guatemalan immigrant to abort her baby. She then proceeded to take the steps needed to see that the abortion was actually committed.[14]

The girl, a ward of the Office of Refugee Resettlement in the Department of Health and Human Services, had been entrusted to the care of Commonwealth Catholic Charities of Richmond—and it was that Catholic Charities office that ensured that the girl had the abortion. When all the facts in this case finally came out, it appeared that the bureaucrats in the Catholic Charities office did not properly inform the bishop and went ahead with an action that brought about the death of the preborn child and untold embarrassment to the bishop.[15]

In fact, Bishop Francis X. DiLorenzo publicly apologized for the incident.

While the press implied that the bishop knew about the abortion in advance and approved it, the bishop's office made it very clear that Bishop DiLorenzo did not know about it and was appalled when he learned the abortion had been carried out. In a statement to the media, Stephen Neill, a diocesan spokesman, said, "Bishop Francis DiLorenzo, after learning late on January 17 of the abortion planned for the next day, specifically said, 'I forbid this to happen.'"[16]

But the damage was done; the bureaucrat acted against Catholic teaching and the scar will forever remain with the bishop. Why such a thing happened in the first place is testimony to the reasons why bureaucrats create problems when they usurp power involving decisions that never were theirs to make in the first place.

Safe Environment

Another of the USCCB's bureaucratic conglomerates is the Safe Environment office, created as a response to the sex abuse crisis.

We can start to unravel the difficulties with the office by taking a moment to meet Teresa Kettelkamp, executive director of that office, and a former colonel with the Illinois state police department.[17] Right after her 2005 appointment, it was reported that Kettelkamp served on the board of advisers of the militantly pro-abortion Feminist Majority Foundation's National Center for Women and Policing.[18]

This feminist organization has an association with Eleanor Smeal, the pro-abortion former president of the National Organization for Women. Kettelkamp denied the association even though the record was clear. The bishops did nothing about it, so Kettelkamp remains in power.

On September 6, 2005, shortly after Kettelkamp took over, bishops across America were telling their religious educators, priests, and bureaucrats that they were now going to be required to provide some sort of "safe environment" program. That is, a program that educates teachers on how to teach children the basics in protecting themselves from sexual predators.

As a result, the directors of religious education (DREs) in many dioceses were up in arms. In the Diocese of Charleston, South Carolina, for example, 12 of 14 DREs sent a letter to Bishop Robert Baker in which they said in part,[19]

> This is a very sensitive issue to cover. There are not counselors or health care professionals in place in the parishes to deal with issues that may arise as a result of this program. The upstate DREs unanimously feel that a better method of presenting this is to have parents teach their children at home using the VIRTUS materials. We suggest having a qualified instructor present the material to the parents at a training session, and the parents would then instruct their children in their homes.

In response, Bishop Baker expressed his understanding for the concerns contained in the letter, but the program remained in place.

But not every bishop was willing to succumb to this mandate. The most outspoken among them was Baker, Oregon's bishop, Robert Vasa, who was applauded by Catholic commentator Domenico Bettinelli, who said of Vasa,[20]

> He's standing up and saying that a bishop is sovereign in his diocese concerning these sorts of things and that no one can order him to do something immoral. The bishop does leave

something ambiguous. He says: "In the diocese, we have indicated that such training must be made available to all children under our supervision in our Catholic schools but have not taken on the nearly impossible task of assuming responsibility for every child in the diocese." If the programs are a problem for children, are they going to stop it in the schools? He leaves that unanswered, but based on his objections it would be very inconsistent if he didn't.

Within the text of Bishop Vasa's 2005 statement are these words: [21]

Are such programs effective? Do such programs impose an unduly burdensome responsibility on very young children to protect themselves rather than insisting that parents take such training and take on the primary responsibility for protecting their children? Where do these programs come from? Is it true that Planned Parenthood has a hand or at least huge influence on many of them? Is it true that other groups, actively promoting early sexual activity for children, promote these programs in association with their own perverse agendas? Do such programs involve, even tangentially, the sexualization of children, which is precisely a part of the societal evil we are striving to combat? Does such a program invade the Church-guaranteed-right of parents over the education of their children in sexual matters? Do I have the right to mandate such programs and demand that parents sign a document proving that they choose to exercise their right not to have their child involved? Do such programs introduce children to sex-related issues at age-inappropriate times? Would such programs generate a fruitful spiritual harvest? Would unsatisfactory answers to any of the questions above give sufficient reason to resist such programs?

By acting in defense of the young children in his diocese and the rights of their parents, Bishop Vasa earned gratitude from national Catholic groups and others, but the biggest blessing Bishop Vasa received—we are sure—is peace of mind. With the USCCB's office producing programs that never get to the root cause of the sex abuse problem, we only wish that other bishops had followed Vasa's lead.

What is it about this mandate from the USCCB's Office of Child and Youth Protection[22] that rankles so many feathers among Catholic parents? Of all those who monitor this, there is one by the name of Mary Ann Kreitzer who has had her finger on the pulse of this project since it started. In 2004, Kreitzer wrote an open letter to all of the United States Catholic bishops and stated,[23]

> How will introducing sexual issues during the latency period in a classroom setting affect children's attitudes toward sexuality? Will placing sexuality in a context of abuse and distrust teach children to fear? Will they see sex as dirty? Will they question every touch? Will they "act out" disturbing ideas and images by inflicting "bad touches" on younger children? These are serious questions. To say, as some bishops have, that materials selected will be "age-appropriate" begs the question. By who's standard? Surely not the secular sex-educators who developed these "touching" programs in the first place.
>
> According to some bishops, the Charter for the Protection of Children and Young People approved by the bishops at their 2002 meeting in Dallas mandates "safe environment" programs for children. That is true. However, the Charter says nothing about **implementation. It does NOT require *classroom* programs** and is silent on who should present the material.
>
> Church teaching, on the other hand, is crystal clear:
>
>> Each child is a unique and unrepeatable person and must receive *individualized* formation. Since *parents* know, understand,

and love each of their children in their uniqueness, *they are in the best position to decide what the appropriate time is for providing a variety of information, according to their children's physical and spiritual growth. . . .* [emphasis added] Therefore, the most intimate aspects, whether biological or emotional, should be communicated in a personalized dialogue. . . . Experience shows that this dialogue works out better when the parent who communicates the biological, emotional, moral, and spiritual information is of the same sex as the child or young person ("Truth and Meaning of Human Sexuality," N. 65 and N. 66).

In other words, it's the parents who should be helping their children understand the environment in which they live and the precautions they should be taking. No bureaucrat, including those from the USCCB, should have the power to rob parents of their rights and interfere with a child's latency period. That period of time is for a child's normal development <u>as a child</u>!

Today, several years after Mary Ann's brilliant letter, and countless other letters from concerned parents across this land, the USCCB's office, complete with its own set of bureaucrats, continues to operate this program, distributing material and demanding compliance. As recently as the USCCB's publication of the 2011 Child Abuse Month material, there is nothing that discusses parental rights or primacy of the parent in teaching children on this very delicate topic.

The office is focused on sex abuser priests and what educators need to share with children about how they can protect themselves. One has to wonder why more attention isn't being paid to weeding homosexuals out of the priesthood than on making sure educators are preparing children for the worst. When you read statements like, "Churches, schools, and youth organizations must ensure that children and youth who worship, study, or participate in activities sponsored by a parish can do so in the safest and most secure setting possible," one is left wondering why the root cause of the problem is not simply confronted and eliminated.[24]

Perhaps it is because, as not a few researchers have pointed out, the entire safe environment project evolved from a pro-homosexual agenda. Christopher Manion pointed out in a well-researched 2006 article,[25]

> From their very inception, "safe environment" programs were diverted from any mention of homosexuality.
>
> When Bishop Fabian Bruskewitz of Lincoln, Nebraska, suggested in 2002 that the bishops conduct a study of the causes of the scandals, his motion did not even get a second. When the John Jay Study, commissioned by the bishops, reported in 2003 that over 80 percent of the crimes committed in the scandals were "homosexual in nature," the bishops buried it like a hot potato.

This does seem to make my point for me, but it still leaves the challenge of dealing with the core cause of this disaster in the hands of bureaucrats who are pandering to the homosexual community.

What is perhaps most devastating about this is that by ignoring or avoiding that so-called "hot potato," men are being denied the help they need to come to know Christ, heal their hearts, and move on. That is the real shame behind the Safe Environment program.

Catholic Campaign for Human Development

Finally, no chapter on Catholic bureaucrats would be complete without talking about the most controversial albatross around the bishops' necks—the Catholic Campaign for Human Development (CCHD). This organization has been accurately defined by many as the best representative of "left-wing radicalism in the Church."[26]

Setting the tone for the massive problems that currently confront the CCHD in Washington, D.C., and nationwide, is this tidbit from the Salt Lake City CCHD offices:[27]

> The new head of the Catholic Campaign for Human Development (CCHD) at the Diocese of Salt Lake City is a former political candidate who supported same-sex "marriage" and the promotion of contraception in the schools; she also opposed attempts to tighten Utah's abortion law.
>
> Jean Welch Hill, who ran as a Democrat for state attorney general in 2008, took over last week as director of the diocesan CCHD and the Peace and Justice Commission. She will also serve as the government liaison, acting as a lobbyist for the diocese.

It is clear to even the most casual observer that, for many years now, CCHD has been pursuing programs that are not so much in the interest of advancing Catholic ideals regarding the human person and his dignity as they are committed to political agendas. When the latest list of CCHD grantees came out in 2011, our friend and ace researcher Mary Ann Kreitzer was Johnny-on-the-spot with analysis. Her report, entitled, "CCHD Continues to Fund Alinsky Organizing with Donations from Patsies in the Pew," is an eye-opener for those who still believe that USCCB bureaucrats are above reproach:[28]

> The bishops' organization has posted its 2010-2011 CCHD (Catholic Campaign for Human Development) grants[29] and surprise, surprise they are once again going in large numbers to Saul Alinsky community organizing groups that agitate for more government funding. The very first group on the list, Connecticut Sponsoring Committee, advertises itself as a community organizing group in the Alinsky model. Here's some info about the group:
>
>> The Connecticut Sponsoring Committee (CSC) is an emerging non-partisan, broad-based, multi-faith coalition based in New Haven and Fairfield Counties. People

from 28 congregations located across 11 urban and suburban municipalities comprise this multiracial representation of over 22,000 Connecticut residents. . . .

The CSC is affiliated with the Industrial Areas Foundation (IAF), a national community organizing network established in 1940. Sixty IAF affiliates nationwide are powerful actors in local and state-level politics; for instance, the Greater Boston Interfaith Organization pushed the legislation for universal health care coverage in Massachusetts, and compelled the state treasurer to divest over $200 million in state funds from the Bank of America. After its official founding in 2011 the CSC will be a member of Metro IAF, which is currently spearheading the "10 Percent Is Enough" anti-usury campaign.

This organization got a $40,000 grant for "organizational development." Now I'm all for anti-usury legislation, but what they don't tell you is that the IAF finds a few issues with broad-based support that they use for organizational purposes. Then they develop a power base that is all about giving power to the organizers for their pet projects and getting their Democratic candidates elected to office. The IAF in many places around the country has engaged in questionable tactics where they bus large groups of people in and intimidate a business or political target. They teach the immoral Alinsky tactics including one that is decidedly anti-Catholic: the ends justify the means.

Worcester Interfaith, another IAF affiliate and grantee ($25,000), brags on its website (2009 newsletter) about all the success they've had getting more government money for an assortment of projects. One of its "recent" accomplishments was:

WI worked with the Worcester/Fitchburg Building Trades Council to create a landmark agreement to give preference to minorities and women for 50 percent of the unions' apprenticeship slots from 1999-2001. This effort was so successful that another agreement was signed in 2003.

Isn't it exciting to know that an organization funded by the bishops systematically discriminates against evil white men! Interesting that the bishops, a group of privileged white men, [don't] mind formalized discrimination against blue collar white men. Well, how many of them have ever had to get their hands dirty?

I could go on and on about the grantees on the latest list. It is the same old same old—promoting liberal positions on "comprehensive immigration reform" and funding groups that lobby for Democrats. Go on and check it out for yourself. Pick a random group on the list and do some searching online. CCHD continues to be a scam that collects money from patsies in the pew who have no idea they are funding this type of "charity."

Shame on the bishops! It's time to cut this program off at the knees.

Kreitzer's analysis is not only revealing, but precise in every aspect. She challenges the bishops, as we all should, for the very reasons that I found it necessary to write this book in the first place. There is something wrong at the offices of the United States Conference of Catholic Bishops. The politics as usual must come to a screaming halt.

Patterning Catholic Church-supported initiatives after the work of community organizing guru Saul Alinsky is simply not something the Catholic bishops should be associated with in any way, let alone be putting their stamp of approval on. Saul Alinsky was a radical political activist whose 1971 book, *Rules for Radicals*, set the stage for many varying forms of community organizing based fundamentally on agitating for change at the local, state, or national level. And I don't mean change for the better!

Alinsky was an enemy of the Church; his programs were and still are the antithesis of Catholic social teaching.

Writing about Alinsky and his fetish regarding the way churches had to be manipulated, Bill Muehlenberg says,[30]

> He fully agreed with Italian Marxist Antonio Gramsci that social institutions must be captured from within, instead of overthrown from without. The long march through the institutions, instead of bloody revolution, was Alinsky's preferred means to achieve the same ends.
>
> And he made it clear that capturing churches was a vital part in promoting the secular left's revolution: "I recognized that if I could win the support of the Church, we'd be off and running. Conversely, without the Church, or at least some elements of it, it was unlikely that we'd be able to make much of a dent in the community."
>
> Thus churches have long been targeted by the radicals, knowing how much easier their task would be if they could infiltrate churches and con gullible believers into doing their dirty work for them.

The sort of philosophy espoused by Saul Alinsky and those who have followed in his footsteps does not comport with the mission of the Catholic Church in America—or any nation for that matter. Social change is not what is needed. What is needed is conversion to Christ and His Word.

Sometimes that vision is not what comes out of places where bureaucrats are striving to either create or implement agendas based on someone else's idea or political framework. Bureaucrats, no matter where they function, can and do have a profound effect on the way any institution, be it government or otherwise, operates. Their personal philosophy can get in the way of the mission, and it is my contention that this is exactly what has happened within the context of the Catholic bishops' bureaucracy, not only in Washington, D.C., but in many states as well.

Without getting too technical, it could be a very good idea for the bishops to consider shutting down the operations that are creating the confusion and then starting over with perhaps a dozen good men and women. Christ had 12 apostles and look what He was able to accomplish!

It didn't take a political party to help Christ along; in fact He died for our sins after living what some would say was a totally politically incorrect life. He set the mark high, but with every bishop doing his part, we might even witness a resurgence in solid Catholic ideals being taught in Catholic colleges. We will explore this in the next chapter. But first, let's examine some actions we can take.

Being a valuable influence

Remember that the USCCB is a bureaucratic administrative structure that has no Church authority and is not a substitute for a bishop. For the most part, the USCCB is "middle management," and its members are working stiffs just like the rest of us. However, they have great opportunity for mischief. This makes the USCCB a most vulnerable portal for outside influences to infect the internal workings of the Catholic Church in America. Pursuing one, or all three, of these actions below will elicit a reaction and will ensure that your voice is heard:

1. Engage your own bishop
2. Grassroots pressure
3. Giving or withholding financial support

Number three is probably the most directly influential. I am not discouraging you from supporting the work of your Church, but rather encouraging you to support its work— with a caveat.

When you give money, "earmark" your donation for a specific purpose if you fear that it could go to support suspect programs. If you withhold your donations from USCCB programs that have gone down the broken path, it is even more effective if you let its members know why. As with any relationship, communication is key. To effect change, you must begin with the truth.

6

CHAPTER SIX:
Catholic School Daze

*Teachers and administrators, whether in universities or schools,
have the duty and privilege to ensure that students receive
instruction in Catholic doctrine and practice. This requires
that public witness to the way of Christ, as found in the Gospel
and upheld by the Church's magisterium, shapes all aspects of
an institution's life, both inside and outside the classroom.*

– Pope Benedict XVI, July 2008,
   in an address to Catholic educators

Where goeth a Catholic college?

Catholic bastions of higher education have become a bit
less than Catholic in far too many instances. It is, in fact, the
case that not every bishop will call attention to a problem
created by a wayward professor or a dissident student group
or even a blatant affront to all that is Catholic—as in the case
of the Notre Dame/Obama fiasco.

The examples of such goings on are numerous, and perhaps the most egregious are the Catholic schools that are in
one way or another aligned with Planned Parenthood.
Planned Parenthood facilities exist in nearly every college
town; they are organizations that pander to perverted

lifestyles, abortion, and birth control for the unmarried. Of course Planned Parenthood is far from the only ally among those Catholic colleges that have fallen into the secular definition of "academic freedom" rat hole.

As Pope Benedict XVI reminded Catholic college presidents a few short years ago, "[A]ny appeal to the principle of academic freedom in order to justify positions that contradict the faith and teaching of the Church would obstruct or even betray the university's identity and mission."[1]

Situation grave

In Pennsylvania, for example, the University of Scranton's "Scranton Inclusion" student group hosted "Sara Bendoraitis, the director of the Gay, Lesbian, Bisexual, Transgender, and Ally Resource Center at American University."

According to the *Scranton Times Tribune*, Bendoraitis "belongs to an abortion rights Facebook group and spoke at a young feminist leadership conference that also featured presentations on abortion rights and birth control. . . . Ms. Bendoraitis spoke at the university . . . about the gay, lesbian, bisexual, and transgender community and how to make the university more inclusive of that community."[2]

The diocese's new bishop, Joseph Bambera, met with the president of the university and expressed concerns, but nothing further was done. This is in sharp contrast to the actions of the previous bishop, Joseph Martino, who issued a statement of absolute disapproval when Misericordia University's Diversity Institute honored pro-abortion, pro-gay-marriage activist Keith Boykin. Upon hearing of the invitation to Boykin to speak, the bishop stated that, in this instance, the university was "seriously failing" to maintain its Catholic identity.[3] According to a Catholic News Agency report,

> "By honoring this speaker through allowing his positions, so antithetical to Catholic Church teaching, to be broadcast on its campus, the university has rejected all four essential characteristics of a Catholic institution of higher learning,"

the diocese said. "These are: its Christian inspiration, its obligation to reflect on knowledge in light of the Catholic faith, its fidelity to Catholic Church teaching, and its commitment to serve the people of God."

Clearly, there is a difference in style among Catholic bishops, even on subjects as serious as student groups giving credence to individuals who are far less than representative of Catholic values.

Sadly there are many states where we can find the same sort of complex examples involving bishops who carry the rod of truth versus those who carry a feather.

Another example is Canisius College in Buffalo, New York, which is a Jesuit institution. The Canisius website boasts a complete selection of GLBT (gay, lesbian, bisexual, and transgender) material.[4] According to CatholicCulture.org, this is the very same college that, in 2009, "helped 'maximize [the] personal and company performance' of Planned Parenthood of Buffalo and Erie County, according to the college's website. Planned Parenthood has taken part in Canisius College's management development program (MDP), which offers participants 'powerful tools and techniques to maximize personal and company performance.' Planned Parenthood is also a past participant in Canisius College's Fundamentals of Fundraising course."[5]

Edward Kmiec, bishop of Buffalo, New York, has been silent.

On the other hand, in Iowa, Bishop Richard Pates fired a local Newman Center's transgendered housekeeper who was quietly offering counseling services and had created a transgendered support group at the Newman Center.[6] Bishop Pates told Susan McIntyre, who had been born a man, that what led to the firing was "your unauthorized representation indicating that you are employed by and operating on behalf of the Newman Center as a counselor or social worker."

In Washington, D.C., things are handled a bit differently, or shall we say not at all. When it was learned that two law professors, Peter Rubin and Julie Cohen, at Georgetown University had worked as counsel to Planned Parenthood, Cardinal Donald Wuerl remained, as far as we have learned, silent, even though these two professors have far more in their biographies than merely helping Planned Parenthood.

Professor Peter J. Rubin, with degrees from Harvard and Yale, states on his official Georgetown biography that he served as counsel in the U.S. Supreme Court for, among others, Dr. Timothy Quill and two other doctors in *Vacco v. Quill*—a case that challenged the constitutionality of New York's ban on physician-assisted suicide. Rubin also served as counsel for Planned Parenthood in *Rust v. Sullivan*—the Supreme Court challenge to the abortion "gag rule" imposed in the 1980s on family planning clinics that received federal funding.

Professor Julie E. Cohen, who has taught at Georgetown since 1999, states on her *curriculum vitae* that, from 1992-1995, she was a "member of pro bono team that represented Bay Area Planned Parenthood affiliates in abortion clinic access litigation."[7]

If we compare these two examples: Bishop Pates—using the rod of truth—who definitively dealt with the transgender Newman Club housekeeper, versus Cardinal Wuerl—using the feather—who has said nothing about the Georgetown professors of law, we have to wonder why such a chasm exists. Aren't all Catholic educational institutions called to follow the same Catholic standard? Aren't all Catholic shepherds called to ensure that the young people who are educated in such institutions realize and recognize the difference between the secular world and the Catholic world of education?

The troubling survey

One of the most trustworthy organizations on the subject of Catholic higher education is the Cardinal Newman Society.[8] In May of 2011, the organization issued an updated report on the status of Catholic colleges and their connections to Planned Parenthood. Entitled, *A Scandalous Relationship: Catholic Colleges and Planned Parenthood*, the report reveals that there are more than 150 such connections on

Catholic campuses in the United States. It also states that, as a result of the report being issued, 29 of those connections have been either removed from college websites or corrected in some fashion. While this is most assuredly a positive sign, it also means that 121 problematic connections remain. According to my math, that means a bit more than 80 percent of the links with Planned Parenthood continue.

But the unfortunate situation is far more serious than simply websites associated with Catholic schools.

Pecksniffian politics

In 2004, the USCCB issued guidelines entitled, *Catholics in Political Life* that state in part: "The Catholic community and Catholic institutions should **not honor** those who act in defiance of our fundamental moral principles. They should not be given awards, honors, or platforms which would suggest support for their actions."[9]

To give you an idea of how bishops interpret their own statements, a few examples are in order. The situations have been handled either with the rod or the feather—as you will see.

At Notre Dame de Namur University in California, Planned Parenthood supporter and pro-abortion Hollywood star Susan Sarandon spoke at a fundraising event. According to *California Catholic Daily*, "Sarandon has been a longtime supporter of Planned Parenthood. She is mentioned in the Planned Parenthood Federation of America's 2007-2008 annual report as one of many Hollywood stars who has lent her name to support the world's largest abortion provider."[10]

George Hugh Niederauer, the Catholic archbishop in whose diocese the school is located, has been silent about this.

In April of 2009, MSNBC "Catholic" pro-abort commentator Chris Matthews gave the commencement address at St. Joseph's University in Philadelphia.[11] Matthews is an avowed Obama supporter and, on one of his programs, suggested that pro-life Americans use "verbal terrorism" tactics.[12]

The cardinal, Justin Rigali, made no comment.

There are bishops who do make their voices heard on occasions when the USCCB guidelines are violated. Among them is Archbishop Jose Gomez who, during his tenure as leader of the Archdiocese of San Antonio, Texas, spoke out firmly in 2008 when abortion rights supporter Hillary Clinton hosted a rally at St. Mary's University—the oldest Catholic college in the archdiocese. According to the *USA Today* article, "The school is an independent liberal arts college with its own president and board of directors but is under the spiritual leadership of the archdiocese."[13]

The archbishop said that he had not been consulted in advance. Further, in a prepared statement in which he said that the university should not send mixed signals, he stated, "Catholic institutions are obliged to teach and promote Catholic values in all instances. This is especially important when people look to our Catholic universities and colleges to provide leadership and clarity to the often complicated and conflicting political discourse."[14]

Now that Archbishop Gomez leads the Archdiocese of Los Angeles, we are hopeful that his voice in defense of clear Catholic teaching will make a positive impact there as it did in San Antonio.

Another bishop who made his voice heard is John Smith of Trenton, New Jersey. When he discovered that Christine Todd Whitman, a pro-abortion Republican, was scheduled to speak at the Catholic Stuart Country Day School, he objected.[15] In a letter addressed to the school's headmistress, Bishop Smith wrote, "Governor Whitman has made it her position over the years that she is pro-choice, and so supports a position totally contrary to official Catholic teaching."[16] Bishop Smith urged that the invitation, which "may well mislead your students, parents, and faculty to falsely conclude that the Church tolerates the pro-choice position," be rescinded. Whitman's speech was canceled.

Along the same lines, Cardinal Raymond Burke made his mark on the Archdiocese of St. Louis during his tenure there when he spoke out against the Cardinal Glennon

Children's Foundation for inviting popular singer Sheryl Crow, who openly supports human embryonic stem cell research, to be part of a fundraising event. Subsequently the cardinal, then archbishop, resigned from the foundation's board.

When St. Louis University basketball coach Rick Majerus made a public statement that he was "pro-choice," the archbishop again spoke out expressing his concern. At that time he said he would speak with a university representative privately about the matter.[17]

But Majerus remained intransigent and the archbishop called on the university to discipline Majerus for his comments. As a result, the *New York Daily News* insulted Archbishop Burke and his authority—which includes leading his sheep and enforcing Church law. Because the archbishop threatened to deny Communion to Majerus unless he repented of his support for abortion, the *Daily News* railed: "No one has denied Burke his right—or anyone's right—to express his opinion on *Roe v. Wade* or stem cell research or any issue. But Burke seemed to overstep his spiritual boundaries when he threatened the First Amendment rights of a private individual in this supposedly free country and the free exchange of ideas in a university community."[18]

In other words, killing a baby is just an "issue" and freedom of speech is supposed to trump defending the innocent from intended death? What sort of freedom is that?

The media bashing of bishops has extremely sad consequences. It is this type of verbal heckling that drives many bishops, in my view, into silence. A Catholic bishop must develop a thick skin and a love of truth that exceeds the popular opinion of the day in order to survive such public derision. Cardinal Burke has always had that ability, but perhaps many bishops do not.

The Obama caper

There is one stunning example of a situation that occurred at the University of Notre Dame that really puts all of this into perspective.

The year was 2009 and President Barack Obama was invited to the University of Notre Dame to deliver the commencement address and receive an honorary degree. The announcement sent shock waves throughout the Catholic community—particularly the Catholic pro-life community.[19]

Once the dust had settled, several different organizations swung into action and many bishops spoke out against the invitation, calling on the president of the university, Father John Jenkins, to withdraw the invitation and end the scandal that would occur if Obama did, in fact, appear.

The significance of the event is not just the fact that it took place, but what we learned about Catholic institutions and their student body—Notre Dame in particular. It came as no surprise when I learned that, prior to Obama's election, a mock election took place on the Notre Dame campus and the majority of students voted for Obama.[20] The actual percentage was 52.6 to 41.1. As CBS reported, "Four years ago, student media groups on campus, not including *The Observer*, conducted a mock election in LaFortune [the student center] a week before the election between President George W. Bush and Sen. John Kerry. . . . With 570 undergraduates and graduate students voting, the vote was 47.5 percent for Bush and 46.8 percent for Kerry."

This is but one example of the tendency among students and faculty at Catholic colleges in America to be in concert with public views and secular ideas about how the world—and the nation—should operate. Where once there was a desire to keep Catholic teaching and a Catholic world view in the curriculum, there is now a tendency to keep it at bay, relegating it to philosophy classes and Sunday Masses. The result is that the Catholic voter, even on a campus as famously Catholic as Notre Dame, is no different than any other voter. This translates into support for those who favor abortion, homosexual marriage, and other subjects which once had no place in a Catholic curriculum and would have been anathema to a Catholic voter.

This is perhaps why the student body at Notre Dame was overwhelmingly in favor of having Obama come, receive the degree, and speak. This is also part of the reason why students hesitated to support any organization that was working to get Obama disinvited. Even the campus pro-life group appeared to be lukewarm about the subject—preferring to host other events on the day Obama spoke rather than confront the problem head on.

But dozens of Catholic bishops did speak out publicly, begging the university to call off awarding the honorary degree. In fact, many bishops urged that Obama's appearance be canceled altogether.[21]

Bishop John D'Arcy

John D'Arcy, bishop of the Diocese of Fort Wayne-South Bend at the time of the Obama debacle, clearly understood what was at stake and did all he could to intervene. What is most shocking is that Father John Jenkins, president of the University of Notre Dame, did not converse with the bishop prior to extending the invitation to Obama. Nor did he seek Bishop D'Arcy's approval. Only after the fact, when the invitation had been accepted, was the bishop informed.

Imagine the outrage resulting from snubbing the leader of the diocese in which you are serving. Bishop D'Arcy issued a public statement, saying,[22]

> On Friday, March 21, Father John Jenkins, CSC, phoned to inform me that President Obama had accepted his invitation to speak to the graduating class at Notre Dame and receive an honorary degree. We spoke shortly before the announcement was made public at the White House press briefing. It was the first time that I had been informed that Notre Dame had issued this invitation.
>
> President Obama has recently reaffirmed, and has now placed in public policy, his long-stated unwillingness to hold human life as sacred. While claiming to separate politics from science, he has in fact separated science from ethics and has brought the American government, for the first time in history, into supporting direct destruction of innocent human life.

This will be the 25th Notre Dame graduation during my time as bishop. After much prayer, I have decided not to attend the graduation. I wish no disrespect to our president, I pray for him and wish him well. I have always revered the office of the presidency. But a bishop must teach the Catholic faith "in season and out of season," and he teaches not only by his words—but by his actions.

My decision is not an attack on anyone, but is in defense of the truth about human life.

Bishop D'Arcy used the graduation day services being hosted by students who opposed the appearance of Obama as his way of affirming that courage, even in the face of media criticism, is to follow Christ without counting the cost.

A voice of love in the midst of a debacle

Among those bishops and their associates who wrote inspiring messages encouraging the University of Notre Dame to be Catholic first, rather than politically correct, was Bishop Kevin Rhoades, whose Respect Life director, Paul Schenck, responded to an e-mail on his behalf. In a manner that was loving toward the problem at hand, while firm regarding the reasons why Obama should not have appeared at Notre Dame, Schenck wrote,[23]

Dear Christina,

Thank you for your note of concern which you recently sent to the bishop's office regarding the University of Notre Dame.

Maria Wood, secretary to Bishop Rhoades, referred your e-mail to me. Bishop Rhoades has discussed this issue with me, as it pertains specifically to my office.

As is clear from Bishop Rhoades' most recent commentary entitled, "Disturbing Advances for the Culture of Death," President Obama's policies, and those of his administration, on abortion and embryonic stem cell research violate the moral law and Church teachings on the sanctity of human life and dignity of the person. Bishop Rhoades concurs with Bishop D'Arcy's statement and position on the matter. (Bishop D'Arcy is the bishop of Fort Wayne-South Bend, the diocese in which Notre Dame is located.) Bishop Rhoades stands firmly with the U.S. Catholic Bishops' statement called "Catholics in Political Life" which unambiguously says, "The Catholic community and Catholic institutions should not honor those who act in defiance of our fundamental moral principles. They should not be given awards, honors, or platforms which would suggest support for their actions."

Bishop Rhoades also supports those who exercise their freedom of conscience and speech to express their opposition to the university's decision to have President Obama as commencement speaker and honoree. In fact, Bishop Rhoades has written to the president of the university to express his disagreement with the university's action.

It is disheartening and distressing when an institution that is regarded as Catholic, such as Notre Dame, fails to follow the guidelines set forth by the bishops of the Catholic Church, especially in these vital moral matters. It is not political or partisan to stand for the sanctity of human life and the dignity of the human person. President Obama clearly does not stand for or advance the cause of the defenseless unborn and their mothers and families. This is the tragic reality we must come to terms with as Catholics living in an increasingly secular environment. It is heartening on the other hand, to see how many Notre Dame students, faculty, and alumni have made their commitment to human life known and how many Catholics and others of good will have done the same.

It is Bishop Rhoades' hope and prayer that all the institutions that bear the name "Catholic" will affirm the Church's teachings, expose the culture of death, and build up the culture of life. Thank you for your selfless commitment to the defense of innocent human life. Please be assured of our prayers.

On behalf of Bishop Rhoades and myself, I am

Sincerely,

Paul CB Schenck, MA (Theol.) LHD Director Office of Respect Life Activities, Roman Catholic Diocese of Harrisburg

What is most inspiring about this letter is that it resounds today as a victory in more ways than one. Within a year of the Obama speech at Notre Dame and the awarding of the honorary degree, none other than Bishop Kevin Rhoades was transferred, in November 2009, to the Diocese of Fort Wayne-South Bend, Indiana, where the University of Notre Dame is located.[24] The pope is indeed a wise man!

Protesting Obama at Notre Dame

During the Obama speech, a group of 88 pro-life Americans peacefully and respectfully protested the event—though that is not how the media portrayed it at the time. These 88 people were arrested for trespassing, and charges were pressed by the university.

Over a year later, when no movement in the case had occurred, Professor Charles Rice wrote a sobering account of the situation in which he said, in part, of those arrested,[25]

How can we explain this vindictive treatment of the ND88? Permit me first to tell you a little about those targets of the university's wrath. Fr. Weslin was 79 and in very poor health when he was arrested at Notre Dame and literally dragged off the campus on a pallet. Born to poor Finnish immigrants in upper Michigan, he joined the Army after high school. He converted from the Lutheran to the Catholic faith and married Mary Lou before earning his commission.

He became a paratrooper and rose to Lieutenant Colonel in the 82nd Airborne Division, earning his college degree en route. When he retired in 1968, he and Mary Lou became active pro-lifers in Colorado. In 1980, Mary Lou was killed by a young drunk driver whom Norman personally forgave. Norman later was ordained as a Catholic priest, worked with Mother Teresa and devoted his life to the rescue of unborn children through peaceful, prayerful direct action at abortuaries. In December, 1990, I was privileged to defend Fr. Weslin when he and his lambs of Christ were arrested at the South Bend abortuary. One does not have to agree with the tactic of direct, non-violent action at abortuaries to have the highest admiration, as I have, for Fr. Weslin and his associates. He is a hero of the faith. Notre Dame should have given Fr. Weslin the Laetare Medal rather than throw him in jail.

The other "criminals" stigmatized by Notre Dame include many whom this university should honor rather than oppress. One is Norma McCorvey, the plaintiff in *Roe v. Wade*, who has become pro-life and a Catholic actively trying to spread the word about abortion. The ND88 include retired professors, retired military officers, mothers of many children, a Catholic nun in full habit, Christian pastors, several Ph.Ds, and Notre Dame grads. They are "the salt of the earth." They came at their own expense, and not as part of any "conspiracy," from 18 states. They came because they love what Notre Dame claims to represent. They themselves do represent it. But it is doubtful that Notre Dame does so anymore. The leaders of Notre Dame ought to be deeply ashamed of their continuing persecution of such people.

Then, nearly two years after the charges had been filed, the charges against the 88 protestors were finally dropped.[26] But as the lead defense attorneys made clear in a public statement,[27]

> The parties remain in profound disagreement over the 2009 commencement, but after prayerful consideration they have decided to put their differences behind them, to cease battling in court, and rather to affirm a commitment to the fundamental proposition that each and every human life is sacred, from conception until natural death, no matter whether rich or poor, humble or exalted, wanted or "unwanted."

> Moreover, both parties have pledged not to re-hash the events of the past, but on the contrary, to recognize each other's pro-life efforts and to work together to find ways to increase those efforts and maximize their impact on the nation's contentious, ongoing debate over abortion policy.

After all is said and done, there is but one thing to say about the Obama fiasco at the University of Notre Dame, and that is what Bishop John D'Arcy wrote in a commentary that was published after the occurrence. In that article, "The Church and the University," he said,[28]

> As bishops, we must be teachers and pastors. In that spirit, I would respectfully put these questions to the Catholic universities in the diocese I serve and to other Catholic universities.

> Do you consider it a responsibility in your public statements, in your life as a university, and in your actions, including your public awards, to give witness to the Catholic faith in all its fullness?

> What is your relationship to the Church and, specifically, to the local bishop and his pastoral authority as defined by the Second Vatican Council?

> Finally, a more fundamental question: Where will the great Catholic universities search for a

guiding light in the years ahead? Will it be the
Land O' Lakes Statement or *Ex Corde Ecclesiae*? The
first comes from a frantic time, with finances as the
driving force. Its understanding of freedom is de-
fensive, absolutist, and narrow. It never mentions
Christ and barely mentions the truth. The second
text, *Ex Corde Ecclesiae*, speaks constantly of truth
and the pursuit of truth. It speaks of freedom in
the broader, Catholic philosophical and theological tradition, as linked to the common good, to the
rights of others and always subject to truth.
Unlike *Land O' Lakes*, it is communal, reflective of
the developments since Vatican II, and it speaks
with a language enlightened by the Holy Spirit.

On these three questions, I respectfully
submit, rests the future of Catholic higher education in this country and so much else.

The *Land O' Lakes Statement* to which Bishop D'Arcy
refers was allegedly designed to bring Catholic principles to
the world through evangelization.[29] However the fatal flaw
was that "the signatories of the *Land O' Lakes Statement*, by
refusing to be shepherded by the Church's bishops, set the
sheep free to roam into whatever error academic freedom
might lead them. Nearly 40 years later, the shepherds are
still trying to gather their scattered flocks."[30]

While it is the mission of the Cardinal Newman Society
to focus attention on *Ex Corde Ecclesiae* as the gold standard
for Catholic institutions of higher learning, it is *Land O' Lakes*
that has created the helter-skelter condition we witness at
Catholic colleges and universities today. *Land O' Lakes* must
be forever buried in the archives of Catholic educational
history if we are ever to see a renewal of Catholic dedication
among Catholic institutions vested with the challenge to be
Catholic first.

Political correctness must become as unpopular as the
plague. It matters not whether the subject is a Catholic
institution, a Catholic bureaucrat, a Catholic bishop, or a
Catholic person. The price of being Catholic requires that we

remain Catholic first, American second, and political only to the extent that we are able to infuse Catholic ideals into every aspect of our daily lives.

What can I do?

As Catholics, we are called to pro-actively and accurately pass on Catholic teaching in our effort to bolster the faithful—and that certainly includes our children.

The best way to achieve this is through authentic Catholic teaching. Avoiding terms that suggest prejudice and intolerance is part of that and should be standard practice at every Catholic college in America today.

This is not always how it actually is. For example, the University of Notre Dame's Core Council for Gay and Lesbian Students uses its published "questions and answers" portion of the website to address alleged "homophobia."[31] This is a politically motivated word that has nothing to do with Catholic teaching.

The inclusion of such language in a document designed to help Catholic students understand the Catholic position on homosexuality leaves the impression that the Church acknowledges homophobia as a legitimate attitude. This is absurd because Catholic teaching does not pander to political agendas.

This is where you come into the picture.

If you are an alumnus of such a school, you have an inherent responsibility to contact the development or advancement office, the alumni association, school hierarchy, the controlling diocese, and even the school newspaper—consistently and repeatedly. Make your voice heard that the school must put Catholicism before politics or anything else.

Most importantly, do not pay tuition to a "Catholic" institution that is not Catholic in character. If you need further clarification, contact the Cardinal Newman Society for a list of excellent Catholic bastions of higher learning.[32]

7

CHAPTER SEVEN:
The Politics of Catholicism

*[W]e should not look on men as lost or beyond hope; we should
not abandon them when they are in danger or be slow to come
to their help. When they turn away from the right path and
wander, we must lead them back, and rejoice at their return,
welcoming them back into the company of those who lead good
and holy lives.*

– From a homily by St. Asterius of Amasea

The four distinguishing marks of the Church are that it
is one, holy, Catholic, and apostolic—not Democrat, Republican, Liberal, and Conservative.[1] But there are times when
it's hard to tell which set of characteristics define the
Catholic Church in America.

It is for this reason that we believe it is time to confront
the elephant in the bishops' collective living room. The
cocktail hour is upon us and nobody is looking at the
enormous brown snuffleupagus[2] sitting in the middle of the
floor. It is apparent that the current problem did not crop up
overnight. As a matter of fact, one could trace the origin, at
least in current times, to the path paved by Catholic Democrat John Fitzgerald Kennedy during his run for the White
House. Thanks to some in the Catholic hierarchy who

ostensibly like their politics more than their vocation, that path is now a full-fledged four-lane highway.

I will always remember how brilliantly Archbishop Charles Chaput put the Kennedy legacy into perspective in his September 22, 2004, column,[3]

> Forty-four years ago this month (Sept. 12, 1960), John F. Kennedy delivered remarks to the Greater Houston Ministerial Association wherein he effectively severed his Catholic identity from his public service. It's OK to elect me president, he argued to a wary Protestant audience, because I won't let the pope tell me what to do.
>
> In pledging to put the "national interest" above "religious pressures or dictates," Kennedy created a template for a generation of Catholic candidates: Be American first; be Catholic second. This was an easy calculus for Kennedy, who wore his faith loosely anyway. And it was certainly what the American public square, with its historic anti-Catholic prejudice, wanted to hear.
>
> The Kennedy compromise seemed to work pretty well as long as the "religious pressures" faced by Catholic elected officials involved issues like divorce, federal aid to Catholic schools, or diplomatic relations with the Holy See. Each of these issues was important, surely, but none involved life and death. None was jugular.
>
> In 1973, by legalizing abortion on demand, the U.S. Supreme Court changed everything. The reason is simple: Abortion is different. Abortion kills. The great Lutheran pastor and theologian Dietrich Bonhoeffer spoke for the whole Christian tradition when he wrote: "*Destruction of the embryo in the mother's womb is a violation of the right to live which God has bestowed upon this nascent life. To raise the question whether we are here concerned already with a human being or not is merely to confuse the issue. The simple fact is that God certainly intended to*

> *create a human being and that this nascent human
> being has been deliberately deprived of his life. And that
> is nothing but murder."*

Noted Catholic theologian Dietrich von Hildebrand
made the same point but with a sharper focus, saying, "The
drivel of the heretics, both priests and laymen, is tolerated;
the bishops tacitly acquiesce to the poisoning of the faithful.
But they want to silence the faithful believers who take up
the cause of orthodoxy, the very people who should by all
rights be the joy of the bishops' hearts, their consolation, a
source of strength for overcoming their own lethargy."[4]

These words may seem a bit harsh until you put things
in the proper perspective.

Think about the perspective of this young priest who
sent us a private e-mail about his quandary. He is part of the
group of priests serving under Cardinal Donald Wuerl of
the Archdiocese of Washington, D.C. Father wrote,

> As a priest in the Washington, D.C. area, I find that
> there is a lot that frustrates us in pro-life work.
> Sometimes I am taken aback, not simply by the
> "business as usual" attitude taken by so many
> people, but by the passivity of the Church's shep-
> herds against the murder of children. In a
> recent gathering of priests who give advice to the
> cardinal, I was <u>the only one</u> who argued for sanc-
> tions against pro-abortion politicians and others
> who have taken a public stance against the sanc-
> tity of life. I am ashamed of the ones who put
> fundraising, other "common" issues, and a false
> compassion above the truth. I know some of the
> guys feel the way I do, but they will not speak out.

The frustration shared by this priest is similar to what is
experienced by many Catholic priests and more than a few
Catholic bishops. When it comes to politicians, Catholic and
otherwise, a simple question such as how to cast a vote can
become overwhelming. There seem to be nearly as many
opinions as there are Catholic bishops.

How should a Catholic vote?

Many years ago, Archbishop John Myers of New Jersey wrote, "Catholics who, because of an incorrectly formed conscience, dissent from this Church teaching, should recognize that they have separated themselves in a significant way from the Catholic community. Such a choice has serious consequences, even if the person acts in the mistaken belief that it is permissible."[5]

That was 1990. In 2004, Bishop Robert Carlson, having become aware of letters to the editor in his local newspaper in Sioux Falls, South Dakota, addressed the same topic. The reason was his heartfelt concern that his flock might be misled by the disjointed rambling of letter writers who really either did not understand Catholic teaching or who were intentionally attempting to confuse the issue.

In Carlson's letter to his flock, he wrote,[6]

It is clear that from the pulpit you cannot endorse a certain political party or speak for or against a particular candidate for office. However, pastors are only fulfilling their duty when they share the teaching of the Church with regard to faith and morals. This is not political activity. . . .

There is a faulty thinking today that all life issues are equal or the same. Even some priests and religious and a few politicians try to promote this. The philosophical fallacy that underpins this argument is called relativism. It teaches that all things and issues are relative and up to the individual to decide which is of greater importance. Some elements in the media favor it as it "squares" in their minds with the sense of strong individualism fostered by the culture. It goes hand-in-hand with the attitude, "whatever I think or believe, whatever I value or want, whatever I feel or desire must be correct." . . .

Opposition to abortion binds every Catholic under pain of mortal sin and admits of no exceptions.

Bishop Carlson left no stone unturned in his outreach to the faithful, setting forth a clear agenda for his priests to follow and for his people to contemplate. His inspiring words are dynamic, true, and logical.

On the other hand, when Bishop Wilton Gregory addressed the 34th Annual Congressional Black Caucus Legislative Conference in September of 2004, his comments did not include a single reference to abortion or any of the other serious threats to vulnerable human persons. His remarks did cover other topics such as "availability of jobs, just compensation for work, guaranteed health care in an era of spiraling costs, and fighting the ever present temptations to racism."[7] Bishop Gregory continued, "And considering that we are a nation of immigrants, it would be particularly tragic if the necessary security measures intended to screen out the few who would do us harm also result in excluding many who can and would otherwise have an opportunity to better their lives and make a real contribution to our society."

There is certainly every reason to be concerned about the social problems Bishop Gregory mentioned, but where are the fundamental things that, for black America in particular, are tearing away the very fabric of their family life? When one out of every three abortions in America is performed on a black baby[8] and black fathers are statistically absent from the family at an alarmingly higher rate,[9] one would think that restoration of the family unit—including defense of the preborn—would have made it into Bishop Gregory's address. He had the perfect audience to deliver such disturbing news. Bishop Gregory and other Catholic leaders must learn to turn the tide with more emphasis on what is genuinely important—to the voter and to those elected to office.

It should be noted that the USCCB sends confusing signals to Catholics in general on the subject of voting. For example, prior to the 2004 elections there were Catholic organizations like Catholic Answers that published excellent material to help voters through the process of equating the choices they had to make at the ballot box with the principle teachings of the Church.

But Catholic Answer's booklet, entitled *Voter's Guide for Serious Catholics*,[10] met with strong public opposition from none other than the United States Conference of Catholic Bishops.[11] The lawyers for the bishops rejected the voting guide, claiming that it was confusing to people and that only its officially approved material should be used.

This is strange, indeed, since the Catholic Answers publication agrees 100 percent with Catholic teaching that identifies five "non-negotiable" subjects by which a politician is to be evaluated: abortion, euthanasia, human embryonic stem cell research, human cloning, and homosexual marriage. The guide makes it clear that any candidate who supports even one of those five non-negotiables would be disqualified from getting the Catholic vote!

The bishops should have been cheering rather than sending out the dogs to make sure the booklet was not used. But when you stop and think about it, agreeing with the Catholic Answers voting guide would require strict adherence to Catholic teaching. And on this, not all bishops concur. If they did, certain Catholic candidates for public office and those already elected would be treated differently; they would all be called to account when they digress from Catholic teaching.

The case of Catholic congressman David Obey

One excellent example of this is retired congressman David Obey, a Catholic Democrat. In 2004, shortly after being admonished by his bishop, Obey wrote an article entitled, "My Conscience, My Vote." The article was published in the Jesuit's *America* magazine. In that article he opines,[12]

> In a democracy, public officials must reserve to themselves prudential judgments about how and under what circumstances to apply moral principles in a pluralistic society. But there are some in my own religion who believe it is the obligation of Catholic public officials to impose, through law, their religious values on issues such as abortion, upon those who do not share our religious beliefs.

Obey conveniently suggests here that killing a preborn baby is really nothing more than a debatable religious belief. Truth apparently means nothing to him. From there he goes on in the same twisted vein, writing,

> [T]he Supreme Court has ruled in numerous cases that there are limits to what government can constitutionally do to limit a woman's range of choices in determining whether to have an abortion.
>
> In trying to deal with those questions over the last 30 years, I have tried to think through how to reflect both my respect for my own religious values and my respect for the constitutional processes of this American democracy. During that time I have voted well over 60 times for limitations of one kind or another on a woman's right to choose abortion. I have, for instance, accepted as a reasonable compromise the Hyde Amendment on Medicaid funding for abortions and have even worked with Representative Henry Hyde (Republican of Illinois) and the U.S. Conference of Catholic Bishops on the question of how to apply that amendment to health services provided under H.M.O.s. I have voted to limit abortion rights in prison and for passage of proposals limiting later-term abortions. I also worked to reach a compromise on the complicated question of how best to persuade the Chinese government to end its policy of forced abortions. So I suppose it is fair to say that my record on abortion is mixed. I make no apology for that. I believe these issues are complicated.

Obey also writes about the time when, in 2003, his bishop, now Cardinal Raymond Burke, told him that he could not receive Holy Communion unless he repented of his support for abortion. Obey issued this statement from his office:

> I have said on many occasions that I agree with the Catholic Church about the undesirability of abortion, but this country is not exclusively Catholic. Bishop Burke has a right to instruct me on matters of faith and morals in my private life and—like

any other citizen—to try to persuade, not dictate how I vote on any public matter. But when he attempts to use his ecclesiastical position to dictate to American public officials how the power of law should be brought to bear against Americans who do not necessarily share our religious beliefs on abortion or any other public issue, he crosses the line into unacceptable territory. The U.S. Constitution, which I have taken a sacred oath to defend, is designed to protect American citizens from just such demands. The U.S. Constitution says, "Congress shall make no law respecting an establishment of religion, or prohibiting the free exercise thereof." That means that in an American democracy no one, not a public official and not a bishop, gets to impose by law his religious beliefs on people of other religions who do not necessarily share those same beliefs.

Further, Obey defiantly wrote, "I very much regret that the bishop saw fit to take the course of action he has chosen. But I make no apology for insisting that he distinguish between his right to try to persuade me on how to vote on any issue and his right to dictate my vote."

This piece of writing details far better than anything we could fabricate what the political problem in the Church is today and how serious it has become. Note that Obey uses the John Fitzgerald Kennedy formula for attempting to conveniently put his Catholic identity in his pocket when he enters the public arena. While a right-thinking person would consider it absurd to have several sets of moral and ethical guidelines on tap, such a scenario does not seem foreign to Obey.

By conveniently relegating abortion to the classification of "religious belief," he avoids the scientific fact that abortion is an act that results in a death. Obey appears to feel good about segmenting his life so that his political views and his Catholic identity remain separate—compartmentalized for convenience, if you will. If there ever were an oxymoron, this is it.

Obey further complicates the situation by asserting that, as a lawmaker, he has to remain within the confines of what the Supreme Court has ruled—using that deadly phrase, "a woman's range of choices." As the father of two, Obey should realize that the problem with the Supreme Court and abortion is that a mother has all the choices, while her baby has none. Thus the Supreme Court's flawed logic should be challenged by lawmakers rather than blindly accepted.

Obey thinks that because his record on abortion is mixed due to his support for some abortion regulation, his support for other types of abortion should not interfere with his ability to function as a Catholic who is also a public servant. I wonder how many would agree with his "logic" if his argument were not about abortion but rather about regulating cocaine distribution at high schools. Would voters elect a man who argued that regulating the dispensing of cocaine to high school students was preferable to an outright ban?

Signs of a contradiction

After the 2004 elections, the "Catholics in politics" fog thickened. Homosexual marriage took center stage and many aspects of the dialogue about Catholics in political life grew even more disrespectful toward Catholic teaching and the authority of the priest or bishop. The smog of innuendo and political posturing abounded.

LifeSiteNews reported an interview with Cardinal Raymond Burke on this topic,[13]

> "There is a tendency to accept same-sex relationships because we do not want to deal with the embarrassment and hurt of recognizing same-sex attraction as disordered," [Burke] said. "The fact that our American culture more and more fails to make any distinction between same-sex attraction and heterosexual attraction does not justify our failure to make the distinction, respecting God's gift of human life in its integrity and helping others to attain the perfection to which we are called as true children of God." . . .

"Bishops will be persecuted," he said, and "also priests and lay people."

Even now those proclaiming the truth are called homophobic and hateful. Yet the archbishop explains, "It's what it means to be a sign of contradiction. We just have to accept that and we have to remain tranquil in proclaiming the truth with charity, but insisting on the truth."

"If we look to the example of Our Lord, we have to take up the cross for the defense of life," he said.

Like Burke, many bishops have grown bolder in their public positions on voting and Catholic obligations. Among them is retired bishop Rene Gracida, who set about explaining the argument that some had used to persuade Catholics that there were proportionate reasons for voting for a pro-abortion candidate:[14]

When a Catholic does not share a candidate's stand in favor of abortion and/or euthanasia, but votes for that candidate for other reasons, it is considered remote material cooperation, which can be permitted in the presence of proportionate reasons strictly defined.

Since abortion and euthanasia have been defined by the Church as the most serious sins prevalent in our society, what kind of reasons could possibly be considered proportionate enough to justify a Catholic voting for a candidate who is known to be pro-abortion? None of the reasons commonly suggested could even begin to be proportionate enough to justify a Catholic voting for such a candidate. Reasons such as the candidate's position on war, or taxes, or the death penalty, or immigration, or a national health plan, or social security, or AIDS, or homosexuality, or marriage, or any similar burning societal issues of our time are simply lacking in proportionality.

Gracida then went on to explain how to prudentially determine who would benefit most from a Catholic's vote, particularly in a close election. While there are ongoing debates about the subject of whether or not a vote for a third party candidate is a mistake, there should be no debate about when it is acceptable to vote for anyone who is committed to abortion, euthanasia, human embryonic stem cell research, or other anti-life actions.

Father John Corapi, SOLT, who is no stranger to controversy, sent a warning to Catholics who vote for pro-abortion candidates. He stated,[15]

> Since a physician needs to be concerned with what's sick, let's get right to the point. It is not morally possible for any Catholic to support abortion, euthanasia, fetal stem cell research, human cloning, or same-sex marriage. There are no ways around this, no justifications whatever. Why? For the simple reason that the Church holds these things to be intrinsically evil. They are evil in themselves, and no circumstances or subjective conditions can ever change that. They are not to be confused with such things as the death penalty and legitimate self-defense, which are not intrinsically evil, and which governments can, and often must, make use of. While the conditions for applying such unfortunate measures as the death penalty and waging war may be open to debate, they are not things evil in themselves, always and everywhere.

And before we get off the subject of signs of contradiction among heroic men in the priesthood, it would be remiss not to mention Samuel Aquila, bishop of Fargo, North Dakota, who spoke in a homily in 2008 on the serious nature of voting. In this homily, he reminded his congregation that each Catholic "will be judged by how we vote."[16] As reported by the Catholic News Agency,

> "An intrinsic evil is anything that is always and at every time wrong—that can never be seen as a 'good.'" [Aquila] noted the intrinsic evils of

abortion, contraception, premarital sex, same-sex acts and the taking of innocent human life during war.

"All of those are intrinsic evils, and no society, and no person if he is Catholic, can ever support an intrinsic evil nor can he or she ever vote for someone who supports intrinsic evil. It is important to understand that, and to understand that truth especially in the upcoming election. Because, yes, all of us will be judged by how we vote. And, yes, there are many Catholics with erroneous consciences who have made prudential judgments that are wrong and have consistently made prudential judgments that are wrong. Either they do not fully understand the teaching of the Church or they choose to ignore that teaching and they choose an evil, and an intrinsic evil."

"For any society to be just, it must reflect the order of God."

Signs of duplicity

Not every bishop prefers to be a flashpoint for contradicting political correctness. Among them is Terry Steib, bishop of Memphis. "He asked [Catholics in his diocese] to follow their consciences and weigh all the moral issues they face before casting their ballots." He further went on to say, "We must recognize . . . that God through the Church, is calling us to be prophetic in our own day. If our conscience is well formed, then we will make the right choices about candidates who may not support the Church's position in every case."[17]

This statement, which might sound innocent enough, could lead a Catholic to think that a vote for a pro-abortion candidate is acceptable if that same candidate is, for example, against the death penalty. Such a conclusion is wrong, but the bishop did not differentiate among the intrinsic evils and the possible wrong actions that can be taken. Steib created confusion similar to that created by the bureaucrats at the USCCB when they issued their statement.[18]

As a matter of fact, some applaud the bishops when they issue statements calling on a state governor to choose either not to enforce the death penalty or to sign a repeal of the death penalty law in his state.[19] And while there is certainly no problem with such statements, it is a bone of contention with Catholics like me that this same Catholic bureaucracy is not at the forefront of issuing calls to states on matters like abortion, homosexual marriage, or birth control programs in schools. Somehow they are silent in far too many cases on such truly controversial subjects.

The same can be said about the manner in which the Catholic bishops have dealt with racism. As I pointed out in a commentary[20] shortly after the bishops issued the guidelines for Catholics and voting entitled, *Forming Consciences for Faithful Citizenship*,[21]

> The bishops tell the reader that, "The direct and intentional destruction of innocent human life from the moment of conception until natural death is always wrong and is not just one issue among many." This is in paragraph 28 and is a fabulous statement. But, in [paragraph] 42 they say, "As Catholics we are not single-issue voters. A candidate's position on a single issue is not sufficient to guarantee a voter's support. Yet a candidate's position on a single issue that involves an intrinsic evil, such as support for legal abortion or the promotion of racism, may legitimately lead a voter to disqualify a candidate from receiving support."
>
> What??? Abortion and racism? Could it be that a hateful attitude and an act of direct murder are equally evil in Church teaching? Where is that written?
>
> And why, pray tell, would the bishops tell us that support for such an evil "may legitimately lead a voter . . ."? Does that mean that a voter could cast a vote for someone who supports such an evil?
>
> What in the world does section 42 really mean? And, believe me, it gets worse.

In [paragraph] 64 the bishops say, "Abortion, the deliberate killing of a human being before birth, is never morally acceptable and must always be opposed," but in [paragraph] 32 they say that "incremental improvements in the law" can be acceptable. One has to wonder if that includes exceptions such as rape, incest, and life of the mother which the bishops have supported for years.

The bishops further state in [paragraph] 33 that, "prudential judgment is also needed in applying moral principles to specific policy choices in areas such as the war in Iraq, housing, health care, immigration, and others." Are we to conclude that like abortion, which is apparently a political issue, these other questions are of equal moral value when examining how a Catholic should vote?

Well, here is your answer. In [paragraph] 34, the bishops advise: "A Catholic cannot vote for a candidate who takes a position in favor of an intrinsic evil, such as abortion or racism, if the voter's intent is to support that position." But they continue in the same paragraph to instruct that, "At the same time, a voter should not use a candidate's opposition to an intrinsic evil to justify indifference or inattentiveness to other important moral issues involving human life and dignity."

If you are now totally confused about what the U.S. Conference of Catholic Bishops is telling the faithful about the murder of innocent preborn babies and the supremacy of this question versus all others, join the club!

I am disgusted with this statement. By the way, tell me why abortion is mentioned by name 15 times, but war is mentioned 21 times and poverty is mentioned 17 times—and the word "murder" which defines abortion is never mentioned.

This is undoubtedly why Catholic commentator Deal Hudson raised questions regarding then Archbishop Raymond Burke's loss of an internal election during an annual bishops' meeting,[22]

> Over the past three years, Burke has assumed the mantle of the late Cardinal John O'Connor in pro-life matters, challenging fellow bishops to take stronger stances in the defense of innocent life. . . .
>
> Burke has been a controversial figure since early 2004 when, as bishop of La Crosse, WI, he began to challenge pro-abortion Catholic politicians publicly on their reception of the Eucharist.
>
> Shortly after moving to St. Louis as archbishop, Burke said he would deny Communion to Sen. John Kerry if he presented himself. Although his position has been backed up by 13 other bishops, Archbishop Burke was clearly straining the boundaries of "collegiality."
>
> Father Reese, former editor of *America* magazine, says the bishops were sending a message: "Most of the bishops don't want Communion and Catholic politicians to be a high-profile issue, and he [Burke] is seen as a man who's pushing that issue. . . . Had he been elected, it could have been interpreted as endorsing his position."

Some bishops denied that this was the case, but as Hudson points out, "In response to the Kerry and Communion controversy, the bishops formed a task force, headed by Cardinal Theodore McCarrick, to study the issue and present a report. That report, *Catholics in Political Life*, differed sharply with Burke, finding that each bishop could decide for himself in such cases."

In point of fact, that June 2004 report by Cardinal McCarrick, entitled *Interim Reflections Task Force on Catholic Bishops and Catholic Politicians*,[23] had its own problems. It created more confusion on the subject addressed in our next chapter.

Opening our hearts and minds

If all this leaves you wondering just what to believe, do not be disheartened. It only means that the USCCB politicrats, along with a few bishops, have accomplished exactly what they intended—giving them free reign.

Such sophistry has existed in the Church since the time of Christ. Paul warns of it in Romans 16:18 when he says, "For such people do not serve our Lord Christ but their own appetites, and by fair and flattering speech they deceive the hearts of the innocent."[24]

Do not be naïve in the teachings of the Church: The teachings are *always* in conformance with Holy Scripture. Remember that we Catholics are called to faith *and reason* and God has given us the ultimate reference book!

As Paul said in 1 Corinthians 2:4, "My message and my proclamation were not with persuasive (words of) wisdom, but with a demonstration of spirit and power."[25]

It's not hard to recognize the difference between partisan pabulum and spiritual power if we really listen. Let's listen with great care.

8

CHAPTER EIGHT:
Holy Souls or Sacred Cows–
The Canon 915 Dilemma

*No one may share the Eucharist with us unless he believes that
what we teach is true, unless he is washed in the regenerating
waters of baptism for the remission of his sins, and unless he
lives in accordance with the principles given us by Christ.*

– St. Justin, martyr, in defense of Christians

Avoiding the obvious

In late 2002, an advertising campaign with the goal of
calling attention to Catholic pro-abortion members of
Congress was launched in consultation with American Life
League's spiritual director. Our hope was that individual
bishops would be inspired to act positively by going
through a series of steps to hopefully persuade pro-abortion
public figures to convert to the Catholic position, repent of
their support for abortion, and become true Catholic heroes
in the public square.

But, if that strategy did not work, we asked the bishops
to deny these public pro-abortion individuals access to the
sacrament of Holy Communion. By doing so, they and their

priests, deacons, and extraordinary Eucharistic ministers would be protecting Christ from sacrilege.

But in June of 2004 we realized that there was a huge problem with our strategy. It became clear that not every bishop viewed Church law as something that he was obligated to obey—at least not the particular law on which we were focused. This law, Canon 915, mandates that those who obstinately persevere in manifest grave sin are not to receive the Holy Eucharist.[1]

What this means is that if a Catholic public figure, such as a politician or member of the media, acts defiantly (manifestly) in advocating, supporting and/or promoting an intrinsic evil like abortion, homosexual acts, or contraception, that individual should be denied Holy Communion until he or she repents publicly. One would think that this Church law is rather easy to understand, but that assumption proved to be an error in judgment.

When the bishops gathered in Denver in June of 2004, we knew our plan was creating division, not harmony, among them. That month America witnessed an obvious contradiction between Cardinal Joseph Ratzinger's June 2004 memo to American bishops and now retired Cardinal Theodore McCarrick's June 2004 document, *Interim Reflections Task Force on Catholic Bishops and Catholic Politicians*.[2]

The Ratzinger memo, "Worthiness to Receive Holy Communion—General Principles," delivered to Cardinal Theodore McCarrick during the bishops' June 2004 meeting, states,[3]

> 5. Regarding the grave sin of abortion or euthanasia, when a person's formal cooperation becomes manifest (understood, in the case of a Catholic politician, as his consistently campaigning and voting for permissive abortion and euthanasia laws), his pastor should meet with him, instructing him about the Church's teaching, informing him that he is not to present himself for Holy Communion until he brings to an end the objective situation of sin, and warning him that he will otherwise be denied the Eucharist.

6. When "these precautionary measures have not had their effect or in which they were not possible," and the person in question, with obstinate persistence, still presents himself to receive the Holy Eucharist, "the minister of Holy Communion must refuse to distribute it" (cf. Pontifical Council for Legislative Texts Declaration "Holy Communion and Divorced, Civilly Remarried Catholics" [2002], nos. 3-4). This decision, properly speaking, is not a sanction or a penalty. Nor is the minister of Holy Communion passing judgment on the person's subjective guilt, but rather is reacting to the person's public unworthiness to receive Holy Communion due to an objective situation of sin.

These words are unambiguous; they leave no room for misinterpretation. But the McCarrick report disagreed. In the June 15, 2004, *Interim Report* he wrote, "[B]ased on the traditional practice of the Church and our consultation with members of our conference, other episcopal conferences, distinguished canonists, and theologians, our task force does not advocate the denial of Communion for Catholic politicians or Catholic voters in these circumstances."

Further in the same report, we find these words,

Other questions were raised about where the process might lead—who would be impacted and what other issues might lead to denial of Holy Communion. We fear that it could further divide our Church and that it could have serious unintended consequences. For example, it could be more difficult for faithful Catholics to serve in public life because they might be seen not as standing up for principle, but as under pressure from the hierarchy. We could turn weak leaders who bend to the political winds into people who are perceived as courageous resistors of episcopal authority. In the past, such actions have often been counter-productive. We also fear it could push many people farther away from the Church and its teaching, rather than bringing them closer.

While the Ratzinger memo laid out five steps that a pastor would take prior to making the decision that denial of Communion was necessary, the McCarrick report sets forth a scenario designed to avoid enforcing canon law.

On the one hand, enforcing Canon 915 could have the desired effect of helping the pro-abortion Catholic public figure understand that his public actions are putting his soul in serious jeopardy. On the other hand, choosing not to enforce the law avoids confronting the flawed public behavior, thus creating even more scandal and harm.

Nothing good ever comes from sidestepping the truth.

I am not suggesting that this latter outcome is what McCarrick was thinking about when he wrote the *Interim Report*, but the language in the report leads one to that conclusion.

Additionally, even though Cardinal McCarrick had the Ratzinger memo in his possession during the June 2004 bishops' meeting, the memo itself was not made public until July of 2004. We wonder why.

It seems that McCarrick's statement could have been so carefully nuanced because of an innate fear among some bishops of public disapproval and media bashing. Such concerns, real or imagined, can have negative effects on the bishops who obviously felt bludgeoned by the press treatment received as a result of the mishandling of the sex abuse scandals. But whether or not that is the case, the obvious outcome of their timidity in confronting public actions that defy Church teaching is that many Catholics in public life continue to deride the Church, insult Christ, and otherwise behave in ways that are fundamentally not Catholic at all.

I find it curious that, while the pro-abortion Pelosi-Biden types are never confronted for their hypocrisy, leaders like me, who clamor for justice, are portrayed as "attacking" bishops instead of defending Christ.

No matter how you slice it, the United States Conference of Catholic Bishops did not, and has not, unanimously agreed to enforce Canon 915.

Communion must not be used as a weapon

Over the years, various bishops have developed many arguments designed to absolve themselves from obeying canon law. For example, Baltimore's Cardinal William H. Keeler said he opposes "an attempt by some bishops to politicize Communion and deny the sacrament to Catholic politicians who support abortion rights." Keeler further stated, "Our position is . . . Catholics have a responsibility to examine their own conscience and see if they are in a state that is appropriate for the reception of the sacrament. . . . We don't need bishops to get into the act."[4]

Such a statement implies that helping an errant Catholic in public life come to grips with his public errors is a political action rather than a healing action. Shepherds are supposed to be concerned, after all, with souls, not politics.

Catholic commentator and analyst Barbara Kralis reported on several bishops who agreed with the Keeler line of reasoning, writing,[5]

> Archbishop Pilarczyk of Cincinnati, former president of the National Conference of Catholic Bishops, said he would not deny [Senator John] Kerry the Eucharist. Pilarczyk asked, "What about the people who do not like the Church's teachings on the death penalty or on homosexual marriages? Are we going to refuse them?"
>
> Using the same flawed theology, Albany's controversial Bishop Hubbard said he would not deny a pro-abortion politician Holy Communion because he would also then have to deny people who favored the death penalty and war, and who neglected care of the poor and the hungry.
>
> This is incorrect. The Church has never condemned war and the death penalty (yet wishes them both to become rare). Instead, the Church teaches *primus est vivere!* The first thing is life! Life is the right that trumps all other rights. Without the right to life, no other rights are possible!

Joliet's Bishop Imesch expressed disagreement with Church law, saying: "Both the good and the wicked can approach the table. You don't question people when they come up here."

And then there is the dissident Catholic group, Call To Action, whose folks wrote,[6]

Asking those who distribute Communion to make a judgment as to the state of any individual's conscience is totally inappropriate. Call To Action is encouraged by St. Cloud, Minn. Bishop John Kinney's statement on this issue:

"I refuse to allow the Eucharistic liturgy to become politicized. . . . I will not allow Holy Communion to be used as a weapon in ongoing political and ideological battles. For this reason, it is not my intention to reject anyone who comes forward in a espectful manner to receive the Body and Blood of Christ. The Church recognizes that it is for each individual to examine his or her own conscience in this regard, and I assume that those who come forward to receive the Body and Blood of Christ have done so and honestly believe they are not in a state of grave sin."

A small group of bishops have been persuaded to use denial of the Eucharist as a coercive tactic to compel adherence to their understanding of Church teachings. This is undermining the Church. By using such methods the bishops further damage their teaching authority which has already been eroded by the clergy sex abuse scandal.

Such statements contribute to confusion not only among Catholics, but the public at large. By evading the truth, large numbers of people are led astray believing that it is perfectly acceptable to be pro-abortion or pro-homosexuality and still be Catholic.

On the other hand, there are many heroic bishops who do enforce canon law because they are more concerned with souls than with public popularity.

Public heroes

In August 2004, Father Joseph Wilson wrote,[7]

> The Eucharist has become the equivalent of a birthday cake. Even if someone has been very naughty, it is really, really mean to say that he cannot have a piece of the birthday cake. Birthday cake is an inclusion ritual, like a party favor or an ice-breaking in-group exercise. It says nothing more than, "You're here. Welcome."
>
> Catholics routinely stream up to Holy Communion who have not approached the confessional in years. The concept of being in a "state of grace," or of "mortal sin," even of "reverent awe" is so abstract as to be meaningless to most of our people (if that seems harsh to you, please remember that 82 percent of us aren't even at Sunday Mass). "Father," I've heard more times than I can count, "I don't come to Mass every Sunday, but I go to Communion because I consider myself to be a good person." Apparently, from the pulpits of many of our churches, there is continually preached an "I'm okay, you're okay" religion of perpetual affirmation, summed up by one wag with this collect: "Lord, help us by your grace to continue to be the good people we really are."

Father Wilson's accurate presentation of how things are in the Church today is part of the reason why some bishops have sought ways to help their fellow bishops see the reality of the situation.

For example, Father William Kuchinsky treated his parish—Our Lady of Grace Catholic Church in Romney, West Virginia—and its progeny, to a lesson on the integrity of Christ in the Eucharist.[8]

On January 7, 2008, the feast of St. Raymond of Pennafort—the patron saint of canon lawyers—Kuchinsky's parish sealed a time capsule that included important Church documents, the *Code of Canon Law*, statements from bishops, articles, and many other items connected to contemporary news regarding Canon 915. Capping the time capsule, at the center of a millstone that is part of a memorial to preborn babies, was a bronze medallion bearing the inscription, "Canon 915."

> Addressing those who might be concerned of the possible ramifications of enforcing Canon 915, Fr. Kuchinsky remarked: "In faith we can hope that by doing what is clearly the right thing this moment may be one when the dark clouds which have descended upon our beloved land can be lifted so that all eyes may see the deception which has brought us as a nation to sacrifice our own children through legalized abortion. We cannot discount the great things God may work when we stand united in faith, in truth, and in justice."

> Father continued: "Those chosen by the Almighty as 'overseers' can help to guide us out of the 'valley of death' by ensuring that a gray fog of confusion does not envelop the faithful and keep them from recognizing the path of life which is clearly marked out in black and white. Canon 915 is Church law written in view of a true understanding of the holy and awesome reality of the Holy Eucharist . . . there is nothing more holy or sacred. Unfortunately, there is also evil this side of eternity. The atrocity of abortion is probably the greatest evil we face in our day."

> Fr. Kuchinsky noted: "It is shameful that many of those who are entrusted with the custody of 'the Mystery of Faith' would permit people so obviously tied up with such a demonic project as the systematic destruction of the unborn to approach the sanctuary to receive the Bread of Life. This scandalous situation is a grievous one

and greatly offensive to the faithful who have any measure of piety for the Holy Eucharist. Yes, we pray for the lost souls who enable the heinous crime of abortion. But, I also pray that one day those who are uncomfortable enforcing Church law in this the most important of issues will also understand the great sorrow, scandal, and confusion they have caused for so many of the faithful by their failure to act and rally the other ministers of Holy Communion to defend the holy of holies from sacrilege."

The significance of the millstone surrounding the 915 Medallion is not lost to those visiting the memorial, as it immediately invokes our Lord's warning: "But he that shall scandalize one of these little ones that believe in me, it were better for him that a millstone should be hanged about his neck, and that he should be drowned in the depth of the sea" (Mt 18:6).

To help with these complex issues, retired bishop Rene Gracida prepared a 12-step program for his fellow bishops.[9] In the introduction, he said, "Recognizing the complexity of the situation in the Church and in our society at the present time I should like to help my brother bishops find their way through the thicket of conflicting opinions and proposals for action. After substantial reflection, I propose a 12-step program for my brother bishops to help them decisively deal with the grave crisis facing our Church and our nation."

His effort to simplify the confusion is, to this day, among the most well-thought-out documents I have seen, but to the best of my knowledge the bishops who might have benefitted from it apparently did not study it.

Bishop Robert Vasa challenged Catholics as well with his explanation of excommunication and the relationship it has to the errant Catholic who should not be receiving Communion, but who should be headed toward the confessional. In referring to public figures known to support such evils as abortion, he explains,[10]

When that moral error is espoused publicly by a Catholic who, by the likewise public and external act of receiving Holy Communion, appears to be in "good standing" then the faithful are doubly confused and doubly discouraged. In that case, the error is certainly not refuted.

Furthermore, the impression is given that the error is positively condoned by the bishop and the Church. This is very discouraging to the faithful. In such a case, private "dialogue" is certainly appropriate but a public statement is also needed. In extreme cases, excommunication may be deemed necessary.

It seems to me that even if a decree of excommunication would be issued, the bishop would really not excommunicate anyone. He only declares that the person is excommunicated by virtue of the person's own actions. The actions and words, contrary to faith and morals, are what excommunicate (i.e., break communion with the Church). When matters are serious and public, the bishop may deem it necessary to declare that lack of Communion explicitly.

There is not enough space in this book to mention all of the shepherds who have set forth equally balanced and inspiring teachings in their role as shepherds of souls. For those we may have overlooked, we publicly extend our apologies, for they, like the following shepherds, inspire us in their unwavering leadership and commitment to Catholic truth:

Gerald A. Gettelfinger - 915*
Joseph Naumann
Charles J. Chaput
John Myers
Robert Vasa - 915
Fabian Bruskewitz - 915
Robert Finn
Raymond L. Burke (Vatican) - 915
Samuel Aquila - 915

Robert Carlson
John Yanta (retired) - 915
Robert Baker - 915
Peter Jugis - 915
John Donoghue (retired) - 915
Michael Sheridan - 915
John Nienstedt
John Smith - 915 (retired)
Joseph Martino - 915 (silenced)
Paul Coakley - 915
Joseph Galante - 915
Gregory Aymond - 915
Rene Gracida - 915 (retired)

* Those with 915 next to their names are bishops who have publicly stated that they will enforce the law.

Currents with Crocodiles

In the list above, two extraordinary bishops are missing because it was their public confrontation with the evils of the day that makes them stand out in a completely different way. They are Bishop Thomas Tobin and Bishop Thomas Olmsted—each a lion for the Lord!

Bishop Thomas Tobin

Bishop Tobin was placed in an untenable position by former congressman Patrick Kennedy, crocodile number one. Kennedy created a media circus out of a private communication between a bishop and a soul for whom the bishop had concerns. As a result, CNN reported,[11]

> "The simple fact is that most bishops don't want to deny Communion to politicians, and we know for a fact that Pope John Paul II gave Communion to pro-choice Italian politicians," said the Rev. Thomas Reese, a senior fellow at the Woodstock Theological Center at Georgetown University. "So the question is, is Bishop Tobin more Catholic than the pope on this?" . . .
>
> In an October interview, Kennedy criticized the bishops for threatening to oppose the health

care bill if it lacked the tough restrictions. In the House debate on the measure, Kennedy opposed a provision with the Church-backed restrictions on federal money for abortions, but voted in favor of final passage of the bill that included that language.

He repeated that criticism and revealed Tobin's earlier admonition in an interview published Sunday, the 46th anniversary of the assassination of John F. Kennedy. Tobin responded by calling Kennedy's position "unacceptable to the Church and scandalous to many of our members."

Most bishops and priests oppose using Communion as a "political weapon," and Kennedy's disclosure of Tobin's admonition may be an attempt to push back against the bishops' support for the abortion restrictions in the House bill, CNN senior Vatican analyst John Allen said.

"The Catholic bishops have been fairly successful, at least to date, at putting abortion at the center of the debate over health care reform, and that obviously has generated some resentment from people who don't share their views," Allen said. Kennedy's decision to come forward "in effect puts the Catholic bishops in a negative light, because it ends up making them look intolerant."

Can you connect the dots? Please allow me to explain the CNN bias. Both John Allen and Father Reese are known to be quite left of center in their Catholic views, yet CNN treats them as experts. Not surprisingly, the CNN interpretation of Bishop Tobin's open letter to Kennedy is biased against the bishop. But, though CNN chose to ignore the truth, CNN nevertheless had access to it—as it came straight from Bishop Tobin. Had CNN used Bishop Tobin's open letter to Congressman Kennedy, made public two weeks prior to the CNN report, the story would have been different. Here is part of what Bishop Tobin wrote to Kennedy:[12]

Your rejection of the Church's teaching on abortion falls into a different category—it's a deliberate
and obstinate act of the will; a conscious decision
that you've re-affirmed on many occasions. Sorry,
you can't chalk it up to an "imperfect humanity."
Your position is unacceptable to the Church and
scandalous to many of our members. It absolutely
diminishes your communion with the Church.

Congressman Kennedy, I write these words
not to embarrass you or to judge the state of your
conscience or soul. That's ultimately between you
and God. But your description of your relationship with the Church is now a matter of public
record, and it needs to be challenged. I invite you,
as your bishop and brother in Christ, to enter into
a sincere process of discernment, conversion, and
repentance. It's not too late for you to repair your
relationship with the Church, redeem your public
image, and emerge as an authentic "profile in
courage," especially by defending the sanctity of
human life for all people, including unborn children. And if I can ever be of assistance as you
travel the road of faith, I would be honored and
happy to do so.

Not only did CNN make an effort to chew up Bishop
Tobin by evading the facts, MSNBC got into the act as well.
Its own pro-abortion Catholic news commentator, Chris
Matthews, acted disrespectfully toward Bishop Tobin while
literally badgering him relentlessly. Keith Fournier, Catholic
analyst and public speaker, wrote about the Matthews
debacle, telling his readers that Matthews[13]

intended to pummel him, browbeat him and try
to persuade him to abandon the truth and excuse
the error which Matthews has embraced. In his
grandiosity and arrogance Matthews proceeded to
talk over the bishop, interrupt him, cut him off,
and try to lecture him in a condescending manner
on "the law." He repeatedly tried to force him to

answer loaded questions. He finally had the audacity to suggest that the bishop needed to rethink his position.

MSNBC should publicly apologize to the bishop and Matthews should be fired for his lack of professionalism. To not give this good and intelligent man, this bishop of the Catholic Church, an opportunity to speak, after inviting him on this show, was inexcusable.

The one thing nobody apparently noticed was that, during the fracas, the United States Conference of Catholic Bishops did not step out and publicly applaud Tobin. Its members remained eerily silent.

Bishop Thomas Olmsted

And then there's the more recent case of Bishop Thomas Olmsted, whose heroic defense of Catholic teaching and subsequent excommunication of a Catholic nun created a national furor. The bishop stood tall through its entirety.

In May of 2010, Bishop Thomas Olmsted took the agonizing step of excommunicating Sister Margaret McBride, the nun who approved of surgically aborting an 11-week-old preborn baby. Since that time, few have reported the case accurately or with a full understanding of Catholic doctrine.

It is the Catholic Church's infallible teaching that there is no circumstance under which a child may be murdered prior to birth by an intentional act of surgical abortion. This doctrinal fact is not, and never has been, Bishop Olmsted's personal opinion. It is, rather, his obligation to defend the teaching of the Church and to make clear the ramifications that follow when a Catholic disobeys a fundamental teaching such as that on abortion.

Bishop Olmsted did everything he could to convince Sister McBride of her error and, when all of his efforts failed, he had no other choice but to excommunicate her.

As a result, the media, including the Catholic media, had a heyday with the coverage and with questions regarding what Bishop Olmsted had done. Catholic News Agency reported,[14]

> Dr. John Garvie, chief of gastroenterology at St. Joseph's Hospital and Medical Center, defended Sr. McBride in an opinion piece published Tuesday in the *Arizona Republic*, calling her a "courageous" and "valued" member of the hospital leadership.

> He characterized the Saturday article in the paper as suggesting that Sr. McBride "violated the Catholic principle of the sanctity of life by condoning an abortion in order to save a mother's life."

> "Let me assure all that there is no finer defender of life at our hospital than Sister McBride," Garvie wrote, saying the sister is considered the "moral conscience of the hospital."

> Calling the sister a "champion of compassionate, appropriate care for the sick and dying," he said he was disappointed that she had been reassigned. "This leaves the impression that she did something wrong," the doctor argued. "What she did was something very few are asked to do; namely, to make a life-and-death decision with the full recognition that in order to save one life, another life must be sacrificed."

However, the truth is that Sister McBride is not God and should not have put herself in the position of making a life or death decision about a vulnerable baby versus a mother with serious heart problems. Perhaps if Sister McBride had taken counsel with Bishop Olmsted, this situation might never have occurred.

But what is most interesting about this case is who took the side of the nun. We are not shocked about the doctor, who apparently felt obligated to defend McBride, suggesting by innuendo that it was the bishop, not the nun, who bore the blood of the dead preborn child on his hands. But far more serious than even this was the fact that the president of the Catholic Health Association, Sister Carol Keehan, came to McBride's defense, arrogantly ignoring the bishop on a question that only he has the moral authority to pronounce.

Keehan e-mailed a statement to the *National Catholic Reporter*, which then wrote a follow-up story on McBride that stated:[15]

> Daughter of Charity Sr. Carol Keehan, CHA president and CEO, said, "St. Joseph's Hospital and Medical Center in Phoenix has many programs that reach out to protect life. They had been confronted with a heartbreaking situation. They carefully evaluated the patient's situation and correctly applied the *Ethical and Religious Directives for Catholic Health Care Services* to it, saving the only life that was possible to save."

Here is but another example of someone second-guessing the moral authority of the bishop. As our next chapter will make very clear, Keehan has her reasons and her own baggage to contend with as a defiant supporter of Obamacare.

The good news is that, in this instance, the USCCB concurred with Bishop Olmsted's decision.[16] Score one for the heroes.

Cardinal Raymond Burke

David Gibson, religion reporter for Politics Daily, wrote in glowing terms about a recent speech given by now Cardinal Raymond Burke in which he clearly found problems with the very public, Catholic funeral of pro-abortion Democrat Senator Ted Kennedy. Gibson stated,[17]

> In a speech last Friday night to a gathering of Catholic conservatives at the Mayflower Hotel in Washington, an outspoken American archbishop

now heading the Vatican version of the Church's Supreme Court said that politicians who support gay marriage or abortion rights cannot receive sacraments without publicly repenting their ways:

"It is not possible to be a practicing Catholic and to conduct oneself in this manner," said Archbishop Raymond L. Burke, whom the pope transferred to Rome in 2008 after Burke's often-stormy tenure as archbishop of St. Louis.

"Neither Holy Communion nor funeral rites should be administered to such politicians," Burke said. "To deny these is not a judgment of the soul, but a recognition of the scandal and its effects."

For more than eight years we literally begged Kennedy's bishop, Sean Patrick O'Malley, to make it clear to the senator that, until he repented of his support for abortion, he should not receive Holy Communion and would be denied the sacrament if he approached a priest. Sadly, that was never done. Kennedy's funeral was but another bone of contention in the long struggle we have had with many bishops to put souls ahead of political concerns.[18] The sacred cow of politics has cost the Church in so many ways—and none of them have been beneficial to souls.

The bottom line

Archbishop Charles Chaput has spoken numerous times on the problematic nature of turning politics into a religion. As he so eloquently stated a couple of years ago, "Where the media see a Catholic politician, Catholic bishops see a soul. For a bishop, the question of Catholics in American public life is only secondarily about electoral politics."[19]

More recently after a speech entitled, "Politics and the Devil," Chaput was asked why there is so much disunity among Catholics on the subject of pro-abortion politicians and Holy Communion. He explained that, because there is no unity among bishops, there can hardly be unity among the faithful themselves, noting,[20] "There is unity among the bishops about abortion always being wrong, and that you can't be a Catholic and be in favor of abortion—the bishops all agree to that—but there's just an inability among the bishops together to speak clearly on this matter and even to say that if you're Catholic and you're pro-choice, you can't receive Holy Communion."

The threads of this disunity have unraveled into a gaping hole. If we peer through it, we get a clue about how it could come to pass that Catholics would—in very large numbers—vote for the most pro-abortion president in United States history, Barack Obama.

How can I be part of the cure?

In addition to what I suggested in chapter seven, I repeat that we must listen closely and critically to what is being said. The distortions in these fine-sounding arguments will make themselves apparent. For example, when someone says "politicizing Communion," that is simply reframing the issue into a straw man to knock down.

This is a favorite tactic for many in politics. The fact that publically promoting sin and advancing anti-Catholic behavior involves a politician does not make it political. This is what is known as "flipping" the argument.

Jesus said, "Whoever has ears ought to hear" (Matthew11:15).[21]

Your greatest defense is to develop critical listening skills. Learn to hear what is really being said and what is being left out. Pay attention to the words chosen and what sources are quoted. Use your ears as God intended.

As you practice this, you might be amazed at how insightful your friends suddenly find you.

ALL's "Lost in the Rockies" ad
addressed the Catholic bishops'
failure to obey Canon Law 915.
The ad ran during the bishops'
Denver, Colorado meeting
in June 2004.

ALL's "Judgment Day" ad ran
in the Washington Times in 2005.

9

CHAPTER NINE:
Obama Plays Catholics for Fools

Are we really a ray of light in the midst of so much darkness, or are we still held fast bound by laziness or human respect? It will help us to be more apostolic and to overcome the obstacles if we consider, in the presence of God, that the people whose paths we have crossed during our lives had a right to expect us to help them to get to know Jesus better.

— *In Conversation with God*, 2:199

Community organizer Barack Obama

The first time I heard that Barack Obama began community organizing activities with the help of a Catholic parish in Chicago that provided him with an office, I have to admit I was shocked. How could such a thing possibly be true, I wondered. But then, just before the 2008 elections, I read an article that stated,[1]

> CB Richard Ellis Inc. is marketing Holy Rosary Church, 11300 S. Martin Luther King Drive, which closed at the end of June, and the adjacent rectory, 351 E. 113th St., for the Archdiocese of Chicago. Sen. Obama, the Democratic presidential nominee, worked out of an office in the rectory in the late

1980s when he was working on the Developing Communities Project.

It had also come to our attention earlier in the campaign that Obama was once Chicago ACORN's (Association of Community Organizations for Reform Now) attorney and worked to train ACORN leaders.[2]

Stanley Kurtz put it all together quite nicely in the *National Review.*[3]

> Before giving us a tour of ACORN's pro-Obama but somehow "non-partisan" election activities, [Chicago ACORN leader Toni] Foulkes treats us to a brief history of Obama's ties to ACORN. While most press accounts imply that Obama just happened to be at the sort of public-interest law firm that would take ACORN's "motor voter" case, Foulkes claims that ACORN specifically sought out Obama's representation in the motor voter case, remembering Obama from the days when he worked with Talbot [former leader of Chicago ACORN]. And while many reports speak of Obama's post-law school role organizing "Project VOTE" in 1992, Foulkes makes it clear that this project was undertaken in direct partnership with ACORN. Foulkes then stresses Obama's yearly service as a key figure in ACORN's leadership-training seminars. . . .
>
> So along with the reservoir of political support that came to Obama through his close ties with Jeremiah Wright, Father Michael Pfleger, and other Chicago black churches, Chicago ACORN appears to have played a major role in Obama's political advance. Sure enough, a bit of digging into Obama's years in the Illinois State Senate indicates strong concern with ACORN's signature issues, as well as meetings with ACORN and the introduction by Obama of ACORN-friendly legislation on the living wage and banking practices. You begin to wonder whether, in his Springfield days, Obama might have best been characterized as "the senator from ACORN."

What this bit of background suggested to us at the time was that Obama knew how to pull the strings and use the right language to ingratiate himself with social justice Catholics—reformers who are not necessarily orthodox Catholics. Believe it or not, there are many well-meaning Catholics who frequently get confused about what the Church teaches regarding the priorities we should have as Catholics. For example, in the Church's hierarchy of concerns, opposition to abortion comes first and working to feed the hungry second.

Catholics for Obama and other contradictions

Once Obama decided to run, things quickly heated up in the Catholic community. For example, at one of Obama's early campaign events at Carlow University in Pittsburgh, hosted by Catholics for Obama, *American Papist* received this from Deal Hudson,[4]

> I received a call from someone who attended the event who told me the "high point was when a Catholic priest urged everyone in the crowd to report any priest to the IRS and to the Diocese of Pittsburgh who preaches from the pulpit that you must vote based on one issue."
>
> There were about 15 sisters present and three priests.

Catholics for Obama describes itself as "representing the Catholic majority" and worked throughout the 2008 campaign on behalf of its candidate and against the fundamental teaching of the Church that human rights begin when a human being begins. As a matter of fact, when one looks back at how the elections turned out that year, there is every reason to suspect that the real victory was not for Obama but for moral relativism. To this very day, Catholics for Obama continues to work on serious questions involving labor unions and health care, but is nowhere to be found when the problem is government subsidy of abortion or denial of conscience rights to Catholics in health care.[5]

Sadly, the organization was not alone in its efforts to advance Obama toward the White House with the Catholic seal of approval. Early on, organizations with similar agendas to those of Catholics for Obama took center stage in the campaign as the majority of bishops looked on silently.

Among the most noticeable of Obama's cheerleaders was former Notre Dame professor of law Douglas Kmiec, whom Obama embraced with open arms. Kmiec became a front man, so to speak, selling the apologetics line that it was perfectly OK to vote for Obama in the general election, even though he did support abortion. Kmiec's line of reasoning was challenged by many, but among those who were most erudite was the now deceased Father Richard John Neuhaus, who wrote,[6]

> Where to begin? Mr. Kmiec has a long history of faithful public service and has been unapologetic in his witness to the sanctity of human life. He has now become a voice for Catholics who wish to back for president a candidate who has a long history of unqualified support for the unlimited abortion license imposed by the *Roe v. Wade* decision of 1973.
>
> His effort to justify his position as a faithful Catholic is, I believe, deeply confused.
>
> Mr. Kmiec argues that we can't rank abortion as greater evil or a more pressing social and legal concern than racism because they are both intrinsic evils. But Mr. Kmiec has misunderstood the meaning of the term intrinsic evil, and the nature of our political moment.
>
> That two actions are both intrinsically evil tells us nothing about the relative gravity of each action. Telling a lie is intrinsically evil. So is rape. They are not equally grave. Except for instances such as perjury or libel, lying is not a crime.
>
> Racism is an attitude that may lead to acts we call racist. But nobody pertinent to our political life today advocates racism or racist acts. The intentional killing of a member of the human family— which is what happens in every abortion—is the

most pressing social justice question of our time. Mr. Kmiec's candidate advocates an unlimited right to abortion. . . .

As I am sure Mr. Kmiec knows, the law also has a pedagogical function. As does the "bully pulpit" of the presidency. Many people believe, wrongly, that if something is legal it is morally acceptable. That is among the reasons why the Supreme Court is so important in this discussion.

And that is among the reasons why it makes a very big difference whether a president takes the position that abortion is grave injustice or takes the position that abortion—including partial birth abortion and the denial of care to a baby who survives the abortion procedure—is a constitutional right. . . .

The archbishop [Chaput] says that he does not believe there is a proportionate reason—a reason he will one day have to give to the aborted babies—to justify support for a pro-choice candidate. Nor has Mr. Kmiec indicated such a proportionate reason. Mr. Kmiec claims his candidate wants to reduce the number of abortions by reducing the incidence of unwanted pregnancy, and he will do that by encouraging "responsible sexual behavior." One may be permitted to point out that four decades of sex education, including the massive promotion of contraception, has not been a great success in reducing unwanted pregnancies or abortions.

I do not know what has prompted Mr. Kmiec's current advocacy, and I take him at his word that he has convinced himself that his position is consonant with being a faithful Catholic.

The fact is, however, that, after all the tortured reasoning and misrepresentation of the positions of others, Doug Kmiec has put himself into the position of supporting for president a candidate whose track record and publicly stated views represent the extreme position of pro-abortion advocacy against the Church's repeatedly stated teaching, at the highest level of magisterial authority, respecting the moral and political imperative to protect innocent human lives.

While Kmiec and his fellow Obama supporters did not address lucid arguments like those made by Father Neuhaus, they did create confusion, tolerance for abortion, and political devastation within the Catholic community. No longer were Catholics interested in serving Christ first and their political obligation second. Folks like Kmiec set an example that convinced an apparent majority of Catholic voters that there was nothing wrong with voting for Obama—and vote for him they did.

As a matter of fact, 54 percent of Catholic voters supported Obama.[7]

The Catholic pick: Obama in the White House

After the election, the fallout and analysis were everywhere. George Neumayr, for example, said, "The Catholic Church in America has bred her own destroyers, graduating from doctrinally corrupt catechetical programs, schools and colleges two generations of pro-abortion politicians. Barack Obama, in his effortless Alinskyite style, has exploited this phenomenon to the hilt, seeking out Catholics such as Joe Biden and Kathleen Sebelius to serve as his agents of destruction."[8]

Anne Hendershott cleverly exposed the facts, telling anyone with an interest in understanding the conundrum of Catholics supporting Obama that "self-described 'progressive' Catholic organizations, such as Catholics in Alliance for the Common Good, Catholics United, and Catholic Democrats . . . along with the Catholic Health Association have created confusion for Catholics."[9]

Of course Father Andrew Greeley, who is another of those priests hostile to Catholic doctrine, had a different perspective. He explained that the reason more Catholics voted for Obama than for anyone else was that Catholics thought that if they had other reasons for voting for Obama, they could use the theory that they had a "proportionate reason" to vote for him.[10]

But that argument was quickly put to rest by Neumayr in another column when he stated, "Obama, early in the race, had shrewdly sized up the opportunity to exploit this Seamless Garment-style sophistry that lingers in the Church in America. He quickly formed Catholic groups, some counting nuns and priests among their members, to support his candidacy."[11]

Further, Neumayr accurately points out,

> According to Father Reese, Obama even enjoyed the benefits of a divided and hesitant episcopate: "Some media outlets estimated the number of vocal anti-Obama bishops at 50 or more. I do not trust these numbers. Some of the bishops included in the tally only spoke out against Nancy Pelosi when she gave an interpretation of Catholic teaching, with which they disagreed. Others simply repeated what *Faithful Citizenship* said, that abortion 'is not just one issue among many.' The document also said, 'As Catholics we are not single-issue voters.'"

> That latter statement was particularly useful to Obama's cause. He benefited both from the false perception that he disagreed with the Church on just a "single issue" and from the intramural squabble among lay Catholics and bishops over whether one could find a "proportionate reason" to offset that "single issue."

For my money, the real reason why so many Catholics voted for Obama can be laid at the United States Conference of Catholic Bishops' doorstep. The bishops prepared a nebulous document on the subject of voting that could be interpreted in any number of ways. Most bishops followed up on the document with little to nothing of substance. Nor did they address the candidates and their positions on vital matters such as abortion, euthanasia, stem cell research, and marriage.

One of the best analyses addressing the root cause of Catholics voting for Obama in the first place was written by Archdiocese of St. Louis moral theologian Msgr. Kevin McMahon:[12]

"Faithful Citizenship" rightly identified the intentional killing of innocent human beings as the prime example of an intrinsic evil that must always be opposed, but then inadvertently allowed a wide range of other moral issues to be treated as equally important. In paragraph 22, the bishops, quoting Pope John Paul II, declared that in our nation "abortion and euthanasia have become pre-eminent threats to human dignity because they directly attack life itself, the most fundamental human good and the condition for all others" (*Evangelium Vitae*, no. 5).

Then, sadly, paragraph 23 obscured this truth by including torture and racism (which no candidate pledged to promote) as intrinsic evils without distinguishing these violations of human life and dignity from the deliberate killing of the innocent. This confusion was repeated in paragraph 45, which seemed to equate capital punishment, torture, racism, and the need to overcome poverty and suffering on the one hand with unjust war, attacks on noncombatants and genocide on the other hand.

The strong affirmation of the primary importance of life itself in paragraph 26 was undercut by paragraph 29, which was interpreted to mean that the protection of innocent human life is no more important than other serious threats to human life and dignity, such as racism, immigration reform, health care, etc.

This "give and take" allowed some to cite the following directive as license to vote for candidates who support deliberate attacks against innocent human life: "There may be times when a

Catholic who rejects a candidate's unacceptable position may decide to vote for that candidate for other morally grave reasons. Voting in this way would be permissible only for truly grave moral reasons, not to advance narrow interests or partisan preferences or to ignore a fundamental moral evil" (no. 35). The lack of concrete examples left the statement unhelpfully vague. . . .

If the exit polls are accurate, then efforts to deliver the "Catholic vote" to anti-life candidates were successful. Those Catholics who, either on their own or on the bad advice of others, misinterpreted "Faithful Citizenship" and voted for candidates dedicated to advancing practices directed against innocent human life may not be culpable for their actions.

However, their votes constituted unjustifiable immediate material cooperation in these same evils. This level of cooperation can be justified only when three conditions are met. First, one opposes the evil agenda of the candidate, but still votes for him to pursue a proportionate good that could not otherwise be attained; second, one makes every effort to avoid giving scandal, which leads others to do evil; third, one acts under duress. None of these conditions was met in the recent election of anti-life candidates.

Sadly, the penalty for our muddled thinking will be visited upon those innocents whose lives will be destroyed by the removal of all restrictions on abortion, by providing federal funding for abortion and destructive embryonic stem-cell research and by lending political support to assisted suicide and euthanasia.

Some would have argued that Monsignor McMahon's analysis was overkill because Obama could not possibly be that rabid in his support of the culture of death. Such folks would be wrong.

Obama's Catholic strategy

From the beginning, President Obama made it a practice to use high profile Catholics as pawns in his game—which to this day is designed to undo any semblance of respect for the Catholic Church. His running mate and vice president, Joe Biden, is among the most ardent Catholic supporters of abortion in the history of the United States Senate. It is my contention that Obama orchestrated many of his selections for pivotal roles in his presidency on the fact that he could use Catholics to his own advantage in pressing forward with his anti-life agenda.

In addition to Biden, we saw Obama's pick for Department of Health and Human Services Secretary, pro-abortion Catholic and former governor of Kansas, Kathleen Sebelius, approved with heartwarming praise after she was nominated.[13] From the moment her nomination was announced, the misguided troops lined up to support her. Catholics for Sebelius was created and moved to motivate Obama Catholics at breakneck speed.[14] These individuals were motivated by the opportunity to get another pro-abortion Catholic into a position of power and influence. Among those who signed the public statement of endorsement for Sebelius are left-wingers Miguel Diaz, Lisa Sowle Cahill, and Douglas Kmiec.

Sebelius was confirmed and has subsequently demonstrated her pride to be on the Obama team. Further, she has approved many draconian regulations, including the removal of safeguards to conscience protection for health care providers who do not want to be involved in providing chemical abortion agents like the morning-after pill.[15]

But Sebelius and Biden were just the beginning in Obama's grand scheme to snare and charm Catholics.

Prior to his early July 2009 meeting with Pope Benedict XVI, Obama hosted a media session with Catholic journalists. Reporter John Allen described the event as a "charm offensive," reporting that upon Obama's arrival at the Vatican it was clear that his strategy had produced the desired results.[16] Many members of the Catholic media fawned all over Obama, applauding his style and grace.

Obama made another curious choice when he appointed anti-Catholic Harry Knox to be an advisor to the White House faith-based initiative office. The uproar over this appointment was immediate. Congressman John Boehner raised the roof, calling attention to the fact that it was Knox who had criticized Pope Benedict XVI for his statements on condoms. During a media briefing, Boehner, a devout Catholic, called for Knox's resignation saying, "We can't have in the White House an anti-Catholic bigot, and that's what this gentleman appears to be."[17] Knox continued to serve his term, with no resignation forthcoming.

Obama picked another pro-abortion Catholic when he nominated Dr. Regina M. Benjamin to be the surgeon general of the United States. Dr. Benjamin shares Obama's commitment to abortion. While she prefers to present herself as someone who is interested in seeking common ground between the two political factions concerned with abortion, her spokespeople have made it clear that she shares Obama's support for "reproductive health issues."[18]

The current United States representative to the Vatican is also a Catholic, Professor Miguel Diaz, whose public position on matters Catholic is far left of center. As the *National Catholic Reporter* stated at the time of the Diaz appointment, "Díaz could be seen as the product of 'divide-and-conquer' politics, meaning an attempt by Obama to mute Catholic criticism of his pro-choice stance by throwing a bone to Hispanics and peace-and-justice liberals."[19]

Obama then selected Notre Dame professor Douglas Kmiec to be his representative in the extremely Catholic country of Malta. Kmiec is the man who defended his support for Obama, and thus for abortion, by writing, "Sometimes the law must simply leave space for the exercise of individual judgment, because our religious or scientific differences of opinion are for the moment too profound to be bridged collectively."[20] Professor Kmiec subsequently resigned his post.[21]

From this small sampling of Obama appointees and nominations it is fairly easy to understand how one could come to the conclusion that there's more to the Obama strategy than meets the eye when the subject is Catholic support for his agenda. In fact, among the most obvious was, and is, his commitment to nationalized health care—which some have defined as socialized medicine. On that subject the support of the Catholic community was staggering.

Obamacare

From the beginning of his presidency, Barack Obama wanted to carve a special place in history for his ideological centerpiece—health care reform engraved in law. Obama sent signals that said one thing as he spewed another. For example, the most obvious sign of Obama's support for health care rationing, or as some defined it, "death panels," was his selection of attorney Thomas Perrelli for a Justice Department post.[22] Perrelli was one of Michael Schiavo's attorneys. As you may remember, Michael Schiavo was Terri Schiavo's husband—the husband who fought his wife's family, in the courts and the media, for the right to authorize withdrawal of Terri's feeding tubes.[23] He won his case and Terri was starved to death.

Perrelli assisted in arguing on behalf of Michael Schiavo's right to have his wife starved to death. Why would Obama make such a controversial appointment at the very moment he was formulating his health care strategy?

Putting such a man on the federal payroll should have been a warning to Catholic leadership, particularly the USCCB. But nobody seemed to know about it. As a matter of fact, the bishops were sold on the idea from the first moment they heard about it. Catholic bishops became the prime supporters, claiming that health care reform had been among their top priorities for years, if not decades.[24]

During the early days of the Obama presidency, when Obama was preparing to launch his health care reform proposal, he welcomed many religious leaders into the White House—among them Cardinal Francis George, who was president of the United States Conference of Catholic Bishops at that time.[25] After speaking with the president for half an hour, the cardinal said that he hoped to establish a "fruitful dialogue" with the White House, making it clear that,

"The common good can never be adequately incarnated in any society when those waiting to be born can be legally killed at choice . . . common ground cannot be found by destroying the common good."

But as the months wore on, the facts in the case of Obamacare began to run a bit contrary to what the cardinal had hoped to accomplish. Obama had other things in mind—even though he constantly lashed out at critics of his health care proposal. He even went so far as to say that those who opposed his proposal and found fault with the culture of death underpinnings of the plan were "bearing false witness."[26]

What is interesting about this particular statement is that Obama made it during a ten-minute conference call with faith leaders of left-leaning religious organizations. As CBN's David Brody pointed out shortly after the comment was made public,

> "When you come out on a FAITH conference call and use the words 'bearing false witness,' that is a direct slap down of conservative Evangelical groups. . . . You can debate the intention behind his words, but it really doesn't matter because it is really only how it is received that matters. In essence he was calling these Christian groups a bunch of liars. It's a serious charge. By ratcheting up the rhetoric, the president just amped up the fight against him and opened up a can of worms."

When Obama hosted a conference call with 1,000 rabbis, he explained to them that he would need their help in "accomplishing necessary reform."[27] He told them, "We are God's partners in matters of life and death." He apparently did not clarify for them that his support in "matters of life" does not include preborn children, the elderly, or the infirm. That is quite an oversight. Furthermore, the arrogance of claiming to be God's partner was another clue in the quest to unpack Obama's real agenda. But not all people of faith who were in positions of leadership were upset with Obama's messianic judgments and pronouncements.

Among those who went to extremes to support Obamacare was the president of the Catholic Healthcare Association (CHA), Sister Carol Keehan, who is no stranger to controversy both inside politics and in Catholic medical ethics. Keehan pulled out all the stops to encourage Catholics to support Obamacare, telling one interviewer that those who found language in the health care proposals that mandated death panels were doing nothing more than "fearmongering."[28]

She went on to explain that she was actually aware of the manner in which the health care law treated abortion, paying for it in many cases, but at the same time she was "tortured by these kinds of issues because it can take forever for poor pregnant women to find someone to vali-

Judie Brown appeared on EWTN's The World Over to debate the Catholic Health Association's support of Obamacare with its president, Sr. Carol Keehan.

date that they're eligible for Medicaid and get them into a maternity program, which is certainly a pro-life tool."

It would be eminently fair to suggest that Sister Carol Keehan is also tortured by the idea of Catholic hospitals divorcing themselves from the millions of dollars in government funding they currently receive. If that were to happen, these hospitals would be able to practice ethically sound, Catholic medicine instead of being hamstrung by government rules and regulations that, in all too many cases, negate human dignity. But Sister Carol likes the money.

Catholic Charities and the St. Vincent DePaul Society joined Sister Keehan in her Obamacare advocacy.[29] Throughout the final six months of 2009 these groups worked in tandem to muddy the waters, deny the problems in the proposals, and basically work as cheerleaders for the Obama overhaul of health care. They were assisted by the USCCB that claimed that health care was a basic human right.[30]

However, this assertion was not unanimously endorsed by every bishop, some of whom publicly distanced themselves from advocacy of the proposal. The *New York Times* reported that Cardinal Justin Rigali spoke out against the plan because he did not think the safeguards against abortion funding were strong enough. In addition, Bishop R. Walker Nickless of Sioux City, Iowa, made a point of telling Catholics, "No health care reform is better than the wrong sort of health care reform." He called on Catholics to contact members of Congress and ask them to oppose it.[31]

In fact, Bishop Nickless clarified,[32]

> [T]he Catholic Church does not teach that "health care" as such, without distinction, is a natural right. The "natural right" of health care is the divine bounty of food, water, and air without which all of us quickly die. This bounty comes from God directly. None of us own it, and none of us can morally withhold it from others.
>
> The remainder of health care is a political, not a natural, right, because it comes from our human efforts, creativity, and compassion. As a political right, health care should be apportioned according to need, not ability to pay or to benefit from the care. We reject the rationing of care. Those who are sickest should get the most care, regardless of age, status, or wealth. But how to do this is not self-evident. The decisions that we must collectively make about how to administer health care therefore fall under "prudential judgment."

Bishop Michael Pfeifer of San Angelo, Texas, wrote to his people about Obamacare,

> In its present form the Obama health plan is indeed deadly for the beginning and the end of human life, but in many ways is deadly for lives who are in between the beginning and the end. There is concern that this plan would also affect, in a deadly way, many mentally ill and incapacitated persons, whose lives could be shortened because their lives are not considered to have value, and they are not considered to be productive people.[33]

Bishop Samuel Aquila of Fargo, North Dakota, struck a similar note. According to CNA,[34]

> He [Aquila] said health care plans must exclude any provisions which deny "the dignity of human life," such as abortion, passive or active euthanasia and embryonic stem cell research. It would be "inherently inconsistent" to expand access to health care without safeguarding human life from conception onward, Bishop Aquila wrote. "True health care begins with the unborn child in the womb," he explained. "When a given plan to provide care fails to protect that life, it is no longer animated by a source of truth and justice, thus it will not, and cannot, flourish."

Why support a massive takeover of health care?

It amazes some that the Church did not take greater care before jumping in to support a proposal that was flawed in so many ways. That bishops and their collaborators in Catholic health care persisted in effectively mustering grassroots support for Obama's plan is a puzzle that may never be easily explained.

For example, the USCCB appeared to be demanding no funding for abortion, but the USCCB health care website never addressed coverage for birth control, human embryonic stem cell research, euthanasia, or in vitro fertilization. Such oversights would have been comical had they not been so deadly serious in the final outcome.

There was a point in the fall of 2009 when the bishops actually stepped forward rather forcefully and said they would not support the legislation if abortion funding were included. That's when Minnesota Democrat Congressman Bart Stupak stepped up, offered a weak amendment to the bill that he said banned the funding and then, at the last minute, backed off his amendment and voted for health care reform with abortion coverage.[35]

Where were the bishops during all this? In the final days of the health care reform battle, the political scene in Washington, D.C. became eerily quiet. All that was left was for Obama to have his moment of glory, sign his flawed proposal into law, and pass out pens to those who had assisted him in the struggle. It is notable that one of those pens was handed to Sister Carol Keehan, who was present for the event.[36]

While Obama said on the day he signed the bill into law that he would issue an executive order "in private" to ensure that no abortion coverage was contained in the law, the actual order he signed merely "limits" which abortions can be subsidized.[37]

There have been many reflections on the reasons why Catholic organizations worked so hard to get health care reform passed, pandering to Obama at every turn. Frankly I think it really is all about the money. If one takes an honest look at the money spigots that run from the government into various Catholic organizations, it does not take a genius to understand the connection.

Is this why Catholic health care is so similar to secular health care these days? The next chapter examines that question. But first, let us reflect on the past for a moment.

A valuable lesson

Barack Obama, defender of partial birth abortion, liberation theology, homosexual rights, and pro-socialism candidate, got over half our votes. Why? Because we let him court, cultivate, and present renegade Catholics as a representation of the Catholic faith while nothing could have been farther from the truth.

Maybe some of us were fooled. Maybe we didn't pay attention. Maybe we didn't vote at all. Maybe we didn't even complain when our wonderful Catholic faith was portrayed as supporting abortion. Maybe we confused Obamacare with social justice.

Obama manipulated Catholics because we let him. Proverbs 26:10 addresses this problem: "Like an archer wounding all who pass by is he who hires a drunken fool."[38]

All we have to do is not let that happen again.

10

CHAPTER TEN:
Perverse Health Care Ethics

Where justice is loved, where the dignity of the human person is respected, where one is not looking to one's own caprice or personal interest, but rather to serve God and others—that's where you'll find peace.

– Bishop A. Del Portillo, *In Conversation with God*

What is Catholic health care?

The first principle of Catholic health care is never to do harm. The second is to care for the poor. In fact, the roots of Catholic health care are best equated with the first nuns who travelled into the wilds of early America to care for those without access to medical treatment.[1] Today those principles are in doubt. Currently, even when Catholics are involved in health care, far too many people are being marginalized and excused from life by health care professionals who should be nurturing them because they are children of God.

Technology in medicine, placed in the wrong hands, has literally become the enemy of life in many cases. On top of that there are federal laws and regulations designed to rob health care professionals of their ability to exercise the right of conscience. Such a combination results in unsuspecting families of desperately ill patients wondering what to do or whom to trust.

Catholic medical ethics run amuck

Over the years we have witnessed a slow-moving embrace of warped ethics in Catholic health care that can only be described as detrimental to respect for the dignity of the human person. This has come about, at least in part, due to society's changing perceptions about death, the desire to avoid suffering at all costs, and personal autonomy. With phrases such as a "right to die" and "death with dignity," it is really not surprising that even some of our Catholic leaders have found it convenient to adopt practices that result in premature death.

Rather than writing about abstract principles, it would be better to focus on a real case involving a lady who wrote to me for advice. I will call her Mary. She wrote:

> Please explain the Catholic Church's teaching regarding the situation that some people I know confronted. My friend's elderly mother had a heart attack and was rushed to the local hospital. From there she was transported to a second hospital by helicopter. By the time her three children got there she was stable and talked to them normally but she was breathing with the assistance of a respirator. She had previously signed a living will but hospitals do not keep these on file in this state.
>
> The Catholic hospital tried unsuccessfully to remove her from the respirator. The woman was mentally functional and stated she wanted to live even if it were on a respirator. She called my mom who is her best friend. She said she was terrified that she had signed a living will. She had just found out that all her family members were coming to see her that afternoon and she was afraid of what that might mean. Her children had been told by the social worker they had to move her, the

> hospital would not keep her and the price of the only facility that would accept her with the respirator was way beyond what her three children could afford and was located far away from where they lived. Insurance would not pay.

> Her three children had financial problems of their own. They were dealing with college tuitions for their children, divorce, and cancer. The children made the decision to disconnect. Does the Church recognize the crushing financial burden that some families are faced with when dealing with elderly? This situation seems so heartbreaking for all concerned.

The fundamental problem with this story is clear. An elderly woman whose life hangs in the balance becomes a bargaining chip for the hospital in a game that pits human dignity against economic disaster. A hospital that takes such a monstrous view of providing breathing assistance to someone following a major heart attack does not have the interests of the patient or the patient's family at heart, but rather has chosen to ignore the patient's wishes because it has put financial concerns first. This is a clear violation of Catholic medical ethics.

As I told Mary,

> In the case you are describing, it is the hospital and its own determination to either suffocate the patient to death or transfer the patient to a costly facility that created the stress on everyone—financial, emotional, and otherwise. The Church teaches that a dying person should be kept comfortable and receive ordinary means of care which includes assisted breathing if needed, not to mention the fact that, in this case, the patient had made her wishes known.

> The hospital personnel should be ashamed; the family is not guilty of murder but the hospital surely is if indeed it withdrew oxygen from this woman.

The basic question in cases like this is a frightening one. When doctors and/or hospital personnel respond to our concerns about a loved one with comments such as, "Are the hospitals supposed to lose money and end up closing their doors and, therefore, not be there for anyone just because elderly, sick patients are demanding more care?" what should we say?

Frankly, the only way to respond to this is with honesty. The crass, brutal attitudes medical personnel use with families of vulnerable patients is a terribly sad sign of the times in which we live. In so many cases, there is no longer respect for the dignity of an individual whose life is waning or whose condition is viewed by hospital ethics committees as unworthy of care. Today it is the "quality of life" ethic that rules decisions and it is, sadly, the families—if not the patients themselves—who are left desolate and abandoned in their hour of need.

Hospital management should be required to explain why its staff or ethics committee members have placed a higher value on the corporate bottom line than on caring for defenseless patients in their hour of need. This is pure, unadulterated evil. Being there for that particular patient is just as important as being there for anyone else. Hospital ethics committees that function on the premise that some lives are unworthy of life have no ethics. A crisis is, indeed, at hand.

A worldwide catastrophe

As stated in a Catholic News Agency article, "Catholic health care workers are facing a worldwide erosion of spiritual and moral standards in their profession." According to Marylee Meehan, president of the International Catholic Committee of Nurses and Medical-Social Assistants, "In the United States, the biggest problem that Catholic nurses are facing is the ability to use their conscience."[2]

According to experts, the Catholic health care professional who applies for a position will be asked outright about his willingness to participate in an abortion, provide contraceptives, or unplug a patient from a respirator if told to do so. If the Catholic says no to such questions, he will not be considered for the position. This would be considered discrimination in most cases, but not when it comes to so-called reproductive health services or cost-saving measures.

In recent years, the Vatican has reiterated the need for Catholics to be outspoken in their defense of proper health care ethics, and to speak clearly in a culture where imposed death is looked upon as nothing more than a charitable act of compassion. Such corrupt ideologies are usurping the very meaning of health care ethics, and it has clearly begun to ooze into the Catholic sectors of health care as well. There is a growing need to be courageously Catholic and un-apologetic for the truth which is, after all, fundamental to the good of the human person, particularly those most at risk—the preborn, the elderly, the terminally ill, and the profoundly disabled.

While many theologians are, with increasing frequency, at odds with the bishops and the teaching magisterium of the Church, the facts have not changed. Opinions do not change truth, whether the subject is contraception, sterilization, abortion, or providing comfort to the dying.

Sterilization, abortion, and other no-nos

It may not come as a surprise to many that even though sterilizations are defined by the Catholic Church as evil, there were more than 9600 of them performed in Catholic hospitals in the state of Texas between the year 2000 and the year 2003. In addition, there were possibly abortions committed in the facilities as well.[3] This is documented in a report that received wide publicity at the time.

Texas is not an isolated case. Bishop Robert Vasa, of the Diocese of Baker, Oregon, severed ties with a Catholic hospital in his diocese because it was performing sterilizations.[4] In 2010, when Vasa made his public pronouncement, he issued this statement regarding his decision: "It would be misleading for me to allow St. Charles Bend to be acknowledged as Catholic in name while I am certain that some important tenets of the *Ethical and Religious Directives* are no longer being observed."

The overriding question in this case was whether or not a Catholic hospital—even one with 92 years of history in a small town like Bend, Oregon—can bend the Church's teachings to suit the clientele. Bishop Vasa said, "No, you cannot." The hospital was not pleased with Vasa's statement, but the underlying question is not who can put up a defense for an immoral practice, but rather why health care providers who pretend to be Catholic would want to contradict Catholic teaching.

One argument put forth in the Oregon case came from the CEO of Cascade Healthcare Community, which runs the hospital. He said the hospital had "an obligation to provide comprehensive health care services to our patients while remaining true to our values of compassion and caring for all."

Well, if the "values" are Catholic, then sterilization is not legitimate health care and that is the end of the argument. There will always be apologists for doing the wrong thing for apparently good reasons, but never do such arguments measure up under scrutiny.

In 2008, the Diocese of Tyler, Texas, saw a repeat aberration of sterilizations in Catholic hospitals. This time it was Trinity Mother Francis Healthcare System that defied the bishop's demand that the performance of sterilizations cease. An independent investigation had revealed that sterilizations were occurring not only in one Catholic hospital, but in two. The outcome, in late 2008, was a mixed bag. While CHRISTUS St. Michael's Hospital in Texarkana acted on the bishop's admonition and stopped sterilizing women, Trinity Mother Francis did not. The latter argued that there were cases where an indirect sterilization could be justified. The hospital further took issue with the bishop's authority to instruct its staff regarding the procedures they could and could not perform.

In response, Bishop Corrada issued a statement for the faithful of his diocese in which he set forth the principles that should govern Catholic health care institutions, saying that the reasons why direct sterilizations are contradictory to Catholic teaching are not based on his personal opinion, but rather "on reason and on the Gospel as infallibly and universally taught by the Catholic Church."[5] He reminded his flock,

> As Catholics, we affirm that human dignity and the Gospel never permit direct abortion, direct sterilization, or euthanasia. Catholics and Catholic institutions who engage [in] such practices commit a grave violation of the Gospel and the human person. If done with personal knowledge and full consent of the will, those involved commit a deadly sin. Teachers of the Catholic faith and Catholic moralists may never condone such actions. Catholic doctors, nurses, and other medical assistants may not participate in such procedures, not even at private or non-Catholic institutions. Catholic institutions may not provide such procedures or tolerate their provision at any facility under their direct control, partial ownership, or administration.

Corrada acted bravely, but most recently we have learned that there are other states with the same situations. For example, the network of Catholic hospitals established by Catholic Healthcare West is deeply involved in providing sterilizations.[6] Of the 41 hospitals in California, Arizona, and Nevada, at least 12 perform sterilizations and provide birth control to patients. Again, a violation of Catholic teaching. But Phoenix, Arizona's bishop, Thomas Olmsted, is the only one to have taken action in that area; we have not heard from the bishops in California or Nevada.

The problems created by defiance of Catholic teaching and Catholic health care ethics are enormous, but are part of the ongoing struggle Catholic health care professionals have with what has become a balancing act pitting Catholic practice against secular demands. Add to this the fact that, for more than 40 years, Catholic medical ethics has been twisting in the wind instead of remaining steadfast to Catholic teaching such as that contained in *Humanae Vitae*, and it is not hard to understand why unethical practices are being carried out as part of Catholic health care. If Catholic health care professionals are at odds with Catholic teaching, the resulting practices will be anything but Catholic.

The roots of this disregard for fundamental Catholic teaching are deeply entrenched due to the silence of most of the hierarchy. Not only have there been cases of intentional sterilizations, but also acts of abortion of preborn children whose existence has been deemed to be burdensome. Tom Szyszkiewicz wrote about one such case in Alaska.[7] At the time he reported, "[S]ome Catholic hospitals perform a procedure called 'early induction for fetuses with anomalies incompatible with life' known by its acronym, EIFWAIL, or simply as 'early induction.' This procedure induces a woman into labor after her unborn child reaches viability around 23 to 26 weeks in cases when the child is known to have a condition that makes death inevitable soon after even a full-term birth. The child born in this way is made comfortable and often held by the mother until death."

According to some supporters of this procedure, early inductions are done to preserve the emotional health of the mother—an argument contrary to Catholic teaching.[8] The fundamental reality in such cases is that the intentional killing of the preborn child, for whatever reason, is still killing. To provide a so-called Catholic medical ethics argument in support of such an act is foolhardy at best.

This would be similar to the arguments given for suggesting that while a Catholic health care facility cannot permit abortions on site, that same facility can send expectant mothers elsewhere to have their babies' lives taken. The evil is still the same, whether one is doing it in-house or sending the victim somewhere else to have the evil done. The bottom line is quite simple: No such action is ever justified.

The problem, however, has become complicated in the United States because of several factors. One is that many members of the Catholic hospital staff are people who do not accept the teachings of the Church in matters of human sexuality and therefore have no problem referring patients for abortion, sterilization, or even abortive chemicals like the morning-after pill or the birth control pill. The second factor

is the looming threat of the Obama administration impos-
ing health care rules and denying conscience protection to
those who, like serious Catholics, do not want to participate
in practices that violate the rights of the human person. As
Father Regis Scanlon has explained, the situation is dire and
needs to be directly addressed by the bishops.[9]

> What did President Obama have in mind when he
> said that we should all work together to "draft a
> sensible conscience clause"? Will he suggest that,
> if medical personnel cannot in good conscience as-
> sist someone seeking an abortion or sterilization
> or administer the "Plan B" morning-after emer-
> gency contraceptive/abortion pill, they will have
> to refer the person to someone who will? This is
> what's known as the "referral solution." . . .
>
> Bishops and administrators of Catholic hospi-
> tals would be wise to direct their medical person-
> nel to stop referring patients who request
> abortions or other immoral procedures to clinics
> that perform these procedures and to insurance
> companies that will refer them to these clinics.
> And such a directive ought to appear in more
> places than just the fine print of the employment
> contracts of healthcare personnel. In fact, the bish-
> ops and Catholic hospital administrators should
> publicly and explicitly state their objections to di-
> rect and indirect referral involving abortions, ster-
> ilizations, and the Plan B pill. We must not give
> President Obama the opportunity to claim in a fu-
> ture "conscience clause" that, by requiring
> Catholic hospitals and medical personnel to refer
> abortions, sterilizations, and Plan B pill requests
> to providers, he is only requiring something
> Catholic hospitals are already doing.

But, collectively, bishops are not addressing the
problem. For example, in Peoria, Illinois, there is a Susan G.
Komen breast cancer center located in the OSF St. Francis
Medical Center. When pro-life Americans brought it to the
attention of the hospital administration, and then the bishop,

the response was nil. Excuses were made for working with the Komen Foundation, which works closely with Planned Parenthood. As of this writing, the Komen relationship with the Catholic hospital remains intact.[10]

Sadly, this is not an exceptional incident. While the Diocese of Lafayette, Indiana, for example, discourages Catholics from supporting the Susan G. Komen programs,[11] the Diocese of Little Rock[12] backed off its warnings and apologized to Komen. This lack of consistency sends a mixed message to Catholics and is a further reflection of the growing confusion among those who really want to know what to do and cannot seem to get a straight answer from the hierarchy.

Tinkering with words

Sometimes this is a problem so deadly that lives are lost due to the inability of some bishops to confront evil and call it by its proper name. Terri Schiavo's brother, Bobby Schindler, has firsthand experience in this matter.

Terri Schiavo collapsed in her home in February 1990.[13] She was subsequently diagnosed with a condition described as encephalopathy—an injury to the brain caused by oxygenation starvation. For the first few weeks, Terri was on a ventilator. She was eventually taken off this mechanical life support and was breathing on her own. However, her condition rendered her unable to communicate verbally. As a result, some described Terri as in a "persistent vegetative state" though those who did communicate with her by eye and finger movement disagreed. After a long and emotionally draining struggle to defend Terri's right to life, her family lost to Terri's husband, Michael. In 2005, Terri was starved to death.

During this long process, Florida's Catholic bishops remained on the sidelines—particularly the diocesan bishop, Robert Lynch. When the bishops finally did make a statement, it was disingenuous at best. The bishops spoke about reconciliation of the opposing parties, never once standing up and proclaiming that, though severely disabled, Terri was not terminally ill and deserved to receive all the care that she would have been given by her parents, her brother, and her sister. In a sense it was as though these bishops had been mummified.

In March of 2007, Bobby Schindler, Terri's brother, wrote a letter to Bishop Robert Lynch in which he set forth the problem. Schindler's letter is a testimony to love, unselfish commitment, and true compassion for the weak and vulnerable in our midst:[14]

> Bishop Lynch:
>
> Speaking on behalf of my family, my intention was to write you a letter subsequent to my sister Terri Schiavo's death in order to explain to you why I hold you more accountable for her horrific death than Michael Schiavo, his attorney, and even the judge that ordered her to die.
>
> In something of a bitter irony, however, it wasn't until I came across your recent article in the *Tampa Tribune*, where your own words succeeded in saying much of what I wanted to say, that I was finally motivated to write.
>
> In the opening paragraph of your commentary, ["St. Petersburg and the Homeless Situation"[15]] you said, "The challenge of the homeless in St. Petersburg has made national news and it has been embarrassing to many people. I am convinced that both on Judgment Day and in history, we will most likely be judged not by the things which we might have considered personally important to ourselves in life but how we took care of others less fortunate." A prophetic statement indeed—and one in complete conformity with the words of our Lord in Matthew 25:31-46.
>
> You then went on to say . . . "The faces which may haunt each of us on Judgment Day may well be those of people who have approached us for assistance and were turned away."

Bishop Lynch, I couldn't have said it better myself. Instead of writing a lengthy letter explaining the hypocrisy of your words, let me just say the following:

The barbarism and nightmare of Terri's two week death by thirst and starvation will be forever seared into my family's memory. It is incomprehensible to us that a nation supposedly built on basic Judeo-Christian principles would allow something so wicked to happen.

That is, until one realizes that just as the culture of death made a triumphal entry into our nation in 1973, via legalized abortion, without so much as a whimper of protest from those with the God-given authority to stop it, so now our disabled and elderly are being targeted for death. The bottom line is, when apostolic grace and responsibility are abdicated, innocent people die.

Fortunately, my family was provided much needed comfort and strength by an enormous outpouring of prayers of support, including the unwavering support of the Holy See, which to this day continues to arrive for our family.

Even more uplifting are the stories we receive almost daily of how my sister has, in a special way, touched the hearts and changed the lives of so many people, not only in our country, but all over the world. So much so that there are efforts being made by people worldwide to promote Terri's cause for beatification.

Terri's legacy is one of life and love. Sadly, your legacy will be that of the shepherd that stood silently by as one of his innocent disabled lambs was slowly and needlessly slaughtered by removing her food and water—while you persistently ignored the cries of her family for help ("her family" being the ones who merely wanted to care for her).

You should not need to be reminded of the many passages of Scripture that condemn the shepherds that "pasture themselves on their sheep," or Christ's admonition to St. Peter to "feed My lambs," etc. As my family and I dedicate the remainder of our lives to saving other innocent lambs targeted by the death culture, I beg the Lord to spare us another successor of the apostles who would exhibit the same scandalous inaction and silence by which you remain complicit in my sister's murder via euthanasia.

I realize that for the sake of my salvation I must come to a point to at least want to forgive you, Bishop Lynch, for aiding and giving comfort to the evildoers who took my sister's innocent and vulnerable life (and yes, she was objectively more innocent and more vulnerable than perhaps any homeless person). The Catholic Church however, has spoken on Terri's case, and she has decreed in favor of Terri's right to life and everything our family did to try to save her.

Your behaviors, in contrast, have brought scandal to the universal Church and to the faithful, particularly here in Florida. Your indifference toward the truth is appalling, but seems to be indicative of the all-too-prevalent corruption of priestly formation in the 1960s and 70s, so perhaps your culpability is somewhat mitigated. Even so, the fact of my sister's murder under your "pastoral care" is a fact you should acknowledge publicly.

This season of Lent is one well suited to seek public forgiveness and make public reparation for public scandal.

At least until that happens, I regret that I must remain, as you said, the face that haunts you as someone that did approach you for assistance and was turned away.

May God have mercy on you, and may my holy sister Terri pray for us all.

Sincerely,

Bobby Schindler

Clearly in this case—which received so much national attention—and in countless others which do not receive the high level of media coverage that the Schiavo case did, it is not infrequent to witness the same sort of disengaged witnessing from bishops. Members of the hierarchy could and should be outspoken and assertive in defense of the most vulnerable in our midst, yet more often than not they remain aloof.

Invitation to prematurely end lives

Hierarchical indifference is leading to instances of quiet, carefully orchestrated efforts to put in place instruments and programs that will give the appearances of being helpful to patients and their families while actually being tools of death. These practices are seeping into the ethics committees and end-of-life care protocols in many Catholic hospitals and nursing homes.

One such problem is POLST—Physician Orders for Life-Sustaining Treatment. According to the website, POLST "is designed to improve the quality of care people receive at the end of life. It is based on effective communication of patient wishes, documentation of medical orders on a brightly colored form, and a promise by health care professionals to honor these wishes."[16]

Sounds innocent enough, but in practice it is anything but—at least according to some experts who have studied the documents, their uses, and the outcomes. One such person is Elizabeth Wickham, Ph.D., who has written,[17]

> The name says "for" treatment but in fact POLST is much more likely to LIMIT life-sustaining treatment. The POLST form becomes part of doctor's orders and is prominently displayed in the patient's medical record wherever the patient goes.

POLST was tested in Oregon in the early 90s and was launched in 1995, one year after Oregon passed legislation legalizing physician-assisted suicide. Now, in 2010, over 30 states have endorsed or are developing POLST programs. . . . In [North Carolina] the MOST form, as it is called, can override your Health Care Power of Attorney agent. The form has a lengthy series of boxes to check indicating levels of treatment. Boxes include "Comfort Measures Only," "No Antibiotics," "No IV Fluids," and "Do Not Attempt Resuscitation."

A trained facilitator, using carefully designed curricula such as the "Respecting Choices" program, may assist in filling out the form which then becomes part of doctor's orders, although it can come into effect with neither the patient's nor a physician's signature.

Do you remember the discussion of death panels in the proposed federal health care bill last summer? Did you know that the "consulting sessions" between physician and patient that were to be encouraged and federally funded involved filling out the POLST form?

Wickham's research has been provided to select Catholic bishops and several Vatican offices. Her concerns that POLST is indeed part and parcel of those Obamacare death panels has thus far failed to make an appearance on the radar screens of either the USCCB or its bioethics advisory groups. But as this apparent lack of concern persists, the danger grows daily. Pressure to save money in health care facilities is escalating, and the Church has yet to mandate ethical guidelines that would negate tragedies like those suffered by Terri Schiavo and others.

The bishops tell us that their *Ethical and Religious Directives for Catholic Healthcare Services* (ERDs)[18] are all that hospital staff and physicians need to make the right decisions, but thus far those directives are little more than words on paper. Language becomes fungible when not supported by direct oversight from those who have the best interests of patients, not balance sheets, at heart.

Researcher Julie Grimstad has seen this happen in her state of Wisconsin. She warns about proposed legislation in the state, making it clear that proposals like POLST contradict the very essence of Catholic teaching on caring for those facing death. In her analysis, she makes several salient points based on the flawed morality of this program. Among her points to consider are these (paraphrased):[19]

1) If a POLST proposal says that withdrawing treatment does not constitute suicide, does that mean that even withdrawing life-sustaining treatment is not to be considered a death wish or a crime against the integrity of the human person?

2) Is death by dehydration a natural process if the patient is subjectively determined to be dying anyway or is in a vulnerable situation similar to Terri Schiavo's?

3) POLST advocacy is based on patient autonomy, asserting that it is paramount in all situations. This is contrary to Catholic moral teaching which states: "A person has the moral obligation to use ordinary or proportionate means of preserving his or her life."

4) While POLST forms suggest that nutrition and hydration can be defined as medical treatment and thus withdrawn or withheld, the Church teaches otherwise.

According to Grimstad,

> In March of 2004, Pope John Paul II addressed the International Congress on Life-Sustaining Treatments and Vegetative State. He unequivocally stated that withholding hydration and nutrition from patients when these will sustain their lives is wrong and that death by starvation and dehydration "ends up becoming, if done knowingly and willingly, true and proper euthanasia by omission."

> . . . In 2007, the Congregation for the Doctrine
> of the Faith strongly reinforced this papal instruc-
> tion, writing to the bishops of the United States:
> "The administration of food and water even by ar-
> tificial means is, in principle, an ordinary and pro-
> portionate means of preserving life. It is therefore
> obligatory to the extent to which, and for as long
> as, it is shown to accomplish its proper finality,
> which is the hydration and nourishment of the pa-
> tient. In this way suffering and death by starvation
> and dehydration are prevented."

5) POLST opens the door for neglect, substandard medical treatment, and cost-saving at the expense of patients'
lives. Although POLST promoters steer clear of mentioning
the money motive, it is undoubtedly a factor in efforts to
limit treatment.

POLST paradigm programs, which are touted as being
successful in avoiding unnecessary "treatment" like
artificially provided nutrition and hydration are the latest in
a long line of programs designed to change the way we think
about death, ask for early death, and help those we love
depart their lives sooner rather than later.[20]

These practices have no place in Catholic health care. But
when leading Catholic organizations are pressing for
compliance with Obamacare, we can expect to see a deluge
of such practices, all in the name of cost containment. Where
are the bishops? Or is financial gain too important to these
Catholic hospitals and those bishops who oversee them?

Making money the bottom line

From the beginning of the Obamacare debates, there has
been a stiff difference of opinion among Catholic organizations. Some have attempted to stay the course and defend
Catholic teaching while others have advocated for nationalized health care reform. The United States Conference of
Catholic Bishops, the Catholic Health Association, Catholic
Charities, and even the St. Vincent DePaul Society have been
among those entities that worked for the passage of some
form of Obamacare.

Now known officially in law as the Affordable Care Act, Obamacare had many faces during its long debate.[21] There were those who said that they would only support it if abortion funding were removed—but when push came to shove, they were happy to see it pass. That's why we found the interview with CHA president, Sister Carol Keehan, so very informative.

Keehan, whose annual salary is nearly $1 million, was asked a question about the relationship between Catholic health care and federal funding for Catholic hospitals:[22]

> [QUESTION:] Considering the difficulty surrounding abortion and other medical interventions that conflict with Catholic teaching, would it be better if Catholic hospitals didn't need public funds?

> [KEEHAN:] From the start, we in Catholic health care have always been not only good members of our church but good citizens of our country, and so we've always worked with government as partners to reach out to our fellow citizens. We haven't said all government is bad, and we haven't said government has no responsibility for the poor.

> If you read the history of why Catholic hospitals are in this or that city, many times it was because elected representatives went to the bishop or to the motherhouse of a women's religious community and asked them to come and run a hospital in that place.

> The charter for the hospital that I ran in Washington for 15 years, Providence Hospital, was signed by Abraham Lincoln because Washington is a federal city. The finance committee for that hospital was the House Ways and Means Committee. The sisters would walk into Congress, go to Ways and Means, and get their annual budget, so we've got a long history of engagement.

> The Ursuline Sisters established the first Catholic hospital in this country in New Orleans.

After the Louisiana Purchase that transferred the territory from France to the United States, they were petrified because they didn't know what it would mean. President Thomas Jefferson visited them, and they still have his handwritten letter in which he promised never to interfere with their work and pledged to help them.

I think the ideal is that we work together, because in many ways we have the opportunity to inform the government about the needs of people and about what works and doesn't work for the people the government is called to serve.

We've been accepting Medicaid for a long, long time, and I can tell you you're never going to get rich by taking care of poor people, not in my lifetime anyway. We have an obligation to our fellow citizens to make our government what it ought to be, and you don't do that by walking away.

Has Keehan forgotten that when Abraham Lincoln signed the charter for Washington's Providence Hospital, there was no government funding for abortion referrals, medical abortions, sterilizations, contraceptives, or other programs that are in direct violation of Catholic teaching?

Thomas Jefferson would be spinning in his grave if he read this interview. After all, leaders like Keehan have welcomed government interference. They have gone along with government regulations in more than a few instances.

For more years than we can count, Catholic hospitals have been on the federal dole. When it came time for the big push to pass Obama's health care reform, the Church was front and center. As of this writing, we are still waiting for the USCCB to outline for the faithful the horrible provisions in that law that pander to organizations like Planned Parenthood Federation of America and euthanasia advocates.

The USCCB has not made it clear that it must not morally witness an alignment of Catholic health care ethics with programs that are fundamentally flawed. Could it be that God's will is trumped by federal funding?

Catholic hospitals that are steeped in practices aligned with Obamacare are not the equivalent of sound health care in the first place.[23] The most egregious of these is the provision of birth control in Catholic settings, by Catholic doctors, and with the approval of far too many Catholic priests, theologians, and ethicists. What is it about birth control that scares bishops into silence?

What can I do?

Like the so-called Catholic colleges we discussed earlier, a hospital with a Catholic identity may not necessarily be Catholic in its health care ethics, policies, or practices. Health care is big business that involves big revenues and salaries. Catholic health care is no different. But the brand of medical ethics applied to practices in a Catholic health care facility should be different.

Ronald Reagan left us with some great advice: "Trust, but verify."[24] So, don't trust me, do yourself and family a favor—read *Humanae Vitae.*

When choosing a Catholic hospital, ask trusted Catholic doctors, clergy, and friends about the hospital staff and practices. Inquire at the controlling diocese and use your critical listening skills. Do not be afraid to press further if you don't like what you hear or get vague answers or platitudes. (Gut check: Does it sound like you're talking to a politician?)

Since by now you have read and understood most of this book, you will be able to ask the right questions and express your concerns to those who, to put it bluntly, rely on you not knowing any better.

You may not have a choice in using a "non-conforming" Catholic health facility, but you have every opportunity to be an *informed* and *prepared* Catholic patient if you take these actions *before* you need emergency or critical care.

11

CHAPTER ELEVEN:
Contraceptive Cowardice

I am not called to be successful. I am called to be faithful.

– Blessed Mother Teresa

Birth control: Cause and effect

The practice of Catholic medicine requires a clear understanding of Catholic health care ethics. As we have just learned, any Catholic facility or practitioner that is aligned with the requirements of Barack Obama's version of health care reform, the Affordable Care Act,[1] cannot be defined as Catholic. Among the most glaring examples of this violation of Catholic ethics would be the prescribing, providing, and recommending of contraceptives of any kind. In fact, it is safe to say that this practice is not only as evil as the provision of abortion, but is the underlying cause of the cultural acceptance of abortion, particularly among Catholics.

As a recent poll reveals, the vast majority of Catholics have no problem with contraceptives. Further, most would deny that Catholic teaching on the matter binds them to obedience.[2] This would be hilarious if it were not so profoundly wrong. But the reasons for this apparent disconnect between what the Church expects of its people and what its people understand about those expectations are really where the dire emergency exists.

Clearly, or at least we hope it is clear, most of those who today call themselves Catholic, particularly between the ages of 10 and 60, have never heard a sermon or learned in Catechism class that the Catholic Church defines the use of contraception, for any reason, as intrinsically evil. In other words, Catholics today, for the most part, do not even consider the possibility that using a form of contraception is the equivalent of writing a one-way ticket to hell.

The fact that the vast majority of Catholic bishops have failed, over the past 50 years, to make it clear to their priests and, through them, their people, the precise Church teaching on this subject is well documented. The most recent poll is just one among many such surveys that have been done. Sadly, those who despise the Church are the very ones making their living marketing various types of products that contribute to "sexual freedom." Such individuals bask in the vacuum the bishops have created; they are all too happy to sell their wares to Catholics while smacking their lips in delight that they are actually poking a finger in the eye of the Church itself.

One would think that the bishops would have wised up over these past 50 years, but their track record proves the opposite to be the case. Perhaps this is best exposed by the words of a heroic Catholic priest, Father Paul Marx, who said, "Future generations will wonder why so many Catholic bishops and priests in the west didn't see contraception as a seminal evil and the chief cause of the Church's swift decline."[3]

This was true when Father Marx said it more than 30 years ago and, sadly, it remains true to this very day. What is it about contraception that appears to drive priests and bishops into silent surrender?

My research and study of this question has brought me to the rather sad conclusion that maintaining the status quo—which means filling the collection plate while helping the folks in the pews feel good about themselves through preaching a watered down version of Catholicism—has led not only to the decline in Catholics but, more specifically, to the decline in vocations to the Catholic priesthood. Two generations of Catholic parents have practiced contraception. This means the number of large families has declined. And since larger families are the fertile ground for many vocations, the ensuing drought has had deleterious effects on the Church, its priesthood, and religious life. Furthermore, sterile relationships within marriage do not a flourishing example of openness to God's will make.

Fundamentally, we could posit this question: If there is no reason to define the Catholic Church and its teachings as unique, heroic, and dedicated to truth, then why even be a Catholic?

Getting it right

What if all the priests, bishops, and laity of the Catholic Church united in living, defending, and teaching indispensable Church teachings regarding human sexuality?

Would the family unit be strengthened in our nation? If one is to accept the analysis of Pope John Paul II on this question, the answer is yes. In his letter to families, he wrote,[4]

> In particular, responsible fatherhood and motherhood directly concern the moment in which a man and a woman, uniting themselves "in one flesh," can become parents. This is a moment of special value both for their interpersonal relationship and for their service to life: they can become parents—father and mother—by communicating life to a new human being. *The two dimensions of conjugal union*, the unitive and the procreative, *cannot be artificially separated* without damaging the deepest truth of the conjugal act itself.

The strength of a couple united totally with God and surrendered completely to His will—including being open to the possibility of children—is nearly unbreakable. One of the reasons why there is an infinitesimally small number of divorces among couples who understand their relationship with God and His gift of children is that they have chosen never to leave God out of any aspect of their married lives. I am not here describing a "perfect" marriage, but am defining one that is grounded in God rather than worldly whim and fancy. And when the going gets tough, as it does in everyone's life, faith can and does make the difference.

Would Catholic young people be more likely to remain sexually chaste until marriage if priests and bishops preached the truth from the pulpit to them and to their parents? Yes! Here again Pope John Paul II lays it out:[5]

> "A grave responsibility derives from this: those who place themselves in open conflict with the law of God, authentically taught by the Church, guide spouses along a false path. The Church's teaching on contraception does not belong to the category of matter open to free discussion among theologians. Teaching the contrary amounts to leading the moral consciences of spouses into error." Pope John Paul II also explained that contraception contradicts and is opposed to true love: "Thus the innate language that expresses the total reciprocal self-giving of husband and wife is overlaid, through contraception, by an objectively contradictory language, namely, that of not giving oneself totally to the other. This leads not only to a positive refusal to be open to life but also to a falsification of the inner truth of conjugal love, which is called upon to give itself in personal totality" (*Familiaris Consortio*, #32).

Parents who are raising children to and through their teenage years with a false sense of what is good, bad, and indifferent about their family are parents who have denied their children proper teaching or who have conveniently avoided the truth themselves. Such parents will not take the difficult road when educating their young in the sensitive area of human sexuality. On the contrary, all manner of perversion is going to occur. This is why the largest market for Planned Parenthood-style sex education is among the children of wayward Catholics. The Catholic teen who does not understand fundamental Catholic truth about his own personal dignity and value is going to be a teen open to the worldly ideals of so-called sexual freedom regardless of the personal cost. Planned Parenthood knows this and delights in the silence of the pulpits from one end of America to the other.

If every Catholic parish had a sound pro-life, pro-family foundation in its catechesis designed to educate parents on how to properly raise Catholic youth to be saints, would Planned Parenthood fail to rob children of their souls? Wouldn't the result be that Planned Parenthood would wither up and disappear? Yes!

In fact, the Church has had that very tool at its disposal since December 31, 1930, when Pope Pius XI issued his remarkable encyclical entitled *Casti Connubii*. In that document he taught,[6]

> [T]he Catholic Church, to whom God has entrusted the defense of the integrity and purity of morals, standing erect in the midst of the moral ruin which surrounds her, in order that she may preserve the chastity of the nuptial union from being defiled by this foul stain, raises her voice in token of her divine ambassadorship and through our mouth proclaims anew: any use whatsoever of matrimony exercised in such a way that the act is deliberately frustrated in its natural power to generate life is an offense against the law of God and of nature, and those who indulge in such are branded with the guilt of a grave sin.

These words were written as part of a much longer document at a time when the first crack in the world's contraceptive dam had occurred. The occasion was Planned Parenthood's founder, Margaret Sanger's, greatest achievement, for she had broken through a solid wall behind which all Christian churches had stood united against contraception. Along with her British cohorts, she pressed the Anglican Church from within until it broke and permitted contraception for limited reasons within marriage. That one action at the Lambeth Conference in 1930 opened the floodgates.[7]

Note that Pius XI acknowledged that single action as "moral ruin." Today his words are ignored, scoffed at as being out of step with modernity, and thought of as totally ridiculous. Yet in those few words resides the key to protecting young people from sexually transmitted diseases and death caused by harmful contraceptive chemicals. Those words show the way to saving marriages, to strengthening the nation, and to shutting down Planned Parenthood.

Jim Burnham puts it quite succinctly when he writes about the deadly blow *Casti Connubii* could bring to Planned Parenthood's culture of sexual insanity. He opines,[8]

> Where the philosophy of Planned Parenthood rejects spouse, fertility, and children, *Casti Connubii* champions all three as inseparably linked. Pius XI understood, as many pro-lifers do not, that we cannot defend the value of children without defending the indissolubility of marriage and the procreative purpose of sex. Many pro-lifers, including many Catholics, have surrendered on divorce and contraception. They are two-thirds conquered. Is it any wonder that their pro-life activities are ineffective?
>
> Some may object that *Casti Connubii* apparently didn't stop the growth of Planned Parenthood. True, but that was because (to borrow G. K. Chesterton's remark about the Catholic Church), "It was not tried and found wanting, it was found difficult and left untried." . . .
>
> Perhaps *Casti Connubii*'s greatest advantage is that its arguments are based on the universal principles of the natural law. The precepts of the natural law don't depend on revelation and are equally binding for believers and unbelievers alike. Many Catholics have adopted the religious skepticism of the surrounding culture. Therefore, arguments based on the natural law are more clear and convincing than arguments that seem based

on religious notions alone. The conclusions presented in *Casti Connubii* are compelling to all men of reason and good will. Let's face it: our culture is more pagan than Christian. If we are going to transform it, we'd better use arguments that will convince even pagans. . . .

Casti Connubii belongs in the hands and hearts of every man and woman who loves the truth and has the courage to fight error. If you are serious about ending abortion, if you are serious about strengthening your marriage, then use *Casti Connubii* to strike the multi-headed hydra of Planned Parenthood a lethal blow.

What are the bishops and their priests waiting for? Pope Pius XI had the antidote to their silence if only they had the will:[9]

57. We admonish, therefore, priests who hear confessions and others who have the care of souls, in virtue of our supreme authority and in our solicitude for the salvation of souls, not to allow the faithful entrusted to them to err regarding this most grave law of God; much more, that they keep themselves immune from such false opinions, in no way conniving in them. If any confessor or pastor of souls, which may God forbid, lead the faithful entrusted to him into these errors or should at least confirm them by approval or by guilty silence, let him be mindful of the fact that he must render a strict account to God, the Supreme Judge, for the betrayal of his sacred trust, and let him take to himself the words of Christ: "They are blind and leaders of the blind: and if the blind lead the blind, both fall into the pit" (Mt 15:14).

The truth is stranger than fiction

To the casual reader, these remarks may seem to be nothing more than complaints about those bishops and priests who have failed to teach and preach the sound, natural law basis for the Catholic Church's admonition that contraception and abortion are fruits of the same evil tree. After all, such a person might think the situation is all but lost anyway, so why mention it?

But my words are not arrows aimed at the heart of the men ordained into the priesthood who have the responsibility to shepherd souls. My words represent sincere sorrow that millions of people, young and old alike, have been misled into believing that Catholic teaching which is hard to accept is Catholic teaching which need not be obeyed.

I have seen countless stories from those who have suffered because of a lack of understanding of the beauty of Catholic teaching, as well as stories from those who do understand and embrace this teaching. Here are insights from four such Catholic women.

Janine's story

Janine was betrayed into believing that the birth control pill was nothing more than a magic potion that would protect her from getting pregnant:

> Dear Judie,
>
> From my personal experience, I believe my child's soul cried before it died; before it breathed its first breath in the creation of my womb.
>
> MR. PILL AND ME
>
> Much reflection has transpired over this life-changing drug and what it has done for me since I read "Golden anniversary of the pill" [*Guestwork*, May 13]. Mr. Pill, you gave me a green light. You gave me the freedom to turn love into lust, and in doing so, I did not wait; I lost dignity, self-respect, and suffered. The fruits that could have been borne from passion harnessed were lost. Yet I continued to go forward with you. You gave me a doctor who, upon my first visit, advised me that I did not have to inform my mother about you. My mother—the person who birthed me, nursed me, loved me—you told me to deny her. Thankfully, I did not listen. One night before I ingested you,

you inspired an instinct that shouted from the depths of my being. It screamed, "Don't. Kill me." I swallowed anyway. You gave me a bald spot on the side of my head. Still, I could not say no to you. Finally, you attacked my heart, giving me palpitations. Horrified by this unnatural beat of life, I stopped. I cut your strings and regained the true freedom of being me.

Good neighbors, if you really want to rejoice, I challenge you to respect and celebrate the wonders of life! Naturally!

Janine

Janine's parents, her local priest, and anyone who might have helped her see the facts in the right perspective abandoned her by their very silence. Nobody ever told Janine the truth about the pill or warned her that the pill could kill an innocent baby while he was still growing within her. Nobody told her that she could suffer serious medical problems, even death. But most importantly, nobody told her that sex outside of marriage was wrong—a sin against God. We are thankful that Janine survived her encounter with "Mr. Pill," but what about all the young women who have yet to learn the truth, either from the pulpit or, frankly, from their doctors?

Why haven't young women been told about saving sex until marriage? Why haven't newly married Catholics learned to understand natural methods of spacing children like natural family planning (NFP)? Well, today, in a society where nearly all Catholics favor contraception, these aren't really questions, but rather serious symptoms of the huge problem created by 50 years of silence in the pulpits.

Gaby's concerns

Gaby sent this note regarding NFP:

I know that the Church would like NFP to be more widely used and [there to be] less [use of] birth control devices and abortions. But to be honest, every show, every article, every person I catch endorsing it on EWTN has more than four children, some eight, some 10! I think, although they love all their blessings and welcomed them, it seems to outsiders, it just doesn't work or it's only for people who really don't care if they have three or eight. I mention this because in watching EWTN this past year with my teenage daughters, they were seeing the same thing and found it "scary." A football player just this week on *Life on the Rock* said they use NFP and have three girls and one on the way—all very young. I'm not being a pessimist, but I want to put my daughters' minds at ease that it could be an option. I didn't myself, unfortunately, so I can't be a good role model there, but I'm trying! Thank you for any advice.

Gaby's honesty about her own failure to follow Catholic teaching is refreshing, but her concerns for her daughters and how they feel about having as many children as God plans for them once they are married tell us a great deal about the culture in which our children and our grandchildren are maturing.

When I responded publicly to Gaby on a public communications forum, I told her this:

We live in such a sexually saturated culture that the very idea of trusting one's fertility to God's will seems a bit frightening to the young. However, if faith in God is cultivated with the proper perspective, and trust in His will is an integral part of that formation for a young person, then the concept of having more than one or two children is actually viewed as a blessing.

Birth control is simply not an option for a Catholic, and there are so many wonderful reasons why this is so. Among the most obvious is the peace of mind and health of body that come about when a married couple decide they will not pollute their bodies or their souls with instruments that are offensive to God.

Doing what God wants is rarely easy, but it is always a blessing.

Cathy

Cathy read Gaby's remarks and wrote:

To say that people with two or three children are not practicing NFP is simply not true. While I myself have eight children, it is not because NFP has failed us in any way (there are five years between child six and seven and five years between child seven and eight). It is because we have on a monthly basis asked ourselves the questions that all couples should ask in regard to [being] open to life at this point in time or not—and, if not, why.

Those questions are something a couple practicing NFP ask themselves on a continuous basis, unlike contracepting couples who ask it once and then never seem to return to the question again. I can't tell you how many times people stop and tell me they wished they had had more children. I surmise it is because they made a plan to have so many and then never ever thought about it again once they reached their "goal."

Bringing life into the world is not something that should be taken lightly or only talked about in the first years of marriage. That is one of the most beautiful things about NFP: it gives you and your spouse an opportunity to continually think about the gifts you have and how you are able to share them, and decide whether . . . to have another child or postpone the decision for another month.

Cecelia

Cecelia, like Cathy, shares words of wisdom:

I found the comments of Gaby on NFP interesting and sad. She said that because many of the people advocating NFP have four or more children, that makes it seem that NFP doesn't

work. Doesn't it ever occur to her or others that
there really are people who truly choose to have
more than one or two children? Gaby's worry is
sad. Why on earth wouldn't a person want a lot of
children? I have five and they are JOY incarnate.

These moms wanted Gaby to receive a message that the
mainstream media is certainly not sending—not to mention
the vast majority of Catholic priests and bishops in our land
today. Perhaps by being exposed to the facts behind the cal-
lous disregard for human life that is detailed in this book,
and others like it, more Catholics, including ordained
priests, will develop the chutzpah to do more than sit back
and ignore Christ's call to follow Him and never count the
cost.

The ultimate dangers inherent in contraceptive cowardice

In one of his most remarkable essays, theology teacher
Thomas Reynolds wrote about the serious problems
Catholics in denial on the subject of contraception must confront. The moral theologians who have led the revolt against
Catholic teaching on matters of a sexual nature have for 50
years said that these teachings are not infallible. They have
been wrong and they are still wrong. This is why Reynolds'
words are germane to this very moment in which we now
live.[10]

According to Reynolds, "[T]he teaching on contraception has been met with widespread private and public
silence and/or rejection among those required to teach and
apply this Church doctrine." This denial of the infallibility of
this teaching reveals to what extent one is imbued with or
motivated by a contraceptive mentality and is a contributor
to the sexual revolution and to the cultivation of lust as a
philosophy of life.

Reynolds continues,

Some, having lost the faith, deny Church authority. . . . Many more, however, are in Catholic
denial: a conscious or unconscious unwillingness
to listen to the Holy Spirit and to identify and ad-

dress their explicit or implicit disobedience to God's will. They are somewhat like Adam and Eve trying to hide from the Lord in the garden. When He finds them, they are unable to accept responsibility for their sin. Only when lovingly and firmly confronted by truth would they begin to face the reality of their sin and accept responsibility for it, a prerequisite for mercy.

There are those who accept the Church's position on contraception, yet are in denial regarding their moral obligation to speak out about this evil. They have a thousand reasons for never addressing this evil in the public or private forum. Many clergy, aware of their own sinfulness, become unduly and inappropriately reticent with regard to identifying the moral evil in the lives of those under their charge. Yet the reality of sin must first be accepted if it is to be cleansed. It is the duty of shepherds to speak this truth remembering that the truth carries the grace of the Holy Spirit with it. Shepherds must become like King David who, only **after** admitting his guilt and begging for mercy and the restoration of a clean heart, proclaims, **"Then I will teach transgressors your ways and sinners will return to thee"** (Ps 51:13). This is not pride; it is zeal for the truth. It will be accepted when it is presented in love, humility, and concern for the salvation of souls.

Other shepherds fear being rejected or ridiculed by parishioners or peers. They fear losing financial support. Many are embarrassed to speak publicly against contraception because they have supported or condoned it so many times privately or in the confessional. Some say they never preach about it because the Scripture readings at Mass do not speak of it, and they must base their homilies on the Scripture readings. Did they not address the tragedy/evil of 9/11 in their homilies? Surely the **entire** Mass is about Jesus' taking our sins upon Himself and reconciling us to the Father.

The homily is a proper place to identify and address existing moral evils for which Jesus died.

Many other shepherds claim they do not want to badger people who already know contraception is morally evil. If that is so, then why are the confessional lines so short or even non-existent while so many are involved in this serious moral evil? Why are the confessional lines so short while virtually everyone goes up to receive Holy Communion? Could it be the widespread denial of sin, a denial that has taken root and pushed out the very awareness of sin and the presence of the Holy Spirit Who leads to all truth? . . .

The dangers for the sheep and lambs are real and growing. The direct and indirect effects of contraception include millions of abortions, a high rate of divorce, spread in use of pornography, and rise in homosexual liaisons. Also deriving from contraception is a critical lack of vocations. Will the Holy Spirit find receptive souls in families whose parents have turned their hearts from God's will (Jn 14:15-17)? Will these young men and women find the models of love and obedience to God's will that give flesh to the Holy Spirit's invitation to the sacrificial obedience of priesthood and religious life? Some of these are the very dangers and evils prophesied and warned of by Pius XI, Paul VI and John Paul II.

Pope John Paul II taught that contraception and abortion are "fruits of the same tree" (*The Gospel of Life* 13). Why? In the act of contraception, God's plan for the unity of the conjugal act is thwarted: the interior and organic connection between love, sex, and new life is broken. The fruitfulness of God's plan for conjugal love is wrested from God's sovereign control and placed under man's "sovereign" control. The effects are manifold: marriage becomes incidental, the conjugal act becomes recreational, selfish, sterile, and

loses its sacred character, homosexual unions are
rationalized into expressions of God's plan for sex,
and human persons are dehumanized and become
objects for pleasure alone.

Results: Blood on their hands

Reynolds has hit the nail right on the head. Today, after
50 years of numerous bishops denying their flock the
precious, soul-saving teaching that sexual sin does exist and
is grave, it is an irrefutable fact that these same bishops are
publicly, and in growing numbers, distancing themselves
from efforts to **REHUMANIZE** the most vulnerable
members of the human family by running, not walking,
away from state and national efforts to recognize human
personhood in the laws of the land. To my mind, this is a
grave, deadly manifestation of what the past 50 years of
laissez-faire attitudes regarding human sexuality and
Catholic teaching has wrought.

Whose brand of politics has driven these bishops into
this wretched state? The answer may surprise you, amaze
you, and perhaps shock you—as it has me.

A valuable lesson

Like the Prodigal Son or Good Samaritan, it does not
matter where you have been, but where you are going.
Whether you have used contraceptives in the past or use
them now, whether you have had an abortion or are considering abortion, what will you do tomorrow?

Pope John Paul II, hopefully someday the patron saint of
the pro-life movement, taught us that freedom is about
doing what we ought, rather than what we want. This is so
counterintuitive to our human nature that even some clergy
and religious do not seem to understand how this feeds our
souls. Encourage, entreat, and demand that our Catholic
health care providers and clergy treat us and lead us to
God's freedom—not to man's pathetic imitation of it.

Meanwhile, teach your sons and daughters and make
them suitable to carry on Christ's mission.

12

CHAPTER TWELVE:
Why Do Bishops Reject Personhood?

There may be occasions when out of prudence or charity we should keep quiet. But prudence and charity are not the result of cowardice or self-comfort. It will never be prudent to keep quiet when keeping quiet may cause scandal or confusion, or when such behavior may have an adverse effect on the faith of others.

— *In Conversation with God,* Volume 4, p. 113

Lessons of the past

Throughout my 40 years of involvement in various aspects of what is commonly referred to as the "pro-life" or, as the mainstream media defines it, "anti-abortion" movement, it has become increasingly clear that the work we do is far more expansive than merely working toward over-turning the 1973 Supreme Court decisions of *Roe v. Wade* and *Doe v. Bolton*. The truth is that these two decisions that combined to decriminalize the killing of the preborn for any reason were the fruits of the sexual revolution of the sixties.

Yes, that's what I said. Sex without responsibility is really the foundation upon which the ethos of contraception, homosexual rights, abortion, in vitro fertilization, human embryonic stem cell research, euthanasia, and human cloning developed. It's a rising river creating a flood of perversity that has flown freely for more than 50 years.

Any logical person can see how this could happen when sexual relations between a man and a woman are mechanized, sterilized, and ultimately divorced from the procreative power that is unique to the human being. As Reynolds said in the previous chapter, the pleasure principle permits anything—anything at all.

So what is the solution? It sure is not to insist that somehow the mere regulation of a particular type of abortion or a specific method of abortion is the goal. Hardly! But apparently these simple facts and conclusions have not occurred to the United States Conference of Catholic Bishops. Its 2011 "respect life" agenda appears to consist mainly of covering the members' backsides.

For example, the USCCB concentrates primarily on ensuring that the federal taxpayer funding of abortion status quo is maintained.[1] The USCCB supports the Hyde-type language that permits taxpayer funding for some abortions in cases of rape, incest, and life of the mother. This law does not address other types of abortion such as medical abortion.

Another example of this backslide is the USSCB's treatment of federal funding for Planned Parenthood. When the pro-life movement began its push in Congress to end taxpayer funding for Planned Parenthood, the USCCB was nowhere to be found. Then all of a sudden, in April of 2011, when the struggle was temporarily lost in the United States Senate, the USCCB made a public statement declaring that it was opposed to the continued funding of Planned Parenthood.[2]

When state legislatures are pressured to pass pro-assisted suicide laws that would, in essence, decriminalize the taking of the lives of the ill and the vulnerable, the USCCB remains aloof. But now it has decided that the bishops should vote on a public statement opposing such actions.[3]

Vote? Why vote on taking a public position on something as clear-cut as the question of whether or not to authorize killing? The USCCB's political structure is fraught with this sort of duplicity.

Having watched the USCCB function in this manner for many years, I can only say that it is still obvious to me that hierarchical politics is hard at work in Washington, D.C. And the shame of it is that Catholic bishops are not politicians; they are spiritual leaders who set examples for the flock by their actions. Sadly, in many instances, those actions give witness to the malaise that has affected so many of our shepherds in recent times.

The best illustration of this is the grassroots drive to achieve legal recognition of personhood for all human beings at risk—born and preborn.[4] Obviously abortion kills, but so do acts of infanticide, euthanasia, and other attacks on the vulnerable. This occurs through acts of commission and omission. In other words, a person can be intentionally deprived of life because a direct action is taken to end that life or because an action that might have saved a life is not taken. The result is the same whether the person is a preborn child, an elderly person with dementia, or anyone else whose only defense is that he is a human being whose life should be protected.

If and when personhood efforts succeed, human beings would be protected and respected as God intended.

This personhood activity has been the foundation of pro-life efforts for nearly 30 years, but in recent years the momentum has picked up and there are now strategies in place in many states, and in Congress, to move toward victory. The various tactics designed to challenge the status quo are bearing fruit, yet the bishops are sadly disconnected.

Why personhood?

The pursuit of constitutional protection of the human rights of every person is mandatory. That is the goal of the personhood effort.

The social and political attitudes in the United States today are out of sync with the natural law and common sense. For more than 35 years Americans have been told that a "right to abortion" is settled law—settled by the *Roe v. Wade* and *Doe v. Bolton* decisions of 1973.

Human embryologist C. Ward Kischer has written of the Supreme Court decisions,[5]

> This landmark decision proved to be the watershed between science and the law. Statements made within the decision, and since, concerning human development, have been disingenuous, irresponsible, or deliberately deceitful.
>
> One would like to believe that Supreme Court Justices, acting as learned and wise servants of our society, exercise great and considerate care in making decisions that not only affect our daily lives, but impact the evolution of our culture in the most moral and responsible way. We also want to believe they seek out all available facts concerning a case before coming to decisions. Alas, such is not the case.

Indeed, history teaches us that when a certain political agenda is in play, the Supreme Court can make decisions based on the preconceived goals of those for whom a favorable decision is desirable. Such was also the case in 1965 when the Supreme Court ruled that contraception could not in any way be controlled by the law.[6] In that decision the winner was Planned Parenthood!

Such politically motivated decisions, which put medical ethics on a collision course with political will, paved the way for folks to do whatever it takes, under cover of law, to shed responsibility for personal behavior. Sexual freedom, in other words, requires the ability to do away with the evidence—which in this case is a baby.

Today, lawmakers, the media, and average Americans live their lives without thinking about the consequences of what the law permits. If this were not the case, the following would not be occurring:

—Women would not be using, and men would not be encouraging the use of, contraceptive chemicals and devices without regard to the fact that these materials are not medicine to treat an illness but rather recreational drugs that permit all manner of promiscuity.[7]

—-Women and men would understand that these contraceptive chemicals and devices can kill people and would reject them.[8] The pharmaceutical companies that market them would go out of business and the deadly medicine would no longer exist.

—Couples who are rendered sterile and cannot bear children when they choose to do so would not seek laboratory scientists to assist them in processes such as in vitro fertilization and other reproductive technologies. They would seek out fertility specialists who can work with the actual problems the couple is facing and solve them in ways that do not involve artificial production of embryonic children.[9]

—Couples would not approve of the practice of treating embryonic children like manufactured goods—meaning that the imperfect ones are killed while only a select few are given the chance to live.[10]

—Scientists would not play God with various types of human cells in an attempt to create clones that can be used for spare body parts.[11] Nor would they make them for the myriad of other goals of biotech companies that only seek to make money and that have no regard for the dignity of the human person.

—-Doctors would not use medical abortion pills like RU-486 (mifepristone) to help an expectant mother rid her body of her baby under the guise of treating some mythical problem such as an interrupted social life or a college career. Instead, doctors would work extremely hard to respect the lives of both mother and child—with a commitment to respect life under all conditions.[12]

—Medical personnel and facilities would not cooperate in efforts to prematurely end the lives of the severely disabled, the aging, and the terminally ill.

In other words, the value of a particular, unique individual would be recognized in the culture and in politics. This is what the personhood movement is all about—striving to restore moral sanity in a culture that has, for too long, treated human persons as chattel rather than the irreplaceable persons they are.

I have listed some of the reasons why personhood is our goal. So why is it that whenever a personhood proposal is considered by a state legislature or as a state or federal constitutional amendment, Catholic bishops find it necessary to publicly oppose it?

What sort of reasons could they possibly have considering the fact that the Church recognizes the value and dignity of the human person without exception and without apology?

The USCCB suffers from a personhood blind spot

The bishops' tendency to be squeamish about human personhood boils down to the very legacy about which this book has carefully attempted to analyze. It has to do with accommodating the world and hesitating to rock the boat—particularly the *sexually saturated society* vessel. The nausea occurs because of a desire to be comfortable with the status quo so political friends or long-time financial supporters are not offended.

What I mean by this is that if the bishops were to publicly advocate for human personhood, they would get under the skin of an awful lot of people. They might lose support or the seat at some political table where they enjoy acceptance. This would happen because, once a personhood amendment passes, each bishop, and the USCCB as a unit, would have to explain the foundational ways in which the culture would change if human rights for every person were protected by the law.

If personhood were recognized in the law, the bishops would be obligated to provide the fundamental reasons why any method of contraception that can potentially cause an abortion would no longer be legal. Once human personhood is recognized at the state or federal level, the government would be obligated to provide equal protection for every person—including those prior to birth. Thus, any threat to that human being would have to be evaluated, and criminal laws would have to be passed to deal with what could be possible crimes against persons. The bishops have been advised not to do this. They have been fed the false argument that it would be imprudent to act in favor of human personhood at this time.[13]

By the same token, the bishops would have to emphasize Catholic teaching on in vitro fertilization. They would have to make it clear that if personhood is acknowledged in the law, IVF and its progeny—including human embryonic stem cell research and human cloning—would be banned.

Finally, the bishops would have to provide education of the fundamental science of the human being whose life can begin either sexually or asexually. Many have not encountered the word "asexually" before, but it is easy enough to understand. An asexually reproduced human being is someone whose life begins as a result of human cloning or by another form of creation that does not directly involve the union of sperm and egg.[14] The point of being specific about this is that regardless of HOW someone comes into existence, he or she is a human being whose life is always and in every case valuable.

There is no way the Church can teach, for example, that human cloning and other kinds of genetic engineering are unethical if it refuses to acknowledge the personhood of asexually reproduced human beings. Even if the Church tries, it loses credibility because others will point out that the Church has taught that only sexually reproduced human beings—in the womb—are persons. This means, quite literally, that the Church has to change its vocabulary.

I pointed out this very thing to the Vatican in a letter many months ago, telling Archbishop Ladaria of the

Congregation for the Doctrine of the Faith,

> The reason we write to you today, however, has to do with the word "conception" as a definition of when a human person's life begins. It has become increasingly clear to us that, with the onslaught of human embryo stem cell research, human cloning, in vitro fertilization and other practices, it is necessary to consider that there are human persons whose lives do not begin at "conception" but rather by other means, which are identified as asexual methods of reproduction.

"Human Embryology and Church Teachings," a 2008 article by Dianne Irving, states the following about asexual reproduction:[15]

> In human asexual reproduction many of these processes operate in reverse to reprogram, or de-differentiate, the DNA in a cell. For example, in cloning by somatic cell nuclear transfer, one can begin with a highly specialized or differentiated human cell (such as a skin cell—in which some or even most of the DNA in that cell's nucleus has been silenced) and then incrementally remove the methylation bars on that DNA to allow it to speak until the DNA in that cell is in the same state of differentiation as the single-cell totipotent zygote—resulting in a new, single-cell human organism, a single-cell embryo, or human being. . . . That is, one begins with just a human cell, but ends up with a new single-cell organism, a human being.

Clearly, the word conception—as it is currently used—does not include human beings who are asexually reproduced. This creates confusion which, in turn, undermines not only our effort to achieve recognition of human personhood, but also our effort to educate the general public.

I have met with several Vatican officials and pressed this point. Why? Because words are important and this question of sexually AND asexually produced human beings is part of the critical evidence that the Church has the capacity to teach if only it chooses to be the defender of each and every human being. The interest that was expressed during my meetings is most encouraging.

Finally, and most importantly, if the bishops placed themselves squarely in the forefront of striving for human personhood, they would have to end their endorsement of legislation that actually permits some abortion (i.e., in cases of rape, incest, and life of the mother). But bad advice has been given to them and, sadly, accepted by them.

That, my friends, is the real problem, though none of the specifics just mentioned are represented in statements the various bishops have put forth when they have enunciated their public non-support for human personhood measures. On this matter, I don't want to point the finger at a particular bishop because the bishops in several states—including Michigan, Florida, Virginia, Georgia, Montana, and Colorado—have issued similar statements that reflect the same mindset. Such comments from bishops have the calculated effect of undermining efforts to evangelize the public on the subject of the humanity of the preborn child and his born, but vulnerable, brothers and sisters. Below are portions of one statement the Montana Catholic conference issued. My rebuttal follows. But please note that Montana is just one example. None of the public statements issued by bishops anywhere on the subject of human personhood have been helpful!

Montana

The Montana statement reads,[16]

> The Roman Catholic bishops of Montana are united with all who embrace the common goal of saving unborn babies, supporting mothers and ultimately putting an end to the tragedy of abortion.
>
> In this battle to protect innocent life, there are many challenges and many different strategies. One strategy we have evaluated is the personhood amendment. We consulted with our brother bishops in Colorado, Michigan, Georgia, and Florida

and elsewhere who have faced, or are currently facing, similar initiatives in their home states. In addition, we met with state and national pro-life organizations, as well as leaders from other faiths who have, like us, agonized over these initiatives.

We have been advised by leading pro-life attorneys that the strategy to pass a state constitutional amendment declaring personhood is problematic, in part, because of its heavy reliance on unpredictable courts and dependence on future legislative actions to define and implement the law. They have also expressed concerns that state personhood amendments might trigger an appellate process that could strengthen *Roe v. Wade*.

The key to advancing the culture of life in Montana is addressing the privacy provision in our state constitution which provides a right to abortion. Therefore, we are working with constitutional experts to develop an amendment which would exclude abortion from the privacy provision in the state constitution.

Passing such a constitutional amendment would open the way to addressing real change in the state. We could then pass laws to enact restrictions such as requiring short waiting periods before an abortion can be performed and requiring parental notification in cases when the person seeking an abortion is under age. These restrictions have been noted in a recent study as being effective in reducing abortion. Passage of such laws would save numerous lives on the way to changing hearts and minds as we work to achieve our ultimate goal of overturning *Roe v. Wade*.

Having placed both competing and compelling opinions in the balance, we, the Catholic bishops of Montana will not support CI-102. No one step along the way is the final destination. Some steps are more significant in

their immediate impact than others. But every step
we take in passing effective pro-life legislation
moves us toward our common goal of complete
protection of human life from conception to natural death. We will combine these efforts to support
unborn life with our ongoing efforts to abolish the
death penalty and to oppose current court actions
that would allow physician-assisted suicide.

There are several points of error in this statement starting with the confinement of the human personhood effort
to nothing more than another effort to do something about
surgical abortion. This is erroneous. Human personhood
efforts are focused on regaining respect and protection of
human rights in the culture and the law for all human
individuals—born and preborn—from the moment of their
biological beginning until death. But once the bishops, or
anyone else for that matter, limit the human personhood
discussion to just another strategy for ending surgical
abortion, the game is over!

The bishops are hung up on legal advice from groups
that are more concerned with crystal balls than they are with
truth. Nobody knows what a given judge or court might do,
and the purpose of the human personhood effort is not
dependent on the whims of judges.[17]

Further, the groups advising bishops are made up of
legal "experts" who are extremely selective in what they
present as authoritative advice! For example, not a single
one of these attorneys has ever publicly addressed the legal
ramifications of the federal government's lie, begun in 1965,
that pregnancy really does not begin at the beginning but
rather at implantation! This was done so that doctors would
not be obliged to tell women the truth about the way a birth
control chemical works to take a preborn person's life. Even
though scientific experts at the time understood that the
baby is alive for seven to eight days prior to implantation,
these people conveniently created a new definition of pregnancy so that women could be duped.

Where are those lawyers on this question? Where have
they been? They are nowhere! Lawyers like this are

obviously the wrong ones to be advising Catholic bishops. The bishops should be relying on the magisterial teaching of the Church, not a legal opinion narrowly written to suit a political mindset that avoids talking about contraception and the illicit nature of reproductive technologies.

Bishops who are concerned with "privacy provisions" should be examining how human personhood would negate any type of privacy that permits killing an innocent person before birth, in a nursing home, or elsewhere where an innocent victim's life is on the line.

Merely restricting when and how a surgical abortion is performed is never going to contribute to society's respect for the dignity of the human person. I am convinced that the bishops have never honestly examined the beauty and power in the human personhood effort.

And while they apparently seek advice from some pro-life experts, I have to say that no bishop has ever contacted me for counsel on what to do about human personhood. Maybe I have just figured out why! The time has come for bishops to stop working to "limit the harm done"[18] and start working on restoring respect for persons in a land that, particularly among Catholics, is steeped in the sleaze of the culture of death.

Politics v. courage

Bishop Paul Swain of South Dakota said in a prepared statement after the defeat of a personhood measure, "That electoral defeat, however, creates the environment in which Initiated Measure 11 is offered. It is the judgment of those who have proposed this law that a total ban on abortions is not politically possible based on that result. It is not for me to make judgments about political realities. We must, however, respond to what is before us."

Note that Measure 11 did not outlaw surgical abortion but regulated which abortions could be committed surgically.[19]

Here we go again! Even though the bishop is a shepherd and a defender of truth, he has made a calculated political statement designed to take a personhood defeat and turn it into an opportunity to support flawed legislative proposals. If indeed he is not in the business of making "judgments about political realities" then why is he taking a purely political position?

These situations challenge those of us in the pro-life movement to remain optimistic even though the men who should be our best friends have, in too many cases, become our foes.

Shortly after the Montana bishops made their public statement in 2009, I wrote an opinion piece that was published online by Renew America. Contained in that article are these words,[20]

> I am not a theologian nor am I an attorney, but I do know what the Catholic Church teaches about the identity of the human person and the dignity inherent in each. This is neither a political nor a legal question. It's a question of whether one accepts or rejects the fundamental truth that human beings all deserve to be equally recognized as human persons endowed with human rights.
>
> For nearly 40 years, the American legal system has been morally imprisoned by a set of U.S. Supreme Court decisions (*Roe v. Wade* and *Doe v. Bolton*) that deny the humanity of the child prior to birth by setting aside all scientific evidence, not to mention common sense. The inanity of these decisions is clear, but apparently to some, how to go about undoing the damage they have done is not.
>
> This is where the human personhood movement comes in, and it's about time Catholic bishops thought about this from a perspective not clouded by the politics of false prudence, legal positivism or incrementalism. Too many dead bodies lie on that road; it's time to change course!
>
> There is no reliance within the human personhood movement on unpredictable courts, Your

Excellencies. There is a firm, undeniable reliance on exact scientific evidence, which leads to the philosophical conclusion that a human being, from his or her beginning, is a human person. This is proven beyond doubt by studying the facts, not by fearing or misrepresenting court decisions. As a matter of fact, the human personhood movement does not address *Roe v. Wade* or *Doe v. Bolton*, for obvious reasons.

Pro-life Americans, including Roman Catholic bishops and their associates in the various state Catholic conferences, have to move beyond the politics and understand that *Roe* and *Doe* are symptomatic of a culture that long ago set out on the path of dehumanizing vulnerable persons. *Roe* and *Doe* were the result of a permissive attitude toward denying the personhood of human beings deemed "inconvenient" or "undesirable."

If we honestly examine the Supreme Court's infamous *Dred Scott* decision, we learn a valuable lesson.[21] The Supreme Court *never* recanted or overturned the prejudice on display in that decision. Citizens took it upon themselves to correct the injustices being perpetrated throughout society and by government against members of the human race. The result was a movement to renew the culture and restore justice by way of a constitutional amendment.

Similarly, it is not the human personhood movement's goal to overturn *Roe* and *Doe*. Our goal is to restore recognition of personhood to all human beings. We do not need the court's permission to do that.

It occurs to me that this fact flies in the face of all that the so-called leading pro-life attorneys have been saying to Catholic bishops nationwide. First and foremost, there is no human being who exists because of the Supreme Court, Congress or any other body of individuals. Each exists by the grace of God, His creative power, and His endowment of personhood at the instant a human being is created. . . .

Further, the human personhood movement relies heavily on a two-pronged educational strategy. We share the science and then we share the reasoning behind the movement. This is why we can state unhesitatingly that not only is legal recognition of human personhood the right goal for pro-life Americans, it is [the] only logical way for society to once again acknowledge the truth of who the human being is and why each is so precious.

We encourage the Catholic bishops of Montana and elsewhere to set aside the disingenuous argument that the passage of a personhood amendment to a state constitution might "trigger an appellate process that could strengthen *Roe v. Wade*."[22] There is absolutely no way that anyone knows whether or not such a trigger would be pulled, but we all know that maintaining the status quo is unthinkable.

We cannot be satisfied, as servants of life and, more importantly, servants of God, with the "common sense restrictions" on abortion that seem to be the standard fare offered by many, including those leading pro-life attorneys relied upon by Montana's bishops.[23] It has never been the pro-life movement's goal to restrict the killing so that it happens less. If one knows that the act of abortion is murder, then how could we ever defend the argument that restricting acts of murder so that fewer people are murdered is a worthy goal? What sort of twisted idea is that?

This perspective is as true today as it was the day I wrote it.

A valuable lesson

Frankly, it is high time for each of us Catholics in the pews to stop being blissfully blind to political shenanigans. We must play our part in the cure that needs only to be administered. We must be convicted in our hearts that, with Christ at our side, there is never a reason—be it political, financial, or otherwise—for us to back away from Him in favor of going along to get along.

Recalling the profound words of Pope John Paul II will help us when we feel tempted to look the other way: "Today, I tell you: continue unflaggingly on the journey on which you have set out in order to be witnesses everywhere of the glorious Cross of Christ. Do not be afraid! May the joy of the Lord, crucified and risen, be your strength, and may Mary most holy always be beside you."[24]

13

CHAPTER THIRTEEN:
Holy Priests Are the Cure

[T]he only legitimate ascent towards the shepherd's ministry is the Cross. This is the true way to rise; this is the true door. It is not the desire to become "someone" for oneself, but rather to exist for others, for Christ, and thus through him and with him to be there for the people he seeks, whom he wants to lead on the path of life.

One enters the priesthood through the sacrament, and this means precisely: through the gift of oneself to Christ, so that he can make use of me; so that I may serve him and follow his call, even if it proves contrary to my desire for self-fulfillment and esteem.

– From an ordination homily by Pope Benedict XVI

The Catholic priesthood has been under attack for some years, and in recent memory the most convenient point of verbal assault has been the sex abuse crisis. But despite this tragedy, the priesthood persists because first and foremost it is of Christ—our first priest, the exemplar for every priest and for every Catholic. The beloved Father John Hardon, SJ, said it best,[1]

Christ . . . lived His priesthood during the nine hidden months within His mother, then through the many years at Nazareth, and while preaching and doing good throughout Palestine. But especially on the cross did He live this priesthood, where He united all the acts of a mortal human being capable of suffering and of death into one supreme sacrifice, by which He became the Mediator par excellence between the human race and God, our priest and pontiff for a sinful mankind. Such was Christ's priesthood in His mortal flesh on earth. But we are not finished. In fact, Christ's priesthood in a profound sense only began during His mortal sojourn which ended on Calvary. Jesus continues His priesthood even now. He had better; otherwise, we could not have a Mass.

As our eternal High Priest He worships, praises, and thanks the divine majesty in His own name and in the name of His people. But, though sinless Himself, He is head of a very sinful human family. So He intercedes before the throne of the Father for us. Being heard by the Father, He keeps sending down blessings on us from His heavenly home. This priesthood of Jesus Christ is the only one fundamental priesthood now in the Church. All other priesthoods are participations in this one. The participation takes place in two different ways. First and mainly, by those ordained to the ministerial priesthood and secondly, by all the faithful as belonging to the priesthood of the faithful.

We have, therefore, because of Christ's priesthood, first of all the ordained ministerial priesthood which we identify with the sacrament of orders. Who belongs to this priesthood? All those who are of the sacerdotal rank: priests, bishops, and the pope at their head. When did this participated ministerial priesthood of Jesus begin? It came into existence at the Last Supper when the Savior did two things. He first changed bread and wine into Himself and already offered, the night before He died, the death He would endure. Then He told the disciples to do what He did "in commemoration of me." It is a defined article of the Catholic faith that the ordained ministerial priesthood, the sacrament of orders, was instituted personally by Jesus at the Last Supper.

Finally, beyond the ordained ministerial priesthood, which is unique and possessed only by those who receive the sacrament of orders, there is a true although subordinate sense in which all the baptized faithful belong to the priesthood of Christ. We begin to share in the priesthood of the Savior when we are baptized into the priesthood of Christ. This sacramental character which we receive at baptism is deepened by the sacrament of confirmation and the Holy Eucharist. It is because of this sharing in Christ's priesthood that the faithful are able to receive any of the other sacraments; without this one no other sacrament can be received. It is because of this share in Christ's priesthood that they are enabled to offer with the priest at the altar the body and blood of the Son of God to His heavenly Father, which is why it is said, "Pray, brethren, that my sacrifice and yours may be acceptable to God, the almighty Father."

It is through the sacrament of holy orders—the union of the priest with Christ—that faithful Catholics receive from their priests education on the teachings of the Church. Through this inspired collaboration with Christ, the ordained priest and the people of the Church can prepare, in faith and through good works, the spiritual salve that is needed to begin the healing process within the Church.

As Pope Benedict XVI said to a group of seminarians who were about to be ordained into the priesthood,[2]

Life is not only given at the moment of death and not only in the manner of martyrdom. We must give it day by day. Day after day it is necessary to learn that I do not possess my life for myself. Day by day I must learn to abandon myself; to keep myself available for whatever He, the Lord, needs of me at a given moment, even if other things seem more appealing and more important to me: it means giving life, not taking it.

It is in this very way that we experience freedom: freedom from ourselves, the vastness of being. In this very way, by being useful, in being a person whom the world needs, our life becomes important and beautiful. Only those who give up their own life find it.

The priesthood, divinely ordained, also exists on a practical level and that is where solid recommendations could be considered for clearing up the crisis. One of my favorite priests, Father Michael Orsi, has studied this question and, as a result, has proposed four steps that could be taken to begin righting the wrongs that are crippling the priesthood in our day.

The vocation crisis solution

Orsi's four recommendations make perfect sense and, in my view, should be evaluated by every bishop who is not already addressing this crisis in his particular diocese.

Orsi's points are these:[3]

1) "Get rid of the priest personnel board." The existence of this structure drives a wedge between the priest and his bishop making it seem as though the bishop is a corporate CEO and the priest is merely an employee. Orsi writes,

The sense of closeness, concern, relationship—family—has been lost. The organization has made a decision that "it" thinks is best for the priest and the parish. The question is often asked by priests what is behind the move? Is this move prompted by my friends or enemies? Or am I just a moveable part? Does the bishop really care about me or know my situation? Am I just filling a slot or is there a genuine pastoral need for my talents? Does anyone care about my needs?

2) "Abandon terms for pastors." The long tradition in the Church prior to recent times was that pastors were lifelong shepherds in their parishes. This created a family atmosphere where the pastor remained, endeared himself to his flock, and nurtured perhaps one or more generations of his parishioners as would be expected of a family leader. And in those days the parish did have a family atmosphere that enriched every member to one degree or another. Not so today, for as Orsi points out,

> The greatest damage caused by terms of office is the instability it has caused in the life of a priest. Most priests are not missionaries. Their parish becomes their family. It provides the man with mothers, fathers, brothers and sisters, and in time, if he stays long enough, he bonds with many spiritual children. A long-term relationship with a parish provides him with love and belongingness. The constant moving or fear of being moved has caused the priest to be more isolated and insecure than ever.

3) "Retirement for a priest is an oxymoron." When I read this for the first time several years ago I cheered out loud, even though I was sitting in an airplane. Father Orsi has made a public statement about a matter I have always found troubling. How can a priest "in the order of Melchizedech" retire? A priest is a priest forever. Orsi makes this point by telling the story of one priest who had reached the age of 75,

> After 50 years of priesthood there he was, alone and at the mercy of another pastor, who could himself be transferred or retire. And all this at 75 years old! Change is hard for anyone, but for old people it is especially traumatic. Does a man at this age deserve the stress and aggravation? Why would a normal person looking to the future opt for this kind of life? Would a family encourage a son to become a priest knowing this possible ending for their son? I doubt it!

4) The bishops' sex abuse policy is harmful. Father Orsi has looked at this for a very long time and his words are as

true today as they were when he first wrote them. They are important enough to include here if we truly want to see a renewal in the Catholic priesthood:

> The recent sexual abuse scandals in themselves are not enough to dissuade vocations. Human beings do fail, sin, and sometimes make poor judgment calls. People do understand this. But how the bishops responded to their recalcitrant priests in this crisis is further indicative of how much they have departed from the family model of priesthood, and therefore more devastating for vocations. The Dallas protocols and the desire at that meeting of many bishops to quickly laicize as many problem priests as possible is symptomatic of the business model they have been working out of for years. When a worker is a problem, business gets rid of him. However, this flies in the face of everything we encourage Christian families to do. We rail against divorce. We proclaim for better or for worse. We tell parents to stick with their children even in tough times. We remind them of the Prodigal Son. But when one of the bishop's sons is in trouble they want to cut him off, get rid of him quickly. Recently Bishop Wilton Gregory, president of the U.S. Conference of Catholic Bishops, sent a letter informing the accused priests of his diocese that they were not welcome at diocesan liturgies. The bishop wrote, "I have decided to exclude all priests on administrative leave from all future diocesan sponsored events. This includes our annual convocation, Clergy Assembly Days, retreats, ordinations, Holy Week Ceremonies, and jubilee celebrations." The bishop should be so firm with pro-choice "Catholic" politicians who continue to act contrary to the faith and show no remorse for their actions or amendment to change!

> No doubt we have some guilty priests and others who are unjustly accused but whatever the case, is it right that they are being shunned by a Church that is their life? I remember when I was

ordained, the bishop gathered the priests in attendance and said to the ordinandi, "Behold your brothers." He didn't add, "until they make a mistake!" In this crisis we have stripped men of their priestly identity, their Church family and, in many cases, their livelihood by giving them a pittance to live on. So much for my loving father the bishop! Why would a young man want to risk his whole life on a family like this?

These concerns, raised by a faithful priest who has done so much to teach the good news, should not be taken lightly. I know there are those in the hierarchy who might say, "Well, this is just one man's opinion." But on the other hand, one of the things this book has attempted to make clear is that the Catholic priesthood today is in crisis and there are ways to right the wrongs that have been done from within the Church due to laxity, secularization, and the Americanism cancer. Sometimes going back to tradition is the best medicine of all, and this is clearly one of those times.

That is not to say that there are not remarkable shepherds in our midst. Quite the opposite.

The Church has heroes walking among us

The Catholic Church in America has many remarkable priests and bishops who light their lanterns and guide us through the dark valleys of this life.

Cardinal Raymond Burke

Cardinal Raymond Burke is one of those leaders who shines. In a speech given a couple of years ago, he told his fellow Catholics,[4]

> While true religion teaches the natural moral law, the observance of the moral law is not a confessional practice. It is rather a response to what is inscribed in the depths of every human heart. Religious faith plainly articulates the natural moral law, enabling men of faith to recognize more readily what their own human nature and the nature of things demand of them, and to conform

their lives to the truth which they recognize. For that reason, the founders of our nation acknowledged the importance of religious faith for the life of the nation. The free exercise clause, in fact, aims to protect the teaching and practice of religious faith for the sake of the common good. In his Encyclical Letter *Caritas in Veritate*, Pope Benedict XVI reminds us:[5]

> The Christian religion and other religions can offer their contribution to development *only if God has a place in the public realm,* specifically in regard to its cultural, social, economic, and particularly its political dimensions. The Church's social doctrine came into being in order to claim "citizenship status" for the Christian religion. Denying the right to profess one's religion in public and the right to bring the truths of faith to bear upon public life has negative consequences for true development. . . . *Reason always stands in need of being purified by faith*: this also holds true for political reason, which must not consider itself omnipotent. For its part, *religion always needs to be purified by reason* in order to show its authentically human face. Any breach in this dialogue comes only at an enormous price to human development.

Presently, in our nation, the Christian faith has a critical responsibility to articulate clearly the natural moral law and its demands. Under the constant influence of a rationalist and secularist philosophy which makes man, instead of God, the ultimate measure of what is right and good, we have become confused about the most basic truths, for example, the inviolable dignity of innocent human life . . . and the integrity of marriage between one man and one woman as the first and irreplaceable cell of the life of society. If Christians fail to articulate and uphold the natural moral law,

Cardinal Raymond Burke met with Paul and Judie Brown in May 2011 to discuss American Life League's Canon 915 Defend the Faith project and the ongoing struggles with pro-abortion Catholics in politics.

then they fail in the fundamental duty of patriotism, of loving their country by serving the common good.

Cardinal Burke's wisdom contributes to understanding the fundamental reasons why Catholics need to be part of the solution rather than contributors to the problems facing our nation—including the disregard for human dignity. Burke, no stranger to controversy, has never allowed negativity—including that of the media—to stand in the way of teaching his flock.

Bishop Samuel Aquila

The same can be said for Bishop Samuel Aquila, whose pastoral letter, "You Will Know the Truth and the Truth Will Set You Free" provided leadership to Catholics in his diocese preparing to cast their votes in the 2004 election.[6] His words are as true today as they were when he wrote them, if not more so. He said many profound things to his flock based on his desire to "address five areas of confusion in the hearts and minds of some of the faithful, in the hope that as a Catholic people we will come to a deeper understanding of the truth that sets us free." He enumerated these areas and provided his people with many resources to further learn

what the Church teaches. One highlight I will give to tease
you into reading the full text is this one from the subsection
entitled, "We must become more deeply convinced that we
can find the truth that sets us free only in Jesus Christ":

> 16. If we choose well and cooperate with grace, we
> orient ourselves to genuine and lasting fulfillment
> both here and hereafter: "Human freedom is a
> force for growth in truth and goodness; it attains
> its perfection when directed toward God" (*CCC*
> 1731). The proper exercise of free will, then, leads
> to freedom in an even fuller sense: the freedom of
> the children of God which is found only in Jesus
> Christ who is "the way, the truth and the life" (Jn
> 14: 6). We can never find this freedom by choosing
> something that is not ordered toward the good—
> toward God. This noblest sort of freedom is found
> only in choosing the good and thereby ordering
> our lives to Jesus and his kingdom.
>
> 17. If, however, we choose what we know is
> gravely wrong and thus fail to cooperate with
> grace, we form our character in a way that is in-
> compatible with the authentic fulfillment that God
> so much wants us to receive. Unless we repent,
> this leads to unhappiness not just here, but also
> hereafter. Whenever a person chooses to go
> against the law of God, "to disobey and do evil,"
> he or she abuses freedom and becomes a "slave to
> sin" (Jn 8: 34-36 and *CCC* 1733).

Bishop Thomas Doran

Bishop Thomas Doran of Rockford, Illinois, upon visiting with Pope John Paul II in 2004 when the Holy Father was
84 years of age and obviously suffering the effects of Parkin-
son's, returned home and wrote of his visit. This illustrates
the beautiful spirit of humility, not to mention a love of being
a shepherd, that exemplifies Bishop Doran. He wrote,[7]

> It is always an experience of course to visit with
> our Holy Father, Pope John Paul II. He is 84 years
> of age and hampered by many infirmities.

Nonetheless, he greets visitors with a smile and demonstrates by the questions that he asks that he is aware of and interested in the problems of each particular diocese as described in the annual reports of the bishops which reach him generally six months before our personal visits to him.

We are rapidly becoming a nation of victims. Victimhood is even a badge of honor and a title to sustenance. Thus it is perhaps difficult for those who are used to our American ethos of independent self-reliance, but under the influence of our culture that independence seems to be a thing of the past. That is why it is inspiring, if unsettling to many, to see the Holy Father who, once possessed of such vigor when he entered upon his apostolic office, and now stricken with infirmities, nonetheless gamely and, I would say, courageously carries on the duties of his office without stint and without complaint, but joyfully and happily.

If we did not have the benefit of his teachings and his writings, but only the example of his persevering and faithful discharge of his duties as priest, bishop and supreme pontiff, we would have to say that he is an extraordinary person and that it has been our privilege to serve Christ with him and under his direction in this challenging age.

Let us pray for our pope, John Paul II: May the Lord protect him and give him life and make him blessed upon earth and not hand him over into the clutches of his enemies.

So many Catholics are touched by Catholic leaders like Bishop Doran who speak of the true meaning of suffering with Christ. His words bring hope to those most in need of inspiration during troubled times.

Father Rawley Myers

The admirable Father Rawley Myers, who was always busy schooling his parish and his friends, constantly inspired people. At one point he wrote a lovely reminder of the reasons why Catholics need to learn more about saints and imitate their virtues,[8]

> Ignorance of the saints is spiritual suicide. If another church had one of our saints, its members would be talking about him or her night and day. Our Church holds in memory the lives of hundreds and hundreds of holy people who have gone before us, but being chronologically prejudiced, we disregard them. It must be true that Catholics today know less about the saints than almost any other generation. And we think we are bright—a flattery advertising constantly casts out to us in order to sell gadgets. The saints were wise, and in ignoring them, we show ourselves to be foolish.

Archbishop Charles Chaput

Archbishop Charles Chaput spends hours teaching the Catholic faith to not only the Catholics in his archdiocese, but anywhere he is invited. In one inspired address at St. Basil's Collegiate Church in Toronto, Canada, on the subject of political responsibilities for Catholics, he laid out various fundamental principles, each of which are in his book *Render Unto Caesar*. Below are some of his words of wisdom,[9]

> The Church in the United States has done a poor job of forming the faith and conscience of Catholics for more than 40 years. And now we're harvesting the results—in the public square, in our families, and in the confusion of our personal lives. I could name many good people and programs that seem to disprove what I just said. But I could name many more that do prove it, and some of them work in Washington.
>
> The problem with mistakes in our past is that they compound themselves geometrically into the future unless we face them and fix them. The truth is, the American electorate is changing, both ethnically and in age. And unless Catholics have a

conversion of heart that helps us see what we've become—that we haven't just "assimilated" to American culture, but that we've also been absorbed and bleached and digested by it—then we'll fail in our duties to a new generation and a new electorate. And a real Catholic presence in American life will continue to weaken and disappear.

More recently, when delivering a speech to the University of Notre Dame's Right to Life Club, Chaput challenged the audience:[10]

"How does one live as a Catholic in the world as it now is?" asked the archbishop. "If we want to 'live as Catholics' . . . we need to learn that lesson in our identity not from the world; not from the tepid and self-satisfied; and not from the enemies of the Church, even when they claim to be Catholic; but from the mind and memory of the Church herself, who speaks through her pastors."

"Nothing we do to defend the human person, no matter how small, is ever unfruitful or forgotten. Our actions touch other lives and move other hearts in ways we can never fully understand in this world," concluded Chaput. "Don't ever underestimate the beauty and power of the witness you give in your pro-life work."

Bishop Robert Vasa

Bishop Vasa, of the Diocese of Baker, Oregon, is a man totally committed to being the shepherd who follows Christ unapologetically. Writer Patrick B. Craine states,[11]

According to Bishop Vasa, statements from bishops' conferences necessarily tend to be "flattened" and "vague," allowing certain teachings to "fall by the wayside through what could be called, charitably, a kind of benign pastoral neglect."

While some call this compassion, "in truth, it often entails a complicity or a compromise with

> evil," he says. "The harder and less popular teach-
> ings are left largely unspoken, thereby implicitly
> giving tacit approval to erroneous or misleading
> theological opinions."

> "I fear that there has been such a steady diet of
> such flattened documents that anything issued by
> individual bishops that contains some element of
> strength," he says, "is readily and roundly con-
> demned or simply dismissed as being out of touch
> with the conference or in conflict with what other
> bishops might do."

Bishop Vasa's assessment may well be accurate, though
I would hasten to add that perhaps because of the singular
quality of the statements made by these remarkable bishops,
the resounding clarity in a sea of politically nuanced
pabulum is the very light that always shines in the darkness
and cannot be extinguished.

This can be said of our next hero as well.

Bishop Joseph Martino

During his tenure in the Diocese of Scranton, Pennsylvania, Bishop Joseph Martino did much to defend Christ
from sacrilege,[12] to require Catholic colleges in his diocese
to either adhere to Church doctrine or stop calling themselves Catholic,[13] and to bring accurate facts to the attention
of many who did not want to hear them and, in fact, worked
against him every step of the way.[14] I admire Bishop Martino most for the manner in which he educated his priests
on the integrity of Catholic teaching—including the real
presence of Christ in the Eucharist. Martino issued a public
document containing official instructions not only to priests,
but to all ordinary and extraordinary ministers responsible
for giving Catholics Holy Communion. According to EWTN,
Martino reminded them of the following:[15]

> 1. To administer the Sacred Body and Blood of the
> Lord is a serious duty which [you] have received
> from the Church, and no one having accepted this
> responsibility has the right to ignore the Church's
> law in this regard;

2. Those whose unworthiness to receive Holy Communion is known publicly to the Church must be refused Holy Communion in order to prevent sacrilege and to prevent the Catholic in question from committing further grave sin through unworthy reception.

Bishop Martino chose early retirement, but his legacy will never be forgotten. In fact, former senator Rick Santorum wrote this of the bishop:[16]

"Many of his brother bishops will look at Martino as they do at other uncompromising defenders of the faith, worrying about the world's reaction," Santorum wrote. "As a Philly guy, though, His Excellency knows something about being booed. He also knows his job and calling: to be the good shepherd who faithfully leads and protects his flock from those who would lead them astray.

"Yes, scores of people are reportedly protesting and threatening to leave the Church. In the end, however, people leaving the Church because of a bishop who enforces its teachings are a blessing compared with the alternative: people leaving because bishops and their priests don't teach, much less enforce, those teachings."

Bishop Joseph Martino of the Diocese of Scranton gifts Judie Brown with an icon of the Holy Mother with Infant Jesus in April 2009.

Obamacare inspired many bishops to teach!

Several bishops with the fortitude to withstand pressure from their peers made excellent statements in opposition to Obamacare for reasons that clarified the truth for Catholics. It was well known from day one that the health care reform law was violating Catholic principles on several levels.

Among those bishops who used this bad law as a teaching moment was Bishop James Vann Johnston of Cape-Girardeau and Springfield, Missouri. LifeSiteNews quoted the bishop as saying, "Health care reform is a very complex issue, with many important peripheral issues, such as cost and how to pay for it, economic impact, the role of the federal government, abortion, euthanasia, tort reform, etc. . . . But as such, health care reform is particularly important in that, as Catholics, we understand the principles that should be at the very heart of this delicate work."[17]

On the principle of subsidiarity, Archbishop Joseph F. Naumann and Bishop Robert W. Finn of Kansas City-St. Joseph note,[18]

> This notion that health care ought to be determined at the lowest level rather than at the higher strata of society, has been promoted by the Church as "subsidiarity." Subsidiarity is that principle by which we respect the inherent dignity and freedom of the individual by never doing for others what they can do for themselves and thus enabling individuals to have the most possible discretion in the affairs of their lives (See: *Compendium of the Social Doctrine of the Church*, 185ff.; *Catechism of the Catholic Church*, 1883). The writings of recent popes have warned that the neglect of subsidiarity can lead to an excessive centralization of human services, which in turn leads to excessive costs, and loss of personal responsibility and quality of care.

On the matter of abortion, they state, "It is inadequate to propose legislation that is silent on this morally crucial matter. Given the penchant of our courts over the past 35 years to claim unarticulated rights in our Constitution, the explicit exclusion of so-called 'abortion services' from coverage is essential."

There were many more such eloquent bishops on this subject and the point here is to remind all Catholics and their shepherds that, in times of crisis, the Church must step forth and proclaim the truth, as these men have done. This is not a matter of politics or popularity, but rather a matter of defending Catholic tradition and teaching no matter the cost. The same can be said for those shepherds and priests who have nurtured souls in other ways, such as retired bishop John Yanta.

Bishop John Yanta, of the Diocese of Amarillo, bravely declared that the anniversary of *Roe v. Wade* should be a day of fast and abstinence, saying:[19]

> "On the anniversary of the Supreme Court decision, *Roe v. Wade* (1973) Jan. 22 shall be observed in all dioceses of the United States as a particular day of penance for violations to the dignity of the human person committed through acts of abortion, and of prayer for the full restoration of the legal guarantee of the right to life (GIRM, no. 373).
>
> "Therefore I, Bishop John W. Yanta, bishop of the Diocese of Amarillo, declare Tuesday, Jan. 22 as a day of fast and abstinence."

Father Denis O'Brien, MM, who served as American Life League's spiritual director for 25 years, wrote many reflections for pro-life Americans including this timeless meditation:[20]

> The disciples of Jesus once asked Him why they had been laughed at by an unclean spirit. The Lord said to them, "This kind can be cast out only by prayer" (Mark 9:29). Some texts read " . . . only by prayer and fasting."
>
> Fasting is one way to atone for our sins and for the sins of others. To atone is to express sincere

repentance, to make up for, to do penance. Our Lord spoke quite bluntly about penance. On one occasion someone told Him about people "whose blood Pilate had mingled with that of their sacrifices. . . . At this He said to them, 'Do you suppose that these Galileans were worse sinners than any others? Unless you repent you will all perish as they did!'" (Luke 13:1-3)

We are all poor sinners. We must all repent....

The Almighty told His people what kind of atonement He wanted: "Is not this the sort of fast that pleases me: to break unjust fetters, to undo the thongs of the yoke, to let the oppressed go free, and to break all yokes? Is it not sharing your food with the hungry and sheltering the homeless poor? If you see someone lacking clothes, to clothe him and not to turn away from your own kin?" (Isaiah 58:6-7)

Difficult? At first. But remember the Chinese proverb, "The longest journey begins with a single step." If I feel that some form of atonement is expecting too much of me when I suddenly feel weak, it may help to remember what the voices said to Joan of Arc: "Who, if not you, and when, if not now?" Or better still, Our Lord's seemingly terse reminder to Paul the apostle: "My grace is sufficient for thee."

A lot of abortionists, a lot of unjust rulers, a lot of lukewarm folks, a lot of folks who think the economy is more important than the Ten Commandments can use our prayer and our fasting. Who, if not us? When, if not now? His grace will see us through.

Closing thoughts

Throughout the pages of this book I have attempted to lay out not only the skeleton of a problem that is massive and destructive to the Church, but to balance it with the wisdom of those who are already part of the cure. There are always going to be those who will complain no matter how much is fixed or needs to be fixed. To them, there is really nothing to be said.

As I have written this book from materials I have been collecting over the last five years, it has become increasingly clear to me that we are called to be people of hope to one another. I, for one, know so many who will never be publicly commended for their defense of the faith, but who have perhaps unknowingly brought souls to Christ by their example, their sacrifice, and the dauntless enthusiasm for their faith.

Among those who have read this volume prior to publication, many have said, "Judie, give us a to-do list! What can we do to help our bishops, to defend our faith, and to be stronger during these difficult times?"

As someone who has spent a lifetime "doing," let me provide a few pointers:

Take every opportunity to speak with your pastor and your parish priests, reaching out to them to make them members of your family. Our good priests enjoy a home-cooked meal, a game with the kids, and simple, relaxing times with families.

Always discuss your concerns with your priests and your bishop with charity, no matter how frustrated you feel. When you sit down to talk with others, you never know what might have just happened in that person's life or where a bit of merciful salve might make a difference that will change a heart.

Teach your family members, your friends, and your enemies what it means to be Catholic by the way you live your life. Speak about your love for Christ and the teachings of the Church that brighten your life even when they are a challenge.

Don't be afraid to call upon your fellow Catholics to join you in prayer, every day of the year, for our dear priests.

They need to know that we care about them and that we know their burden is great. After all, as one wise priest once said to me, "We are only human!"

In closing, please share this prayer with all those who, as concerned Catholics, know the mighty power of God's grace.

A Prayer for Priests and Bishops[21] (Taken from the Roman Missal)

O God, who hast appointed Thine only-begotten Son to be the eternal High Priest for the glory of Thy Majesty and the salvation of mankind; grant that they whom He hath chosen to be His ministers and the stewards of His mysteries, may be found faithful in the fulfillment of the ministry which they have received. Through the same Christ Our Lord. Amen.

Appendix

To find the articles listed below, go to
http://www.all.org/. Type the name of the article into the
search box and you will be able to read the article in its
entirety.

"Who's Minding the Store at the Catholic Bishops' Shop?"
by ALL staff

"Politics Does Not a Bishop Make," by Judie Brown

"Saint John Fitzgerald Kennedy or the Devil in Disguise?"
by Judie Brown

"Pope John Paul II and Excusing Abortion," by Judie
Brown

"Pugnacious Pelosi v. Befuddled Bishops," by Judie Brown

"Dear Catholic Bishops: The Time for Bravery is at Hand,"
by Judie Brown

"Catholic Bishops and True Charity," by Judie Brown

"Sleeping with the Enemy: Conference of Catholic Bishops
Cooperation with Pro-Abortion Organizations,"
by Michael Hichborn

For the following articles, go to
http://www.renewamerica.com/. Type the article title into
the search box and you will be directed to the article.

"Catholic Charities: Just Say 'No' to Blood Money!" by Judie
Brown

"Pandering to Pelosi," by Judie Brown

Follow the links below for more information on topics
discussed in this book. You may need to type the article's
title into the website's search box.

"What Ardent Practicing Catholics Do: Correcting Pelosi,"
by Father John de Celles, STL
http://www.nationalreview.com

"Saving Catholic Health Care Ethics," by Nancy Valko, R.N.
http://www.wf-f.org/11-1-Valko.html

Catholic Teaching Documents on Contraception
*Type the name of the document into the site's search box

"Address to Midwives on the Nature of Their Profession," by Pope Pius XII (10/29/1951)
http://www.catholicculture.org

Vatican II: *Gaudium et Spes* (12/7/65)
http://www.vatican.va/archive/hist_councils/ii vatican_council/

Pope Paul VI, *Humanae Vitae* (7/25/68)
http://www.newadvent.org

John Paul II, *Familiaris Consortio* (11/22/1981):
http://www.wf-f.org/FamCons.html

Pope John Paul II, *The Gospel of Life* (1995):
http://www.wf-f.org/EvangeliumVitae.html

Catechism of the Catholic Church (1997): http://www.scborromeo.org/ccc/para/2370.htm

Notes

Chapter 1

1. Rev. John A. Hardon, SJ, "The Discovery of Catholic America" (oral presentation, 1992, transcribed as "Transcript of Talk on Christopher Columbus"), The Real Presence Association, http://www.therealpresence.org/archives/ Christopher_Columbus/Christopher_Columbus_001.htm.

2. *Longinqua*, (encyclical of Pope Leo XIII on Catholicism in the United States), January 6, 1895, http://www.vatican.va/holy_father/leo_xiii/encyclicals/ documents/hf_lxiii_enc_06011895_longinqua_en.html.

3. *Testem Benevolentiae Nostrae, (Concerning New Opinions, Virtue, Nature and Grace, with Regard to Americanism, an encyclical of Pope Leo XIII)* promulgated January 22, 1899, http://www.papalencyclicals.net/Leo13/l13teste.htm.

4. *New Advent Encyclopedia Online*, s.v. "Tradition and Living Magisterium," accessed August 22, 2011, http://www.newadvent.org/cathen/15006b.htm.

5. *beginningCatholic.com*, s.v. "Catholic Tradition: Life in the Spirit," accessed August 22, 2011, http://www.beginningcatholic.com/catholic-tradition.html.

6. Russell Shaw, "Vatican II and the Culture of Dissent," May 20, 2009, http://www.catholicity.com/ commentary/rshaw/06045.html.

7. *Humanae Vitae*, (encyclical of Pope Paul VI on the regulation of birth), July 25, 1968, http://www.vatican.va/holy_father/paul_vi/ encyclicals/documents/hf_p-vi_enc_25071968_humanae-vitae_en.html.

8. Cardinal James Francis Stafford, "In 1968, something terrible happened in the Church," July 29, 2008, California Catholic Daily, http://www.calcatholic.com/news/newsArticle.aspx?id=2782389d-da2c-40ce-8d7f-071d2345291c.

9. *Veritatis Splendor*, (encyclical of Pope John Paul II on questions of the Church's moral teaching), August 6, 1993, http://www.newadvent.org/library/docs_jp02vs.htm.

10. *New Advent Encyclopedia Online*, s.v. "secularism," accessed August 22, 2011, http://www.newadvent.org/cathen/13676a.htm.

11. 2 Timothy 4:2-5, *New American Bible*, http://old.usccb.org/nab/bible/2timothy/2timothy4.htm.

Chapter 2

1. Zeno, "The Latest Form of American Atheism," (comment on David Carlin, blog) August 11, 2007, http://zenoferox.blogspot.com/2007/08/atheism-gets-militant.html.

2. Mary Jo Anderson, "Neo Gnostics at the End of the Age," CatholicCulture.org, accessed August 23, 2011, http://www.catholicculture.org/culture/library/view.cfm?recnum=4635.

3. Bishop Rene Henry Gracida, DD, "The Arian Heresy Revisited," CatholicCulture.org, accessed August 23, 2011, http://www.catholicculture.org/culture/library/view.cfm?recnum=6251.

4. Ibid.

5. Rev. Anthony Brankin, "Americanism as Our Own Little Heresy Still Burrows Its Way Into Our Hearts," (transcript of talk given by Fr. Brankin at Catholic Citizens Forum Luncheon on July 13, 2007), CatholicCitizens.org, http://www.catholiccitizens.org/press/contentview.asp?c=41521.

6. Ibid.

7. John J. Pilch, "American Catholicism's Bicentennial," 1989, (originally published in *The Catholic Review,* the newspaper of the archdiocese of Baltimore), http://www9.georgetown.edu/faculty/pilchj/carroll.htm.

8. Ibid.

9. Rev. Anthony Brankin, "Americanism as Our Own Little Heresy Still Burrows Its Way Into Our Hearts," (transcript of talk given by Fr. Brankin at Catholic Citizens Forum Luncheon on July 13, 2007), CatholicCitizens.org, http://www.catholiccitizens.org/press/contentview.asp?c=41521.

10. Biography of John Tracy Ellis, author of *The Life of James Cardinal Gibbons,* http://archives.lib.cua.edu/findingaid/ellis.cfm.

11. Canon Aaron Huberfeld, "Catholics and True Love of Country," (reproduced from a sermon given at St. Francis de Sales Oratory), October 28, 2010, http://stlouis-catholic.blogspot.com/2010/10/catholics-and-true-love-of-country.html.

12. Rev. Anthony Brankin, "Americanism as Our Own Little Heresy Still Burrows Its Way Into Our Hearts," (transcript of talk given by Fr. Brankin at Catholic Citizens Forum Luncheon on July 13, 2007), CatholicCitizens.org, http://www.catholiccitizens.org/press/contentview.asp?c=41521.

Chapter 3

1. Michelle Boorstein and William Wan, "After Child Abuse Accusations, Catholic Priests Often Simply Vanish," *The Washington Post,* December 4, 2010, http://www.washingtonpost.com/wp-dyn/content/article/2010/12/02/AR2010120206646.html?hpid=more-headlines.

2. Msgr. Charles Pope, "Article in Washington Post on Clergy Sexual Abuse Misses the Mark," Archdiocese of Washington website, December 5, 2010, http://blog.adw.org/2010/12/article-in-washington-post-on-clergy-sexual-abuse-misses-the-mark/.

3. Voice of the Faithful, http://www.votf.org/.

4. SNAP (Survivors Network of those Abused by Priests), http://www.snapnetwork.org/.

5. "Credibility Gap: Pope Needs to Answer Questions," *National Catholic Reporter*, March 26, 2010, http://ncronline.org/news/accountability/credibility-gap-pope-needs-answer-questions.

6. "Onward Catholic Soldiers?" Letters to the website First Things about the U.S. in Afghanistan, August/September 2002, http://www.firstthings.com/article/2007/01/onward-catholic-soldiers-19.

7. Rachel Zoll, "Jesuit Official Protesting Expected Vatican Ban on Gay Priests," FreeRepublic.com, September 30, 2005, http://www.freerepublic.com/focus/f-religion/1494760/posts.

8. Jerry Filteau, "Sex Abuse Report Pays Special Attention to Homosexual Priests," Catholic News Service, March 2, 2004, http://www.catholicnews.com/data/abuse/abuse01.htm.

9. Hilary White, "Sex Abuse in Catholic Church Was Homosexual Problem, not Pedophilia: Vatican," LifeSiteNews.com, September 29, 2009, http://www.lifesitenews.com/news/archive/ldn/2009/sep/09092910.

10. Rev. Michael Orsi, "Abusive Bishops and the Destruction of Priests' Reputations," *Homiletic and Pastoral Review*, (January 2009): 48.

11. Bishop Rene Henry Gracida, "It Is a Matter of Justice!" FreeRepublic.com, June 19, 2011, http://www.freerepublic.com/focus/ f-religion/2736815/posts.

12. Deacon Greg Kandra, "Statement from Fr. Corapi's Superior—Updated," *The Deacon's Bench* (blog), March 21, 2011, http://www.patheos.com/community/deacons-bench/2011/03/21/statement-from-fr-corapis-superior.

13. SOLT (Society of Our Lady of the Most Holy Trinity), http://www.societyofourlady.net/welcome.html.

14. Msgr. Charles Pope, "Turning Back the Tide: One Pastor's Attempt to Assert the Biblical Teaching on Homosexuality in an Age of Confusion," Archdiocese of Washington website, March 31, 2011, http://blog.adw.org/2011/03/turning-back-the-tide-one-pastors-attempt-to-assert-the-biblical-teaching-on-homo-sexuality-in-an-age-of-confusion/.

15. "Archbishop Niederauer Apologizes for Giving Communion to 'Sisters of Perpetual Indulgence' at San Francisco Parish," Catholic News Agency, October 12, 2007, http://www.catholicnewsagency.com/news/arch-bishop_niederauer_apologizes_for_giving_communion_to_sisters_of_perpetual_indulgence_at_san_francisco_parish/.

16. Tom Zabiega, "The Tale of Two Bishops: Archbishop of San Francisco, George Niederauer, and the Anglican Archbishop of Kenya, Benjamin Nzimbi," CatholicCitizens.org, October 9, 2006, http://catholiccitizens.org/platform/platformview.asp?c=36548.

17. "San Fran. Archbishop 'Very Happy' about Plan Regarding Homosexual Adoptions," Catholic News Agency, February 7, 2007, http://www.catholicnewsagency.com/news/san_fran.archbishop_very_happy_about_plan_regarding_homosexual_adoptions/.

18. "Newspaper: Bishop Steib allowed accused priest to minister in Mexico," CatholicCulture.org, April 8, 2010, http://www.catholiccuLture.org/news/headlines/index.cfm?storyid=5954.

19. List of parishes in the Diocese of Memphis, http://www.parishesonline.com/scripts/hostedsites/org.asp?ID=20959.

20. "U.S. Ordination Class of 2010: 31% Foreign-Born; 10% are Converts," CatholicCulture.org, April 19, 2010, http://www.catholicculture.org/news/headlines/index.cfm?storyid=6064.

21 Jeff Ziegler, "Priestly Vocations in America: An Updated Look," *Catholic World Report*, (June, 2006), 30-32, http://www.ignatius.com/Images/Products/USVocations.pdf.

Chapter 4

1. Matt C. Abbott, "Current Catholic Controversies, Part 1," Renew America, July 30, 2008, http://www.renewamerica.com/columns/abbott/080730.

2. The USCCB's 2007 document, *Forming Consciences for Faithful Citizenship* states, "Two temptations in public life can distort the Church's defense of human life and dignity: The first is a moral equivalence that makes no ethical distinctions between different kinds of issues involving human life and dignity. The direct and intentional destruction of innocent human life from the moment of conception until natural death is always wrong and is not just one issue among many. It must always be opposed. The second is the misuse of these necessary moral distinctions as a way of dismissing or ignoring other serious threats to human life and dignity." http://www.priestsforlife.org/elections/initial-statement-on-bishops.htm.

3. Blase Cupich, "Racism and the Election," *America*, October 27, 2008, http://www.americamagazine.org/content/article.cfm?article_id=11161.

4. Cathy Lynn Grossman, "Bishops: Faith Should Shape How People Vote in '08," *USA Today*, November 14, 2007, http://www.usatoday.com/news/religion/2007-11-14-bishops-meeting_N.htm.

5. "Bishop Hubbard Approves Free Distribution of Needles to Drug Abusers," CatholicCulture.org, January 29, 2010, http://www.catholicculture.org/news/headlines/index.cfm?storyid=5290.

6. Ibid.

7. Thomas Peters, "[Bishop] Lori Issues Clarification on CT Plan B Decision," FreeRepublic.com, October 3, 2007 (originally posted October 2, 2007 on Bishop Lori's blog), http://www.freerepublic.com/focus/f-religion/1905953/posts.

8. "The Truth About the 'Morning-After Pill,'" (Statement on the So-Called "Morning-After Pill" by the Pontifical Academy for Life, October 31, 2000), American Life League, accessed August 24, 2011, http://planbkills.com/catholic-teaching.html.

9. "Catholic Hospitals in Conn. to Allow Plan B," MSNBC.com, September 27, 2007, http://www.msnbc.msn.com/id/21018908/.

10. John-Henry Westen, "Wisconsin Bishop Breaks from Conference and Opposes Emergency Contraception in Catholic Hospitals," LifeSiteNews.com, December 19, 2007, http://www.lifesitenews.com/news/archive/ldn/2007/dec/07121906.

11. John Connolly, "Wisconsin Requires Catholic Hospitals to Provide Contraception," LifeSiteNews.com, January 25, 2008, http://www.lifesitenews.com/news/archive/ldn/2008/jan/08012504.

12. Paul Mitchell, "Cardinal George Welcomes Hillary Clinton to Chicago," *Thoughts of a Regular Guy* (blog), May 4, 2007, http://regularthoughts.blogspot.com/2007/05/cardinal-george-welcomes-hillary.html.

13. "Pro-Life Group Begs Bishop to Stop Pro-Abortion Speaker from Church Engagement," LifeSiteNews.com, February 7, 2003, http://www.lifesitenews.com/news/pro-life-group-begs-bishop-to-stop-pro-abortion-speaker-from-church-engagem.

14. Bill O'Reilly, "Living Legends," BillOReilly.com, March 4, 2010, http://www.billoreilly.com/newslettercolumn?pid=28968.

15. Rebecca Millette, "Controversial Pro-Obama Priest Would Leave Church Rather Than Take Position at High School," LifeSiteNews.com, April 12, 2011, http://www.lifesitenews.com/news/controversial-pro-obama-priest-would-leave-church-rather-than-take-position.

16. Kathleen Gilbert, "Cardinal George Suspends Controversial Obama-Supporting Rev. Pfleger," LifeSiteNews.com, April 28, 2011, http://www.lifesitenews.com/news/cardinal-george-suspends-controversial-obama-supporting-rev-pfleger.

17. Stefano Esposito, "Cardinal Francis George: Ball in Michael Pfleger's Court," *Chicago Sun-Times*, April 29, 2011, http://www.suntimes.com/news/5098796-417/cardinal-george-ball-in-pflegers-court.html.

18. John Garcia and Michelle Gallardo, "Archdiocese Reinstates Rev. Pfleger to St. Sabina," abc7chicago.com, May 21, 2011, http://abclocal.go.com/wls/story?section=news/local&id=8142916.

19. "Cardinal Mahony Says Abortion Should Not Be Funded by Health Care Bills," Catholic News Agency, September 24, 2009, http://www.catholicnewsagency.com/news/cardinal mahony says abortion should not be funded by health care bills/.

20. Mary Ann Kreitzer, "Fr. Sparks to Scandalize Catholics in California!" *Les Femmes—The Truth* (blog), September 12, 2010, http://lesfemmes-thetruth.blogspot.com/2010/09/fr-sparks-to-scandalize-catholics-in.html.

21. Tim Louis Macaluso, "Religion Interview: Bishop Matthew Clark and a Changing Church," *City Newspaper*, March 2, 2011, http://www.rochestercitynewspaper.com/news articles/2011/03/RELIGION-INTERVIEW-Bishop-Matthew-Clark-and-a-changing-church/.

22. "Instruction Concerning the Criteria for the Discernment of Vocations with Regard to Persons with Homosexual Tendencies in View of Their Admission to the Seminary and to Holy Orders," (Congregation for Catholic Education), posted on the official Vatican website, approved by Benedict XVI on August 31, 2005, http://www.vatican.va/roman curia/congregations/ccat heduc/documents/rc con ccatheduc doc 20051104 istruzione en.html.

23. Ibid.

24. Kathleen Gilbert, "Rochester Bishop: Vatican Isn't Against Homosexuals Entering Priesthood," LifeSiteNews.com, March 7, 2011,

http://www.lifesitenews.com/news/rochester-bishop-vatican-isnt-against-homosexuals-entering-priesthood.

25. Eric Giunta, "Miami Archdiocese Again Features Prominent Gay-Activist Priest," Renew America, January 31, 2010, http://www.renewamerica.com/columns/giunta/100131.

26. Rev. John Zuhlsdorf, "Dominican Sister Associates B.V. Mary with Pro-'Choice' Position…No…Really!" *Fr. Z's Blog—What Does the Prayer Really Say?* (blog), December 9, 2009, http://wdtprs.com/blog/2009/12/dominican-sister-associates-bv-mary-with-pro-choice-position-no-really/.

27. Rev. John Malloy, "More on 'Sister' Donna Quinn," *A Shepherd's Voice* (blog), October 27, 2009, http://johnmalloysdb.blogspot.com/2009/10/more-on-sister-donna-quinn.html.

28. Patrick B. Craine, "Bishop Vasa to Doctors: Faith Trumps Supposed Medical Norms," LifeSiteNews.com, February 16, 2011, http://www.lifesitenews.com/news/bishop-vasa-to-doctors-faith-trumps-supposed-medical-norms?utm_source=LifeSiteNews.com+Daily+Newsletter&utm_campaign=6c08fc84e3LifeSiteNews_com_US_Headlines02_16_2011&utm_medium=email.

29. Patrick B. Craine, "Nebraska Bishop: Don't Make 'Prudence' an Excuse to Avoid Preaching Boldly on Homosexuality," LifeSiteNews.com, April 15, 2011, http://www.lifesitenews.com/news/nebraska-bishop-dont-make-prudence-an-excuse-to-avoid-preaching-boldly-on-h.

30. "Biden's New Bishop Blasts Candidate on Abortion," CatholicCulture.org, October 27, 2008, http://www.catholicculture.org/news/headlines/index.cfm?storyid=898.

31. Archbishop Charles Chaput, "Thoughts on a New Knighthood," (transcript of speech given to Catholic cadets at the United States Air Force Academy on October 25, 2010), http://www.archden.org/index.cfm/ID/4771.

32. Quote by Edmund Burke, http://www.quotedb.com/quotes/870.

Chapter 5

1. "Ask the Register" is a question and answer forum of the *South Nebraska Register*. All questions are answered by priests from the Diocese of Lincoln. This newspaper is no longer being published.

2. Rev. Ray Blake, "Pope: Bishops' Conference Doesn't Replace Bishop," *Fr. Ray Blake's Blog* (blog), November 16, 2010. http://marymagdalen.blogspot.com/2010/11/pope-bishops-conference-doesnt-replace.html.

3. The Saint Joseph Foundation, http://www.st-joseph-foundation.org/newsletter/2000/cfd18-1.htm.

4. "Report to the NCCB," (A report on the Liberty and Justice for All program given by the Ad Hoc Committee for the Bicentennial during the 1976 U.S. Catholic Bishops' Call To Action Conference in Detroit), November 1, 1976, http://www.cta-usa.org/whobishconference/A_reporttoNCCB.html.

5. Stephanie Block, "The Underground Call To Action," CatholicCulture.org, accessed August 24, 2011, http://www.catholicculture.org/culture/library/view.cfm?id=1318.

6. S.L. Hansen, "Vatican Affirms Excommunication of Call To Action Members in Lincoln," Catholic News Service, December 8, 2006, http://www.catholicnews.com/data/stories/cns/0606995.htm.

7. "Vatican Supports Excommunication of Call To Action Group," Catholic News Agency, December 8, 2006, http://www.catholicnewsagency.com/news/vatican-supports-excommunication-of-call-to-action-group/.

8. "Bishops Merge Organizations," Diocese of Gaylord, July 2, 2001, http://www.dioceseofgaylord.org/inside/ 170/index.phtml?artid=84.

9. Charles Wilson, "Domus Dei: A House Built on a Weak Foundation," The Saint Joseph Foundation, March 19, 2000, http://www.st-joseph-foundation.org/newsletter/ 2000/cfd18-1.htm.

10. "History of the Catholic Charities Network," Catholic Charities USA, accessed August 25, 2011, http://www.catholiccharitiesusa.org/Page.aspx?pid=290.

11. "Catholic Charities Receives Large Federal Contract for Disaster Relief," Catholic News Agency, August 4, 2009, http://www.catholicnewsagency.com/news/catholic charities receives large federal contract for disaster relief/.

12. Mobilize the Immigrant Vote website, http://mivcalifornia.org/docs/Mobilize the Immigrant Vote.

13. Mobilize the Immigrant Vote "November 2008 Voter Guide," http://mivcalifornia.org/docs/Voter guide.

14. Peter J. Smith, "Bishop in Center of Catholic Charity Scandal Says He Forbade Minor's Abortion," LifeSite-News.com, July 3, 2008, http://www.lifesitenews.com/news/archive/ldn/2008/ jul/08070315.

15. Dionne Walker, "VA Catholic Bishop Sorry for Abortion Mix-Up," FOXNews.com, July 1, 2008, http://www.foxnews.com/wires/2008Jul01/0,4670,AbortionInvestigation,00.html.

16. "Bishop DiLorenzo Forbade Charity's Assistance in Girl's Abortion, Diocese Says," Catholic News Agency, July 3, 2008, http://www.catholicnewsagency.com/news/bishop_dilorenzo_forbade_charitys_assistance_in_girls_abortion_diocese_says/.

17. See Kettelkamp biography at the United States Conference of Catholic Bishops website, http://www.usccb.org/about/child-and-youth-protection/who-we-are.cfm.

18. Paul Likoudis, "Return to Platform," CatholicCitizens.org, October 15, 2005, http://catholiccitizens.org/platform/platformview.asp?c=29119.

19. Ibid.

20. Domenico Bettinelli, "Kudos to Bishop Vasa," *Bettnet.com* (blog), October 9, 2005, http://www.bettnet.com/blog/index.php/weblog/comments/kudos_to_bishop_vasa/.

21. Bishop Robert F. Vasa, "To Make Sure We Really Protect Children, We Need Answers," CatholicCulture.org, accessed August 25, 2011, http://www.catholicculture.org/culture/library/view.cfm?recnum=6691.

22. Child and Youth Protection, on the website of the United States Conference of Catholic Bishops, http://www.usccb.org/about/child-and-youth-protection/.

23. "Keep 'Touching' Programs Off Our Children: An Open Letter to the United States Catholic Bishops," April

13, 2004, (letter written by Mary Ann Kreitzer, president of Catholic Media Coalition),
http://www.catholicmediacoalition.org/touching.htm.

24. See the USCCB website's Child and Youth Protection page,
http://www.usccb.org/issues-and-action/child-and-youth-protection/safe-environment.cfm.=

25. Christopher Manion, "'Safe Environment' Programs Began as Pro-Homosexual Propaganda," CatholicCulture.org, accessed August 24, 2011,
http://www.catholicculture.org/culture/library/view.cfm?id=6649&CFID=77776141&CFTOKEN=80675041.

26. Matthew Vadum, "Left-Wing Radicalism in the Church: CCHD and ACORN," Human Events, October 26, 2009,
http://www.humanevents.com/article.php?id=34070.

27. Patrick B. Craine, "New Utah CCHD Head Supported Gay 'Marriage,' Promoting Contraception in Schools," LifeSiteNews.com, April 18, 2011,
http://www.lifesitenews.com/news/new-utah-cchd-head-supported-gay-marriage-promoting-contraception-in-school.

28. Mary Ann Kreitzer, "CCHD Continues to Fund Alinsky Organizing with Donations from Patsies in the Pew," *Les Femmes—The Truth* (blog), April 14, 2011,
http://lesfemmes-thetruth.blogspot.com/2011/04/cchd-continues-to-fund-alinsky.html.

29. List of 2010-2011 CCHD Grantees on the USCCB website,
http://www.usccb.org/about/catholic-campaign-for-human-development/grants/upload/cchd-grantees-2010.pdf.

30. Bill Muehlenberg, "Capturing the Churches," CultureWatch, March 10, 2010,
http://www.billmuehlenberg.com/2010/10/03/capturing-the-churches/.

Chapter 6

1. Quote by Pope Benedict XVI on the website Guarding the Grotto: Alumni Protecting Notre Dame's Catholic Identity, http://www.projectsycamore.com/academic/.

2. Laura Legere, "Bishop Raises Concern about University of Scranton Speaker," *The Scranton Times Tribune*, May 7, 2010, http://thetimes-tribune.com/bishop-raises-concern-about-university-of-scranton-speaker-1.768404#ixzz1LkIn-rlEn.

3. "Bishop Martino Voices 'Absolute Disapproval' for University Inviting Gay Activist," Catholic News Agency, February 19, 2009, http://www.catholicnewsagency.com/news/bishop martino voices absolute disapproval for university inviting gay activist/.

4. GLBT Resource Library—an online list of resources for Canisius College, http://www.canisius.edu/campus leader/glbt resources.asp.

5. "Jesuit College's Management, Fundraising Programs Benefited Planned Parenthood," CatholicCulture.org, December 4, 2009, http://www.catholicculture.org/news/headlines/index.cfm?storyid=4810.

6. "Anger at Iowa Newman Center after Bishop Fires Transgendered Employee," CatholicCulture.org, January 18, 2010, http://www.catholicculture.org/news/headlines/index.cfm?storyid=5186.

7. Georgetown Law website containing biography of Julie E. Cohen, Professor of Law, http://www.law.georgetown.edu/faculty/facinfo/tab faculty.cfm?Status=Facult,y&ID=232.

8. "Catholic Colleges Remove Planned Parenthood Connections from Websites Following CNS Report," Cardinal Newman Society, May 2, 2011, http://www.cardinalnewmansociety.org/Home/tabid/36/ctl/Details/mid/435/ItemID/859/Default.aspx.

9. "Committed to helping others?" California Catholic Daily, March 14, 2011, http://www.calcatholic.com/news/newsArticle.aspx?id=4420943e-c48b-42f7-b1b1-15c0c5937f35.

10. Ibid.

11. "St. Joseph's University Joins Our Lady's," *The Practicing Catholic* (blog), April 5, 2009, http://thepracticingcatholic.wordpress.com/2009/04/05/st-josephs-university-joins-our-ladys/.

12. Steven Ertelt, "MSNBC Host Chris Matthews Says Pro-Life Advocates Use 'Terrorist' Methods," LifeNews.com, March 3, 2009, http://www.lifenews.com/2009/03/03/nat-4880/.

13. "Archbishop Objects to Clinton Rally at Catholic University," *USA Today*, February 14, 2008, http://www.usatoday.com/news/politics/election2008/2008-02-14-clinton-archbishop_N.htm.

14. "San Antonio Archbishop Not Happy about Hillary's College Visit," Catholic News Agency, February 13, 2008, http://www.catholicnewsagency.com/news/san antonio archbishop not happy about hillarys catholic college visit/.

15. Wally Edge, "Catholic Bishop Bars Whitman from Speaking to Students," PolitickerNJ, October 7, 2008, http://www.politickernj.com/wallye/24245/catholic-bishop-bars-whitman-speaking-students.

16. Kathleen Gilbert, "New Jersey Bishop Persuades Princeton Catholic School to Disinvite Pro-Choice Former Gov. Whitman," LifeSiteNews.com, October 7, 2008, http://www.lifesitenews.com/news/archive/ldn/2008/oct/08100707.

17. "Majerus Abortion Rights Comment Gets St. Louis Bishop's Attention," Associated Press article on ESPN.com, January 23, 2008, http://sports.espn.go.com/ncb/news/story?id=3210049.

18. Dick Weiss, "Rick Majerus Standing by His Beliefs," Free Republic, January 27, 2008, http://www.freerepublic.com/focus/f-news/1960436/posts.

19. Thomas Peters, "Obama to Give Commencement at Notre Dame!" *American Papist* (blog), March 20, 2009, http://www.americanpapist.com/2009/03/breaking-obama-to-give-commencement-at.html.

20. Kaitlynn Riely, "Notre Dame Students Vote Obama in Mock Election," CBSNews, February 11, 2009, http://www.cbsnews.com/stories/2008/10/27/politics/uwire/main4546989.shtml.

21. Kathleen Gilbert, "79: More Bishops Condemn Obama Honor in Final Days before ND's 'Day of Shame,'" LifeSiteNews.com, May 15, 2009, http://www.lifesitenews.com/news/archive/ldn/2009/may/09051515.

22. Kathryn Jean Lopez, "South Bend's Bishop John D'Arcy Will Not Attend Notre Dame's Commencement," *National Review Online*, March 24, 2009, http://www.nationalreview.com/corner/179262/south-bends-bishop-john-darcy-will-not-attend-notre-dames-commencement/kathryn-jean-lo.

23. Keith Fournier, "Paul Schenck for Bishop Rhoades on Notre Dame Scandal," Catholic Online, April 14, 2009, http://www.catholic.org/politics/story.php?id=33146.

24. Biography of Bishop Rhoades from the Roman Catholic Diocese of Harrisburg, http://bishoprhoades.com/.

25. Charles E. Rice, "Notre Dame 88," The American Catholic, October 5, 2010, http://the-american-catholic.com/2010/10/05/notre-dame-88/.

26. Kathleen Gilbert, "Charges Dropped against 'Notre Dame 88,'" LifeSiteNews.com, May 5, 2011, http://www.lifesitenews.com/news/breaking-charges-dropped-against-notre-dame-88.

27. "Thomas More Society's Relentless Legal Defense Wins Justice for Pro-Life Activists at Notre Dame," Christian Newswire, May 5, 2011, http://www.christiannewswire.com/news/9413116925.html.

28. John M. D'Arcy, "The Church and the University: A Pastoral Reflection on the Controversy at Notre Dame," *America*, August 31, 2009, http://www.americamagazine.org/content/article.cfm?article_id=11840.

29. The entire text of the *Land O' Lakes Statement* can be found at http://consortium.villanova.edu/excorde/landlake.htm.

30. "The Land O' Lakes Statement," Catholic Answers, accessed August 25, 2011, http://www.catholic.com/thisrock/2005/0511fea1sb5.asp.

31. See the University's of Notre Dame's Core Council for Gay, Lesbian, Bisexual & Questioning Students website http://corecouncil.nd.edu/questions-about-sexual-orientation/.

32. The Cardinal Newman Society http://www.cardinal-newmansociety.org/.

Chapter 7

1. Ronald A. Knox, "The Four Marks of the Church," IgnatiusInsight.com, accessed August 25, 2011, http://www.ignatiusinsight.com/features2007/rknox fourmarks_may07.asp.

2. Read the biography of Mr. Snuffleupagus at Wikia, http://muppet.wikia.com/wiki/Mr._Snuffleupagus.

3. "Let's Make a Deal: Catholic Conscience and Compromise," Archbishop's column in the *Denver Catholic Register*, week of September 22, 2004, http://www.archden.org/dcr/news.php?e=97&s=2&a= 2293.

4. "Say No to CCHD-Catholic in Name Only," *Les Femmes—The Truth* (blog), accessed August 25, 2011, http://www.lesfemmes-thetruth.org/v83twilight.htm.

5. "The Obligations of Catholics and the Rights of Unborn Children," A Pastoral Statement by the Most Reverend John J. Myers, Bishop of Peoria—June 1990, Women for Faith and Family, http://wf-f.org/Myers-90-cooperation.html.

6. Bishop Robert J. Carlson, "The Responsibility to Have a Well Informed Faith Life," ewtn.com, August 2004, http://www.ewtn.com/library/bishops/informfa.htm.

7. Remarks of Bishop Wilton Gregory at the forum "Great Voices of Faith in a Time of Crisis," 34th Annual Congressional Black Caucus Legislative Conference September 10, 2004, posted to The National Institute for the Renewal of the Priesthood on October 23, 2004, http://www.jknirp.com/wilton2.htm.

8. John R. Lott, Jr. and Sonya D. Jones, "Abortion Rate among Black Women Far Exceeds Rate for Other Groups," FOXNews.com, April 9, 2008, http://www.foxnews.com/story/0,2933,348649,00.html.

9. Joyce Kelly, "Father Absence 'Decimates' Black Community in U.S.," Reuters, June 14, 2007, http://www.reuters.com/article/2007/06/14/us-usa-fathers-idUSN0419185720070614.

10. Catholic Answers Action, *Voter's Guide for Serious Catholics*, (San Diego, CA, 2006), www.caaction.com/pdf/Voters-Guide-Catholic-English-1.pdf.

11. "U.S. Bishops' Lawyers Reject Catholic Answers Voter Guide," EWTN News, August 25, 2004, http://www.ewtn.com/vnews/getstory.asp?number=48969.

12. David R. Obey, "My Conscience, My Vote," *America*, August 16, 2004, https://americamagazine.org/content/article.cfm?article_id=3708&comments=1.

13. "Archbishop Burke Warns of Upcoming 'Persecution' Over Abortion and Homosexuality. . ." LifeSiteNews.com, February 9, 2005, http://www.tldm.org/News7/abortionBurke2.htm.

14. "Statement of Bishop Rene Henry Gracida on Voting for Pro-Abortion Candidates," Catholic Online Exclusive, September 9, 2004, http://www.catholic.org/featured/headline.php?ID=1321.

15. John A. Corapi, "Form Your Conscience. Vote Your Conscience!" CatholicCulture.org, accessed August 25, 2011, http://www.catholicculture.org/culture/library/view.cfm?recnum=6063.

16. "We 'Will Be Judged by How We Vote,' Says Fargo Bishop," Catholic News Agency, November 4, 2008, http://www.catholicnewsagency.com/news/we_will_be_judged_by_how_we_vote_says_fargo_bishop/.

17. Thomas C. Fox, "Memphis Bishop Calls Upon Catholics to Avoid 'One Issue' Votes," *National Catholic Reporter*, October 21, 2008, http://ncronline.org/node/2238.

18. "A Culture of Life and the Penalty of Death," Statement of USCCB on the death penalty, http://www.usccb.org/deathpenalty/.

19. "U.S. Bishops Urge New Mexico Governor to Sign Repeal of the Death Penalty," USCCB News Release, March 16, 2009, http://www.usccb.org/comm/archives/2009/09-057.shtml.

20. Judie Brown, "Politics Does Not a Bishop Make," American Life League, November 15, 2007, http://www.all.org/article/index/id/MzY0NA.

21. For this document and others, visit the Faithful Citizenship home page at http://faithfulcitizenship.org/.

22. Deal Hudson, "Did the Bishops Punish Archbishop Burke?" CatholiCity.com, November 19, 2007, http://www.catholicity.com/commentary/hudson/01572.html.

23. Barbara Kralis, "Bishop Vasa—A Shepherd for Our Time," Renew America, July 18, 2004, http://www.renewamerica.com/columns/kralis/040718.

24. Romans 16:18 (New American Bible), http://old.usccb.org/nab/bible/romans/romans16.htm.

25. 1 Corinthians 2:4 (New American Bible), http://old.usccb.org/nab/bible/1corinthians/1corinthians2.htm.

Chapter 8

1. American Life League's Canon 915 Project, http://www.canon915.org/.

2. Barbara Kralis, "Bishop Vasa—A Shepherd for Our Time," Renew America, July 18, 2004, http://www.renewamerica.com/columns/kralis/040718.

3. Cardinal Joseph Ratzinger, "Worthiness to Receive Holy Communion—General Principles," CatholicCulture.org, accessed August 25, 2011, http://www.catholicculture.org/culture/library/view.cfm?id=6041.

4. Frank Langfitt, "Cardinal Keeler Calls for Keeping Politics out of Communion," *The Baltimore Sun*, May 28, 2004, http://articles.baltimoresun.com/2004-05-28/news/0405280277_1_catholic-politicians-communion-bishops.

5. Barbara Kralis, "Prohibition is Worthless Without Enforcement," lifeissues.net, accessed August 25, 2011, http://www.lifeissues.net/writers/kra/kra_13prohibitionno.html.

6. "Denial of Communion to Politicians: A CTA Policy Statement," churchwatch.org, June 2004, http://www.cta-usa.org/watch2004-06%20/communion.html.

7. Rev. Joseph F. Wilson, "The Price of My Soul's Salvation," CatholicCulture.org, accessed August 25, 2011, http://www.catholicculture.org/culture/library/view.cfm?recnum=5964.

8. "Canon 915 Millstone Memorial Dedicated," Children of God for Life, January 8, 2008, http://www.cogforlife.org/kuchinsky915.htm.

9. Bishop Rene Henry Gracida, "A Twelve Step Program for Bishops," EWTN News, October 4, 2004, http://www.ewtn.com/vnews/getstory.asp?number=50110.

10. Bishop Robert Vasa, "Excommunication is a Declaration of Acts that Severs Ties," Catholic Online, January 8, 2010, http://www.catholic.org/national/national story.php?id=35150.

11. Tom Cohen, "Kennedy Abortion Debate Puts Politics, Religion Back in Spotlight," CNN, November 24, 2009, http://edition.cnn.com/2009/POLITICS/11/23/kennedy.abortion/.

12. Judie Brown, "Bishop Thomas Tobin: A Lion for the Lord," American Life League, November 22, 2009, http://www.all.org/article/index/id/NTQwNA/.

13. Deacon Keith Fournier, "Opinion: Chris Matthews Should Be Fired for His Offensive Interview of Bishop Tobin," Catholic Online, November 24, 2009, http://www.catholic.org/politics/story.php?id=34908.

14. "Sister Violated More Than Catholic Teaching in Sanctioning Abortion, Ethicist Says," Catholic News Agency, May 19, 2010, http://www.catholicnewsagency.com/news/sister-violated-more-than-catholic-teaching-in-sanctioning-abortion-ethicist-says/.

15. Jerry Filteau, "Catholic Health Association Backs Phoenix Hospital," Faith in Public Life, December 22, 2010, http://faithinpubliclife.org/content/news/2010/12/catholic_health_association_ba.html.

16. "US Bishops Back Olmsted in Arizona Abortion Drama," Catholic News Agency, June 24, 2010, http://www.catholicnewsagency.com/news/us-bishops-back-olmsted-in-arizona-abortion-drama/.

17. David Gibson, "Vatican Official: Church Erred in Holding Kennedy Funeral," Politics Daily, accessed August 26, 2011, http://www.politicsdaily.com/2009/09/22/vatican-official-cardinal-erred-in-holding-funeral-for-kennedy/.

18. Judie Brown, "The Kennedy Funeral: Spitting on Christ," American Life League, August 31, 2009, http://www.all.org/article/index/id/NTAxNw/.

19. "Media Risks Making Politics a Religion by Marginalizing the Church, Archbishop Chaput Says," Catholic News Agency, March 17, 2009, http://www.catholicnewsagency.com/news/media_risks_making_politics_a_religion_by_marginalizing_the_church_archbishop_chaput_says/.

20. Rebecca Millette, "Archbishop Chaput: Refusing to Act on Pro-Abort Catholic Politicians Hasn't Worked," LifeSiteNews.com, April 11, 2011, http://www.lifesitenews.com/news/archbishop-chaput-refusing-to-act-on-pro-abort-catholic-politicians-hasnt-w.

21. Matthew 11:15 (New American Bible), http://old.usccb.org/nab/bible/matthew/matthew11.htm.

Chapter 9

1. "Obama's Old Office for Sale," *Huffington Post*, September 4, 2008, http://www.huffingtonpost.com/2008/09/04/obamas-old-office-for-sal_n_124079.html.

2. Phil Sevilla, "ACORN, CCHD, and the Principle of Subsidiarity," *The Warrior* (blog), September 30, 2009, http://thewarriorspost.blogspot.com/2009_09_01_archive.html.

3. Stanley Kurtz, "Inside Obama's Acorn," *National Review Online*, May 29, 2008, http://www.nationalreview.com/articles/224610/inside-obamas-acorn/stanley-kurtz.

4. Thomas Peters, "Sisters of Mercy Host Catholics for Obama Event," *American Papist* (blog), October 2, 2008, http://www.americanpapist.com/2008/10/sisters-of-mercy-host-catholics-for.html.

5. See Catholics for Obama website at http://www.catholicsforobama.blogspot.com/.

6. Rev. Richard John Neuhaus, "A Response to Doug Kmiec," *National Catholic Register*, July 16, 2008, http://www.ncregister.com/site/article/15476.

7. Brian Kelly, "54% of Catholics Voted for Obama," Catholicism.org, November 6, 2008, http://catholicism.org/54-of-catholic-voters-voted-for-obama.html.

8. George Neumayr, "Touchdown Obama," *The American Spectator*, March 27, 2009, http://spectator.org/archives/2009/03/27/touchdown-obama.

9. Anne Hendershott, "Who Are These Fake Catholic Groups?" Catholic Advocate, March 18, 2010, http://www.catholicadvocate.com/2010/03/who-are-these-fake-catholic-groups/.

10. Rev. Andrew Greeley, "Why So Many Pro-Life Catholics Backed Obama," Andrew M. Greeley: Author, Priest, Sociologist, November 5, 2008, http://www.agreeley.com/articles/110508.htm.

11. George Neumayr, "A Web of Confusion," *The Catholic World Report*, April 27, 2011, http://www.catholicworldreport.com/Item/450/a_web_of_confusion.aspx.

12. Msgr. Kevin T. McMahon, "Commentary: Confusion and the Catholic Vote," *St. Louis Review*, December 4, 2008, http://stlouisreview.com/article/2008-11-13/commentary-confusion.

13. Jennifer Giroux, "Obama Nominates Abortion Industry's Top Governor," *Human Events*, March 2, 2009, http://www.humanevents.com/article.php?id=30903.

14. "26 Catholic Leaders, Scholars and Theologians Offer Support for Sebelius," Catholics United, March 1, 2009, http://www.catholics-united.org/?q=node/241.

15. Rev. John Zuhlsdorf, "Obama Administration Cancels Conscience Protections for Health Care Workers," *Fr. Z's Blog—What Does the Prayer Really Say?* (blog) February 21, 2011, http://wdtprs.com/blog/2011/02/obama-administration-cancels-conscience-protections-for-health-care-workers/.

16. John L. Allen Jr., "Obama Charm Offensive Ahead of Pope Meeting Seems to Be Working," *National Catholic Reporter*, July 4, 2009, http://ncronline.org/blogs/ncr-today/obama-charm-offensive-ahead-pope-meeting-seems-be-working.

17. Karen Schuberg, "Boehner Says We Can't Have 'Anti-Catholic Bigot' in White House, Calls for Obama Adviser to Resign," CNSNews.com, February 4, 2010, http://www.cnsnews.com/news/article/60999.

18. "Surgeon General Nominee Regina Benjamin Pro-Abortion," *California Catholic Daily*, July 16, 2009, http://www.calcatholic.com/news/newsArticle.aspx?id=1c9e5b98-4d08-45bc-88fe-5cbae6f86298.

19. John L. Allen Jr., "A New Face of Catholicism," *National Catholic Reporter*, June 8, 2009, http://ncronline.org/news/vatican/new-face-catholicism.

20. Steven Ertelt, "Obama Picks 'Pro-Life' Catholic Sellout Douglas Kmiec for Malta Ambassador," LifeNews.com, July 2, 2009, http://www.lifenews.com/2009/07/02/int-1254/.

21. Michael Sean Winters, "Douglas Kmiec, U.S. Ambassador to Malta, Resigns," *National Catholic Reporter*, April 16, 2011, ncronline.org/news/politics/douglas-kmiec-us-ambassador-to-malta-resigns.

22. Kirk, "Obama Brings Back Terri Schaivo [*sic*] Fight Thru Attorney Pick," *Drudge Retort* (blog), December 8, 2008, http://www.drudge.com/archive/115665/obama-brings-back-terri-schaivo-fight-thru.

23. Terri Schiavo Life & Hope Network home page http://www.terrisfight.org/.

24. USCCB documents on health care http://www.usccb.org/healthcare/.

25. "Cardinal George Meets with President Obama to Advance 'Common Good,'" Catholic News Agency, March 18, 2009. http://www.catholicnewsagency.com/news/cardinal_george_meets_with_president_obama_to_advance_common_good/.

26. Adrienne S. Gaines, "Obama Says Health Plan Critics 'Bearing False Witness,'" *Charisma*, August 20, 2009, http://charismamag.com/index.php/news/23038-obama-says-health-plan-critics-bearing-false-witness.

27. Ed Morrissey, "Obama to Rabbis on Health Care: 'We Are God's Partners in Matters of Life and Death," *Hot Air*, August 19, 2009, http://hotair.com/archives/2009/08/19/obama-to-rabbis-on-health-care-we-are-gods-partners-in-matters-of-life-and-death/.

28. "It's Time to Take Our Medicine: An Interview with Sister Carol Keehan, DC," U.S. Catholic, March 26, 2010, http://www.uscatholic.org/culture/social-justice/2010/03/its-time-take-our-medicine?page=0,1.

29. Katie Walker, "Collateral Information: Catholic Charitable Organizations Supporting Obamacare," American Life League, August 3, 2009, http://www.all.org/article/index/id/ODcx/.

30. Deal Hudson, "The Risks of a 'Right' to Healthcare," CatholiCity, August 10, 2009, http://www.catholicity.com/commentary/hudson/06635.html.

31. David Kirkpatrick, "Some Catholic Bishops Assail Health Plan," *The New York Times*, August 27, 2009, http://www.nytimes.com/2009/08/28/health/policy/28catholics.html.

32. Bishop Robert Morlino, "Seeking Ethical Health Care Reform," *Catholic Herald* (Diocese of Madison), August 27, 2009, http://www.madisoncatholicherald.org/bishop/13-bishopcolumn/861-seeking-ethical-health-care-reform.html.

33. Bishop Michael Pfeifer, "Obama Plan Deadly for Those at Beginning, End of Life," San Angelo Diocese, September 3, 2009.

34. "Bishop Aquila Outlines Four Principles for Genuine Health Care Reform," Catholic News Agency, September 1, 2009, http://www.catholicnewsagency.com/news/bishop_aquila_outlines_four_principles_for_genuine_health_care_reform/.

35. Mark Sappenfield, "Bart Stupak Vows 'Yes' in Health Care Vote. What Comes Next?" *The Christian Science Monitor*, March 21, 2010, http://www.csmonitor.com/USA/Politics/2010/0321/Bart-Stupak-vows-yes-in-health-care-vote.-What-comes-next.

36. "Sr. Keehan Receives Presidential Pen for Supporting Health Care Despite Bishops' Objections," Catholic News Agency, March 24, 2010, http://www.catholicnewsagency.com/news/sr._kehaan_receives_presidential_pen_for_supporting_health_care_against_bishops_decision/.

37. CNN Wire Staff, "Obama Signs Executive Order on Abortion Funding Limits," CNN Politics, March 24, 2010, http://articles.cnn.com/2010-03-24/politics/obama.abortion_1_offer-abortions-abortion-funding-abortion-opponents?_s=PM:POLITICS.

38. Proverbs 26:10 (New American Bible), http://old.usccb.org/nab/bible/proverbs/proverb26.htm.

Chapter 10

1. Nancy Frazier O'Brien, "What Makes Health Care Catholic? Panelists Point to Service to the Least," Catholic Online, March 6, 2007, http://www.catholic.org/national/national_story.php?id=23295.

2. Alan Holdren, "Catholic Nurses Seeing Rise in Threats to Consciences, Association Reports," Catholic News Agency, February 7, 2011, http://www.catholicnewsagency.com/news/international-catholic-nurses-seeing-rise-in-threats-to-consciences/.

3. "Texas Catholic Hospitals Did Not Follow Catholic Ethics, Report Claims," Catholic News Agency, July 3, 2008, http://www.catholicnewsagency.com/news/texas_catholic_hospitals_did_not_follow_catholic_ethics_report_claims/.

4. Patrick B. Craine, "Bishop Vasa Severs Church's Ties with Hospital over Sterilizations," Catholic Online, February 17, 2010, http://www.catholic.org/national/national_story.php?id=35449.

5. Bishop Alvaro Corrada, SJ, "Statement on Human Dignity, Conscience, and Healthcare to the Catholics and People of East Texas," Given to the Diocese of Tyler, TX, December 1, 2008, www.dioceseoftyler.org/documents/HumanDignityBpCorrada.pdf.

6. Steven Ertelt, "Report Shows Catholic Healthcare West Promotes Abortions," LifeNews.com, http://www.lifenews.com/2010/12/20/nat-6948/.

7. Thomas Szyszkiewicz, "Where to Draw the Line? Prenatal Ethics," lifeissues.net, March 7, 2004, http://www.lifeissues.net/writers/szy/szy_01prenatalethics.html.

8. John-Henry Westen, "Ontario Bishop Says 'Early Induction' Policy at Catholic Hospital Under Vatican Review," LifeSiteNews, March 5, 2009, http://www.lifesite-news.com/news/archive/ldn/2009/mar/09030511.

9. Regis Scanlon, "Abortion Referrals at Catholic Hospitals," bNet, October, 2009, http://findarticles.com/p/articles/mi_7672/is_200910/ai_n42043296/pg_2/?tag=mantle_skin;content.

10. See OSF HealthCare site for relationship between Susan G. Komen Breast Center and OSF St. Francis Medical Center, http://www.osfsaintfrancis.org/services/ WomensServices/SusanGKomenBreastCenter/.

11. Karen Malec, "Susan G. Komen's Funding of Planned Parenthood Causes Diocese to Discourage Support— Coalition on Abortion/Breast Cancer Praises Decision," ChristianNewsWire, March 31, 2008, http://www.christiannewswire.com/news/ 820676110.html.

12. "Diocese of Little Rock Backtracks from Warning about Komen Foundation," Catholic News Agency, March 12, 2008, http://www.catholicnewsagency.com/news/ diocese_of_little_rock_backtracks_from_warning about_komen_foundation/.

13. See the Terri Schiavo Life & Hope Network for a timeline of Terri's life following her collapse, http://www.terrisfight.org/timeline/.

14. Bobby Schindler's letter to Florida bishop, Robert Lynch, March 9, 2007, http://www.lifesite.net/ldn/2007_docs/ SchindlerLetter.pdf.

15. Bishop Robert N. Lynch, "St. Petersburg and the Homeless Situation," Roman Catholic Diocese of St. Petersburg, accessed August 27, 2011, http://home.catholicweb.com/Bishop_DOSP/index.cfm/ NewsItem?ID=195580&From=Home.

16. See the POLST (Physician Orders for Life-Sustaining Treatment Paradigm) website, http://www.ohsu.edu/polst/.

17. Elizabeth D. Wickham, Ph.D., "Repackaging Death as Life: The Third Path to Imposed Death," American Life League, November 16, 2010, http://www.all.org/article/index/id/ODIxMA.

18. Ethical and Religious Directives for Catholic Health Care Services (Fourth Edition, June 15, 2001) can be found at the USCCB website, http://old.usccb.org/bishops/directives.shtml.

19. Julie Grimstad, "Selective Killing Fields: POLST in Action," American Life League, March 21, 2011, http://www.all.org/article/index/id/ODcxMw/.

20. Susan E. Hickman, Ph.D., et al., "Use of the Physician Orders for Life-Sustaining Treatment (POLST) Paradigm Program in the Hospice Setting," *Journal of Palliative Medicine*, (February 2009), http://www.ncbi.nlm.nih.gov/pmc/articles/PMC2966836/.

21. See HealthCare.gov for information on how to understand the Affordable Care Act, http://www.healthcare.gov/law/introduction/index.html.

22. "It's Time to Take Our Medicine: An Interview with Sister Carol Keehan, DC," *U.S. Catholic*, March 26, 2011, http://www.uscatholic.org/culture/social-justice/2010/03/its-time-take-our-medicine?page=0,1.

23. Robert Knight, "Playing God with Catholic Hospitals," *The Washington Times*, January 5, 2011, http://www.washingtontimes.com/news/2011/jan/5/playing-god-with-catholic-hospitals/print/.

24. Quote by Ronald Reagan found at http://www.brainyquote.com/quotes/quotes/r/ronaldreag147717.html.

Chapter 11

1. See HealthCare.gov for information on how to understand the Affordable Care Act, http://www.healthcare.gov/law/introduction/index.html.

2. Lauren Keiper, "Most Catholic Women Use Birth Control Banned by Church," Reuters, April 13, 2011, http://www.reuters.com/article/2011/04/13/us-contraceptives-religion-idUSTRE73C7W020110413.

3. For information on Natural Family Planning see http://www.thedefender.org/Natural%20Family%20Planning.html.

4. Pope John Paul II, *Letter to Families*, 1994, http://www.vatican.va/holy_father/john_paul_ii/letters/documents/hf_jp-ii_let_02021994_families_en.html.

5. "Contraception is Intrinsically Evil . . .," These Last Days Ministries, accessed August 27, 2011, http://www.tldm.org/news6/contraception.htm.

6. *Casti Connubii* (encyclical of Pope Pius XI on Christian marriage), December 31, 1930, http://www.vatican.va/holy_father/pius_xi/encyclicals/documents/hf_p-xi_enc_31121930_casti-connubii_en.html.

7. See the "History of the Pill," on American Life League's The Pill Kills website, accessed August 27, 2011, http://thepillkills.com/history.php.

8. Jim Burnham, "Casti Connubii: The Church's Answer to Planned Parenthood," Family Life Center International, accessed August 27, 2011, http://www.familylifecenter.net/article.asp?artId=182.

9. *Casti Connubii* (encyclical of Pope Pius XI on Christian marriage), December 31, 1930, http://www.vatican.va/holy_father/pius_xi/encyclicals/documents/hf_p-xi_enc_31121930_casti-connubii_en.html.

10. Thomas M. Reynolds, "Contraception and Catholic Denial," included in a letter from Julie Grimstad to supporters of the Life is Worth Living organization, July 7, 2009 (letter is not found online).

Chapter 12

1. "USCCB Welcomes House Passage of 'No Taxpayer Funding for Abortion Act,'" PR Newswire, May 5, 2011, http://www.prnewswire.com/news-releases/ usccb-welcomes-house-passage-of-no-taxpayer-funding-for-abortion-act-121351403.html.

2. "Planned Parenthood Funding Ban Fails in Senate," EWTN, April 14, 2011, http://www.ewtn.com/vnews/getstory.asp?number=112767.

3. "Bishops to Vote on Physician-Assisted Suicide Document at Seattle Meeting; Statement Says Practice Does Not Advance Compassion, Choices," PR Newswire, June 1, 2011, http://www.prnewswire.com/news-releases/ bishops-to-vote-on-physician-assisted-suicide-document-at-seattle-meeting-statement-says-practice-does-not-advance-compassion-choices-122952018.html.

4. Dianne Irving, Ph.D., "Can Either Scientific Facts or 'Personhood' Be Mediated?" lifeissues.net, March 15, 1994, http://www.lifeissues.net/writers/irv/ irv_13personmediated.html.

5. C. Ward Kischer, "A New Wave Dialectic: The Reinvention of Human Embryology and a Futuristic Social Policy for Humankind," (reproduced from the book, *The Human Development Hoax*) lifeissues.net, accessed August 28, 2011, http://www.lifeissues.net/writers/kisc/kisc_14newwave dialectic1.html.

6. "Contraceptive Compromise," American Life League, January 1, 1997, http://www.all.org/article/index/id/MjQ5OA.

7. Judie Brown, "The Pill and 50 Years of Misery," Renew America, May 6, 2010, http://www.renewamerica.com/columns/brown/100506.

8. Michael Hichborn, "Abortifacient Effects of Birth Control Pills Pro-Life Video," *The American Life League Report*, July 7, 2008, http://www.youtube.com/watch?v=Z96eKLwnJ2s.

9. To find out more about NaProTECHNOLOGY, visit this website: http://www.catholicinfertility.org/naprotechnology.html.

10. Katie Walker, "ALL Joins International Call for Ban on In Vitro Technologies," American Life League, June 21, 2010, http://www.all.org/article/index/id/Njk0Mw/.

11. "Human Cloning: The Myths vs. the Facts!" Children of God for Life, modified on July 14, 2011, http://www.cogforlife.org/cloningfact.htm.

12. "PFLI Condemns FDA Approval of Chemical Cousin of Abortion Pill Mifepristone (RU486)," *Deacon for Life* (blog), August 16, 2010, http://deaconforlife.blogspot.com/2010/08/pharmacists-for-life-condemn-abortion.html.

13. Clarke D. Forsythe, "The Blackmun Myth," *National Review Online*, September 16, 2009, http://www.nationalreview.com/articles/228252/blackmun-myth/clarke-d-forsythe?page=1#.

14. Dianne N. Irving, "Analysis of Legislative and Regulatory Chaos in the U.S.: Asexual Human Reproduction and Genetic Engineering," lifeissues.net, October 4, 2004, http://www.lifeissues.net/writers/irv/irv_81chaosasexgen9.html.

15. Dianne N. Irving, "Human Embryology and Church Teachings," lifeissues.net, September 15, 2008, http://www.lifeissues.net/writers/irv/em/ em_132embryologychurch5.html.

16. "The Roman Catholic Bishops Will Not Support CI-102, the Personhood Amendment," Statement by the Roman Catholic bishops of Montana, Montana Catholic Conference website, November 19, 2009, http://www.montanacc.org/directors_pages/ 11_2009_Personhood.html.

17. Paul Benjamin Linton, "State 'Personhood' Proposals," *The Human Life Review*, Fall 2009, http://www.humanlifereview.com/index.php?option= com_content&view=article&id=96:state-personhood-proposals&catid=46:2009-fall&Itemid=6.

18. Bob Ellis, "Bishop Swain Issues Statement in Support of Initiated Measure 11," Dakota Voice, September 30, 2008, http://www.dakotavoice.com/?p=9964.

19. "South Dakota Abortion Ban, Initiated Measure 11 (2008)," *Ballot Pedia*, last modified August 19, 2011, http://ballotpedia.org/wiki/index.php/ South_Dakota_Abortion_Ban_Initiative_%282008%29.

20. Judie Brown, "Human Personhood and Ill-Advised Catholic Bishops," Renew America, December 10, 2009, http://www.renewamerica.com/columns/brown/091210.

21. *Dred Scott v. Sanford* (1857), ourdocuments.gov, accessed August 28, 2011, http://www.ourdocuments.gov/ doc.php?flash=true&doc=29.

22. "The Roman Catholic Bishops Will Not Support CI-102, the Personhood Amendment," Statement by the Roman Catholic bishops of Montana, Montana Catholic Conference website, November 19, 2009, http://www.montanacc.org/directors_pages/11_2009_Personhood.html.

23. Jonquil Frankham, "Pro-Life Group Asks Obama Why He Supports Removing All 'Common Sense' Restrictions on Abortion," LifeSiteNews.com, October 29, 2008, http://www.lifesitenews.com/ldn/2008/oct/08102906.html.

24. Quote by Pope John Paul II http://sspeterpaul.com/PopeJohnPaulII.htm.

Chapter 13

1. Rev. John A. Hardon, SJ, "The Priesthood," Real Presence Eucharistic Education and Adoration Association, accessed August 27, 2011, http://www.therealpresence.org/eucharst/priesthd/priest.htm

2. Homily of His Holiness Benedict XVI at a Mass for the ordination to the priesthood of 15 deacons of the Diocese of Rome, May 7, 2006, http://www.vatican.va/holy_father/benedict_xvi/homilies/2006/documents/hf_ben_xvi_hom_20060507 priestly-ordination_en.html.

3. Rev. Michael Orsi, "The Real Reason for the Vocation Crisis," Ignatius Insight, accessed August 27, 2011, http://www.ignatiusinsight.com/features2005/orsi_vocationcrisis1_jan05.asp.

4. Archbishop Raymond Burke, "Reflections on the Struggle to Advance the Culture of Life," CatholiCity, September 26, 2009, http://www.catholicity.com/commentary/burke/06937.html.

5. *Caritas In Veritate* (encyclical by Pope Benedict XVI), June 29, 2009, http://www.vatican.va/holy_father/benedict_xvi/ encyclicals/documents/hf_ben-xvi_enc_20090629 caritas-in-veritate_en.html.

6. Rev. Samuel J. Aquila, DD, *You Will Know the Truth and the Truth Will Set You Free* (A pastoral letter on deepening our understanding of the truths of the Catholic faith), November 30, 2004, http://www.fargodiocese.org/Bishop/Homilies/ PastoralOnTruth.pdf.

7. "We Are Rapidly Becoming a Nation of Victims," CatholicCitizens.org, June 13, 2004, http://catholiccitizens.org/press/ contentview.asp?c=16594.

8. Rev. Rawley Myers, "The Saints Must Guide Us," Catholics United for the Faith, accessed August 27, 2011, http://www.cuf.org/Laywitness/LWonline/SO06Myers.asp

9. Archbishop Charles Chaput, "Rendering unto Caesar: The Catholic Political Vocation," Archdiocese of Denver website, February 23, 2009, http://www.archden.org/index.cfm/ID/1511.

10. Rebecca Millette, "Archbishop Chaput: Refusing to Act on Pro-Abort Catholic Politicians Hasn't Worked," CatholicCitizens.org, April 16, 2011, http://catholiccitizens.org/press/pressview.asp?c=52854.

11. Patrick B. Craine, "U.S. Bishop Vasa: Individual Bishops Trump Conference Every Time," Deep Calls to Deep, September 22, 2010, http://abyssum.wordpress.com/2010/09/23/ bravo-bishop-robert-vasa/.

12. Matthew Cullinan Hoffman, "Scranton Bishop Says He will Refuse Communion to Joseph Biden," LifeSiteNews.com, September 2, 2008, http://www.lifesitenews.com/news/archive/ldn/2008/sep/08090212.

13. "Bishop Martino Tells Catholic Colleges: Student Health Services Must Follow Church Teaching," CatholicCulture.org, April 7, 2009, http://www.catholicculture.org/news/headlines/index.cfm?storyid=2560.

14. "Bishop in PA Battles for Orthodoxy," Faith on msnbc.com, April 13, 2009, http://www.msnbc.msn.com/id/29680844/page/2/.

15. "Scranton's Bishop Instructs Ministers: No Communion for Public Sinners," EWTN News, February 27, 2009, http://www.ewtn.com/vnews/getstory.asp?number=94008.

16. Kathleen Gilbert, "Pro-Life Leaders Hail Bishop Martino's Courageous Outspokenness for Pro-Life, Pro-Family Values," LifeSiteNews.com, February 27, 2009, http://www.lifesitenews.com/news/archive/ldn/2009/feb/09022713.

17. Peter J. Smith, "Another Bishop Says ObamaCare Violates Catholic Social Teaching," LifeSiteNews.com, September 18, 2009, http://www.lifesitenews.com/news/archive/ldn/2009/sep/09091811.

18. Archbishop Joseph F. Naumann and Bishop Robert W. Finn, "Kansas City Bishops Issue Joint Health Care Reform Pastoral Statement," *The Catholic Key Blog* (blog), September 1, 2009, http://catholickey.blogspot.com/2009/09/kansas-city-bishops-issue-joint-health.html.

19. "Catholic Bishop John Yanta Encourages Catholics and Christians to Morally Vote Pro-Life," Christian News Wire, accessed August 28, 2011, http://www.christiannewswire.com/news/ 824088431.html.

20. Rev. Denis O'Brien, MM, "Writings of Fr. Denis E. O'Brien M.M. Spiritual Director, ALL," Semper Fi Catholic Forum, accessed August 28, 2011, http://www.semperficatholic.com/page3.html.

21. "A Prayer for Priests and Bishops," (A prayer taken from the Roman Missal), CatholicCulture.org, accessed August 28, 2011, http://www.catholicculture.org/culture/ liturgicalyear/prayers/view.cfm?id=989.

Index

the Broken Path

How Catholic Bishops Got Lost in the Weeds of American Politics

———————————————————

Judie Brown